SHAPING AN AMERICAN INSTITUTION

I could not have this feeling
of pride if Sears had simply
made good profits and sales.
Sears has been a clean business,
an honest business, it has performed
a real service to the American
people, it has sincerely tried
to guard the welfare of its
employees, it has performed its
obligations to the communities
of our country. In short, it is
not merely a business—it is
a great institution.

—ROBERT E. WOOD
*Address to company-wide meeting
of Sears executives, 4 May 1950*

Shaping an American Institution

Robert E. Wood and Sears, Roebuck

James C. Worthy

UNIVERSITY OF ILLINOIS PRESS

Urbana and Chicago

This book is printed on acid-free paper.

Library of Congress Cataloging in Publication Data

Worthy, James C.
  Shaping an American institution.

  Includes bibliographical references and index.
    1. Wood, Robert Elkington, 1879–1969. 2. Sears,
Roebuck and Company—Biography. 3. Executives—United
States—Biography. I. Title.
HF5467.S4W67 1984   381′.45′0006073   83-18157
ISBN 0-252-01051-5 (alk. paper)

To my wife, Mildred Leritz Worthy,
who made this and many other things possible.

Contents

Acknowledgments

Six years in the writing, this book would not exist were it not for the help I received from many individuals along the way.

I am indebted to the current management of Sears, Roebuck and Co., who displayed keen interest in the project from the beginning. While the company neither sponsored nor supported my undertaking, senior officers gave me their wholehearted encouragement and cooperation throughout. Portions of the text were submitted to various Sears personnel to check for factual accuracy, but the manuscript was not reviewed by Sears or by any member of General Wood's family. I was allowed to work and write with complete independence, for which I am deeply appreciative, and I accept full responsibility for the final result.

All information I requested from the company—and it was considerable—was made available to me. I enjoyed unrestricted access to the official Sears Archives, whose staff—notably chief archivist Lenore Swoiskin—provided invaluable assistance in locating needed materials, verifying factual statements, and otherwise supporting the research essential to my task. Especially useful were the transcripts of interviews recorded by Diana Seidel as part of an oral history project she conducted for the company a number of years ago. Future historians will find a rich mine of information in the documentary resources of its well-organized archives.

During the early stages of my research, Dean W. Webbles, then administrative assistant to Sears chief executive officer, took the time to identify sources of information, make necessary contacts, and provide examples of Wood's management style from his own personal experience. I am grateful for his aid.

A large portion of the materials used in this book originated in conversations and tape-recorded interviews with retired Sears officers and executives who knew and worked with the General and took part in many of the events described herein. I was privileged to talk with the following individuals, among others: Frederick P. Boynton, Jr., Robert E. Brooker, James W. Button, J. C. Haynes, Carol W. Jones, Arthur J. Lowell, Gordon M. Metcalf, Charles A. Meyer, Robert V. Mullen, Douglas J. Peacher, Louis C. Pfeiffle, Arthur Rosenbaum, Ralph Schindler, W. Wallace Tudor, and Arthur M. Wood. I report with sadness and a sense of personal loss that some of those named are now deceased.

The series of interviews conducted over a three-year period with Edward Pennell Brooks, who was closely associated with Wood from his Montgomery Ward days until well after World War II, merit special mention. The frequency with which Brooks is cited as the authority for facts and revealing anecdotes gives some indication of the extent of my indebtedness to him.

I had the singular honor of interviewing Mary Hardwick Wood, the General's widow, in her home in her ninety-ninth year. Her recollections of the Panama Canal and World War I periods of her husband's life, offered freely and graciously, were vivid and uniquely useful.

Others who afforded me valuable insights into General Wood and his career included his longtime personal friend (but no relation) J. Howard Wood, former publisher of the *Chicago Tribune*, and Robert S. Adler, son of Max Adler, Julius Rosenwald's merchandising vice-president.

Burleigh B. Gardner conducted extensive studies of Sears organization and management during the years immediately following World War II, originally as executive secretary of the Committee on Human Relations in Industry of the University of Chicago and subsequently as president of Social Research, Inc. He furnished me with a number of reports from his files, in addition to his personal reminiscences of Wood and his ways, both of which added to the factual and interpretive material at my disposal.

David G. Moore, at one time my assistant in the research and planning unit of the Sears corporate personnel department and now chairman of the Department of Business Administration at the University of North Florida, also went into his files on my behalf. I was able to obtain from him a number of reports which had disappeared from my own files over the years.

Justus Doenecke of the University of South Florida, who has studied the American isolationist movement that preceded World War II, helped me to better understand this significant phase of General Wood's public career.

Sanford Cobb, who once headed the Sears book department and is highly knowledgeable about publishing, not only served as the source of much useful information from his own Sears/Wood experience but also gave me expert counsel during the years I spent preparing this book. I am grateful for his assistance in the difficult task of devising an orderly plan for organizing and presenting the complex array of materials of which it is comprised.

Fortunately for my purposes, both General Wood and one of his principal aides, James M. Barker, on separate occasions recorded their "Reminiscences" with the Oral History Collection of Columbia University. My thanks go to The Trustees of Columbia University in the City of New York for permission to quote liberally from both documents. I am equally obliged to Dale Mayer and the staff of the Herbert Hoover Presidential Library of West Branch, Iowa, for their courtesy in giving me access to their collection of General Wood's personal papers.

This book was readied for publication during a period of major technological innovation in the publishing industry. While early versions of the manuscript were typed in traditional fashion by Julia Taylor, subsequent versions, including the final one, were prepared on a sophisticated word processor by Stuart Halliday. Instead of a typed manuscript, the University of Illinois Press received a set of floppy disks from which type was set by electronic means, thereby materially reducing the time and costs of manufacturing this book. Both Taylor and Halliday are staff members of the J. L. Kellogg Graduate School of Management of Northwestern University. I am grateful for their help. Hard copies of a late version of the text, generated by high-speed photocopying equipment, were provided to advance readers through the good offices of Patricia Mottram of my old firm, Cresap, McCormick and Paget.

Three individuals took time away from their busy schedules to read the manuscript in its entirety: J. Michael Lennon, my former colleague at Sangamon State University; Harold F. Williamson, my present colleague at Northwestern University; and Burleigh B. Gardner, my long-time friend identified above. I benefited immeasurably from their critical advice.

It was my great good fortune to have as my editor Pamela Lee Espeland, to whose keen editorial judgment this book owes much and for which I am deeply grateful.

Finally, I wish to express my appreciation to the staff of the University of Illinois Press for their patience and encouragement during the latter stages of completing this book.

PROLOGUE

D URING THE THIRTY years of General Robert E. Wood's leadership, Sears, Roebuck and Co. grew to become not merely a major
economic enterprise but also a unique American institution. In part, the
company's course during those years was shaped by powerful underlying
trends—economic, social, and political. But the company's response to
these trends, the manner in which it converted problems into opportunities, was largely the work of a single man. Because of General Wood,
Sears * response differed materially from that of other major corporations.

What distinguished Wood from most leading businessmen of his time
was a special concern for human values. Entering the merchandising field
from a military background, he devised a plan of organization and a style
of management based essentially on the principle of encouraging and developing people. In doing so, he had no formal body of theory to draw
upon nor any significant predecessor to emulate, for at the time most accepted theory and prevailing practice pointed in contrary directions.

Wood was one of the major American businessmen during the first
half of the twentieth century, but his career is of more than historical interest. Today's—and tomorrow's—managers can learn much from studying
the ways Wood dealt with the challenges he faced. Modern managers con-
front different problems in different frameworks, and actions which were
appropriate and effective for Wood may be inappropriate and dysfunctional
today. But the values which underlay and guided his actions are as valid

---

* Sears official style manual sternly forbids use of the apostrophe to denote the pos-
sessive case of the company's name. From long habit, I have followed that style throughout
this book.

now as they were then and will remain so many long years hence. It is instructive, therefore, to observe these values as they were expressed in the complex interactions among a man, his company, and his era. There was obviously a close relationship among the three. Wood joined Sears at a highly propitious time; the company was at the end of one stage of its evolution, and it and the country were ready to move in new and untried directions. If Wood and Sears had come together twenty-five years earlier or twenty-five years later, the course each took might have been markedly different.

Sears helped shape Wood in many important ways. It is interesting to speculate on what Wood might have done and become if the Du Ponts had made him an offer sufficiently attractive to induce him to remain in that family-dominated company, or if World War I had not intervened and he had stayed in the asphalt business after leaving Du Pont. Many of Wood's distinctive personal traits would undoubtedly have surfaced in these other settings, but they probably would have expressed themselves in ways quite dissimilar from the ways they expressed themselves at Sears. His concern for people, his feelings about business's obligations to the community, his recognition of the dependence of a retail enterprise on a stable and prosperous body of consumers, his instincts for building public acceptance and support—these and other characteristics which were so prominent in Wood found a singularly encouraging environment in Sears and proved singularly useful to it. How they might have fitted into and developed within another environment can only be guessed.

A pair of companies and a pair of men offer interesting contrasts: Montgomery Ward and Sears, Roebuck; Sewell Avery and General Wood. Both Avery and Wood headed companies which to outward appearances had much in common. Both were combinations of mail-order plants and nationwide systems of retail stores; both were headquartered in Chicago. And the two men were contemporaries. But there the resemblances ended. Avery was one of the most autocratic big businessmen of this century; Wood, one of the most democratic. Ward's under Avery was tightly centralized and rigidly controlled; Sears under Wood was highly decentralized and permissive to a degree unique in large-scale organizations.

The contrasts between the two companies and the men who headed them are made more intriguing by the fact that Wood worked five years for Ward's before joining Sears. Had he eventually assumed the presidency, Ward's would have been a vastly different company from what it was under

Avery. But it still would not have become what Sears became. At Sears, Wood inherited the warm, friendly, humane traditions established by his predecessor, Julius Rosenwald—traditions Ward's lacked. Absent these, Sears, too, would have turned out otherwise. And even given them, it goes without saying that Sears under Avery would not have been the same.

It is often said that an organization is the lengthened shadow of a man. It would be truer to say that an organization seeks out men who are compatible with its traditions and culture—or that men move most readily to the top in organizations whose traditions and culture fit best with their own personalities and values. It is telling that in their few years together General Wood and Montgomery Ward were very uncomfortable with each other and the relationship did not last. Wood and Sears, on the other hand, got along extremely well from the start and stayed together for many years—as did Avery and Ward's, once they found each other. What is significant for present purposes is that both Sears and Wood were fortunate in coming together, that each helped shape the other, and that Sears was a better company and Wood a better man because by historic accident their paths converged.

It was my own good fortune to join Sears as General Wood was approaching the peak of his career and to hold positions which brought me into frequent contact with him, enabling me to observe his actions and their consequences firsthand. I was in such positions, in fact, for over half the period during which he was the company's chief executive officer. On more than one occasion, I sought to persuade him to set down in an orderly and systematic fashion the body of principles which informed and guided his practice as a businessman. But my efforts were entirely without success; the notion of putting forth his ideas in any complete fashion left him cold.

Wood had a superb mind. He thought long and deeply on the work in which he was engaged, but he left only a fragmentary record of his thoughts. For a man in his position he made relatively few speeches, and these he always wrote himself. They were not always models of syntax, but they were invariably clear and intelligible; he had no difficulty making himself understood. Almost without exception, his speeches were brief—even his formal addresses on major occasions—and restricted to a single topic or a narrow range of topics. When he spoke or wrote, he was interested only in what was directly relevant to the particular situation. His letters and internal memoranda usually dealt with highly specific matters and gave the sketchiest, if any, rationale behind his decisions and directives. In other words, nowhere is there a systematic statement of the whole body of his thought—and yet his practice reveals that such a whole body of thought did exist, and that its elements were organically related. It was not part of Wood's temperament to spell these out in any consistent, coherent way; rather, it was his instinct to act according to his principles, and it is in his actions that his whole body of thought is revealed. He was first and always a man of action, and his spoken and written words were in fact themselves simply one of his means of acting.

Actions are ephemeral, however, and leave few enduring footprints. It has been said of Wood that Sears was his monument. But Sears is no marble statue, and in any event an organization makes a poor monument. Built of fragile, malleable materials, it does not stay the same. It shifts and changes as conditions shift and change, as new hands take over. The Sears, Roebuck thirty years after Wood retired is a very different organization from what it was when Wood was in his prime. There are many evidences of Wood still around, but they are overlaid with heavy accretions and difficult to recognize.

It is unfortunate that Robert Wood did not write *My Years at Sears, Roebuck*, as Alfred Sloan wrote *My Years at General Motors*;[1] if he had, the literature of management would be richer. In writing this book, I have sought to do for Wood what he did not do for himself—and, in a sense, what John McDonald, Sloan's editor, did for Sloan. Regrettably, I did not enjoy the advantage McDonald did of having his subject alive and personally involved in the writing. Time and again, it would have been enormously helpful to ask Wood what the true facts of a certain situation were, or what his real reasons were for doing some of the things he did. But this is a luxury I did not have.

Toward the close of Wood's active business career, a member of the Sears headquarters personnel staff wrote in an internal memorandum addressed to me:

> What has been achieved at Sears this last quarter century is not just a business success. It is a development of a way of life, of principles and beliefs, of a "constitutional system," if you will. Our success and standing in this country, including even our business success, surely depend as much on our leadership here as they depend on our merchandising ability.
>
> Yet this Sears way of life, this "Sears Constitution," is lived rather than expressed. Of course, principles are not good unless they

are being lived, and nothing could be further from our way of doing things—or less effective—than pious lip service to great principles. But fundamentals, once they have been realized in living, also need verbal formulation. A religion needs both saint and dogma, a society both morality and law. Without actual living, principles become empty hypocrisy. Without formulation, they become fond memories.

Those of us who have been so fortunate as to work close to General Wood need no formulation to know what it is he and the Sears he built stand for. But how many of us are there? And how long will we be here? Yet, the General himself has primarily acted rather than spoken. For this reason it is important that we formulate the principles, the experience, and the meaning of Sears. When those who can bear personal testimony are no longer here, it may stand as a testament and a guide.[2]

As noted above, Wood's total lack of interest in setting forth his body of thought precluded his leaving behind such a testament and guide. Thus, when his successors faced their own problems of running the company, they had nothing concrete to which to refer and had to feel their way. At first gradually and then inexorably, Sears drifted away from much that Wood personified. He himself remained the saint, but the dogma was missing. And because the principles on which he acted were never systematically formulated, they became in time little more than fond memories.

As one of the remaining few who had the privilege of working with General Wood, I have set my hand at this very late date to describing in reasonably orderly fashion the principles embodied in Wood's business career. This study does not purport to be anything remotely resembling a "Sears Constitution"—the day when such a document might have served a useful purpose is long since gone—but it does seek to record the managerial values and methods of a major American business leader who should be remembered not only for what he accomplished but for the uniquely creative ways he did so.

This is not a biography in the usual sense of the term. Rather than tracing Wood's life in a purely chronological fashion, it focuses on his managerial philosophies and practices. Since these had distinct characteristics, they are treated here distinctly, as individual topics and not as events on the timeline of the General's life. When introducing and developing a new topic, it was often necessary to go back in time to a period previously discussed and view it again from another perspective or to move forward into the future to consider its eventual scope and impact. As a result, this book is built around a structure that differs in a number of respects from those found in other biographies. The reader may find it helpful to begin by reviewing the following description.

Part I, "The Chronology," establishes a chronological framework for the body of the book.

Chapter 1 sketches in broad outline the major features of General Wood's life up to the time he joined Sears, Roebuck in late 1924. It emphasizes those events and influences which shaped his mature business and managerial character, specifically: his early habituation to command responsibilities; his exposure during the building of the Panama Canal to men of remarkable administrative capabilities; his learning to handle successfully the intricate service-of-supply problems in Panama and during World War I; and the emergence of the idea of integrating mass production and mass distribution to serve better the rapidly diversifying needs of the American people. One of Wood's most striking characteristics was his ability to learn from experience, and much of what proved most significant in his later career traces back to these early years.

Chapter 2 encapsulates the history of Sears, Roebuck and Co. under Richard Sears and Julius Rosenwald, and Chapter 3 recounts the principal events of Wood's life during his Sears years and after.

Part II, "The Strategies," presents Wood's basic ideas about the kind of company he wanted Sears to be.

Chapter 4 describes the goal he set for the company: in his words, "lowering the costs and raising the standard of living of the American people." To achieve this goal, he fashioned a dual strategy: a buying strategy to integrate mass production and mass distribution, and a selling strategy to penetrate the rapidly growing urban middle-class market. Through the buying strategy—described in Chapter 5—he built a system of efficient, reliable sources of supply based on the recognition of the mutuality of interests between producer and distributor and the need for stable, long-term buyer-seller relationships. Through the selling strategy—described in Chapter 6—he created a nationwide (and eventually hemisphere-wide) network of retail stores and catalog plants closely geared to the changing demographic and economic characteristics of consumer markets.

Part III, "The Policies," details the operating policies Wood skillfully crafted in five key areas to accomplish his defined business purpose.

Chapter 7 focuses on the measures Wood fashioned to build a very large organization unique for its remarkable degree of decentralization and reliance on individual initiative and judgment. Such a structure placed a premium on having people at all key points in the organization who were capable of carrying the significant levels of responsibility required to make the system work. This, in turn, called for major innovations in management personnel policies and practices—the subject of Chapter 8.

Wood recognized early the need for close and continuing attention to employee relations in a widely dispersed organization where authority and responsibility were broadly delegated. Knowing that employee goodwill and support were essential, he structured and managed the organization to foster these attitudes. Sears became noteworthy not only for its high level of performance but also for the humane values it represented. Chapter 9 examines the means by which these ends were accomplished.

General Wood was among the small minority of business leaders in his generation who recognized the pivotal nature of corporate public policies. He was one of the first major business leaders to have a concept of corporate social responsibility and to develop practices specifically designed around it. He recognized Sears stake in a sound and vigorous economy and deliberately shaped company policies to help strengthen the industrial base of the communities and regions important to Sears. His approach to public relations was not the typical one of seeking to change public attitudes to suit business purposes; rather, he sought to change business practices to merit public support. These issues are discussed in Chapter 10.

Chapter 11 treats Wood's entrepreneurial policies. His entrepreneurial spirit was expressed not only in his Sears career proper but also in the launching of the Allstate Insurance Company, in Sears penetration of the Latin American and Canadian markets, and in the company's great post–World War II domestic expansion.

Dealing with the manager necessitates dealing with the man; in Part IV, "The Man," the emphasis shifts from the strategies and policies, principles and practices to the unique individual behind them.

While the General would have been offended to be called a "politician," he exhibited an extraordinarily high level of political skill and astuteness in the way he identified and mobilized the support of constituencies, internal and external, necessary to accomplish his purposes. His methods and achievements in this regard are examined in Chapter 12. Chapter 13 presents a series of vignettes—personal sketches—of a very human being with a full share of personal idiosyncracies.

Chapter 14 seeks to place General Wood in the context of his times and to evaluate the significance of his contributions to business enterprise and managerial practice. While not all of his contributions were positive, on balance they fall strongly on the positive side.

Finally, given the dramatic recent developments at Sears, this book would not be complete without an Epilogue placing these developments within their historic context and evaluating their significance for the company's future.

PART I

THE CHRONOLOGY

1

Robert E. Wood: The Early Years

ALTHOUGH HIS CAREER spanned a large part of the world, Robert Elkington Wood's roots were firmly planted in the midwestern United States. He was born in June 1879 in Kansas City, Missouri, the eldest of five children.[1] His mother, Lillie Collins, was the daughter of an Irish immigrant who fought as a captain in the Civil War. His father, Robert Whitney Wood, was successively a farm boy in central New York State, a Kansas homesteader, a fighter in the bloody struggle to bring Kansas into the Union as a free state, a lieutenant in John Brown's raiders, a gold prospector in Colorado, a captain in the Union Army with a distinguished combat record, and finally a coal and ice merchant in Kansas City, where he was known as a staunch Republican.

When Robert Wood was a boy, the frontier was still not far from Kansas City; he often saw the covered wagons going down to Oklahoma, and watched with admiration as the town marshal and his deputies practiced pistol shooting outside their office in the central part of town.

These were years of intense agricultural unrest, especially in that part of the country. Farmers were struggling under heavy loads of mortgage debt and defenseless against the exactions of the railroads on which they depended for the movement of their crops. Eastern financial interests, the bête noire of the populist movement then sweeping the prairies, were perceived as the villains on both counts. As the son of a man who all his life was involved in the concerns of his times, young Wood must have been aware of and was probably sympathetic with the demands of the Grangers, then at the height of their power, for laws limiting railroad rates and warehouse charges. He must have been familiar with the agitation for the bimetallist monetary policy designed to improve farm prices and ease the burden of debt service. The year of his graduation from high school was the year William Jennings Bryan electrified the grain belt of the country with his ringing cry, "They shall not crucify mankind upon this cross of gold"; one did not have to be a Democrat to be moved.

Robert Wood's mother, much younger than his father, had once taught school and inculcated in her children a love of reading and a keen desire for education. In an era when few young men thought of attending college, and in a part of the country where few of these thought of attending one of the great Ivy League schools, Wood set his sights on Yale, where his father promised to send him. Unfortunately, the senior Wood's business suffered in the hard times which followed the panic of 1893 and the cost of Yale posed difficulties, particularly because the other four children indicated strong desires for college educations as well.

To ease the burden on his father, of whom he was very fond, Robert proposed that he attend tuition-free West Point. Under law, appointments to the military academy are made by members of Congress, and at the time these were customarily handled on a straightforward patronage basis. Robert called on the congressman from his district, who happened to be a Democrat, and was told, "Wood, I can't appoint you, you're a Republican and I may have some good Democrat who wants the appointment." In an early demonstration of his powers of persuasion, Robert prevailed upon the reluctant congressman to make his selection through the then unorthodox procedure of competitive examination. The examination was held, Robert bested his opponents, and the congressman appointed him to the academy, where he enrolled in 1896.

Wood was not one of the academy's star cadets chiefly because, in his own words, he "detested the discipline." On the other hand, he later recalled, "the studies came easy to me because I liked math and so I stood high except for my demerits. I was very careless and got plenty of demerits. But I've always felt very grateful to the military academy, because I was a raw, and undisciplined kid. I was the youngest man in my class, and it made a man of me. I felt the impress of that education all my life. . . . I still think, it's a narrow education, but it's a thorough education." [2]

The academic demands were rigorous. Because of the small size of the Army at that time, there was no great demand for officers; instead of helping students who might need it, the faculty deliberately sought to eliminate as many as possible. Wood was one of those who survived and in 1900 graduated thirteenth in a class of fifty-four.

Rather than receiving the customary ten-week graduation leave, he was ordered to join his regiment immediately and within a matter of days was on a transport bound for China and the Boxer Rebellion. En route, it was learned that Peking had fallen, and the group was diverted to the Philippines and the Aguinaldo insurrection. Here Wood spent two years "up in the bush, 150 miles north of the railroad . . . chasing these guerillas through the mountains." A year later, Aguinaldo was captured and the insurrection collapsed. Meanwhile Wood had been promoted to first lieutenant and at twenty-one found himself in command of a troop of cavalry, 100 men and 100 horses strong. "I've never felt so important since," he subsequently reminisced. "I sort of fancied myself a second Napoleon." He seems not to have minded the role: "In my little town of 6,000 people, the troop commander was the mayor, the judge, he decided the ownership of chickens, of animals, even of wives. So it was a great experience for a young man, and I enjoyed it thoroughly."

Despite the prevalence of fever and dysentery, Wood remained in good health. On being ordered home in 1902, he and his men marched 200 miles down to Manila, turned in their horses, and boarded a transport bound for the States.

He was next posted to Fort Assiniboine, Montana, where he found himself with little to do and plenty of time on his hands. Still,

> for a young man it was a fascinating life. You could drop your reins on your horse's neck and you could ride 100 miles in any direction with no fences. We were only 15 miles from the Canadian line, and that was before the immigration to Canada, Western Canada, and the country was all virgin prairie. The plow had never touched it. We used to ride up to a Mountie post at Medicine Hat. But there were no people there. Plenty of game, geese, prairie chickens—so that again was interesting.

Much as Wood loved hunting and fishing, "I didn't want to spend my life doing that." He considered taking a job building a railroad in Mexico, but decided against it after meeting the promoter for whom he would work. He was next detailed to West Point as an instructor in French ("I had a thorough knowledge of the grammar of the language and I could read it, but I couldn't speak it.") Although he enjoyed being back at the academy, he soon concluded he "wasn't cut out to teach." However, one rewarding feature of this period of his life was his meeting Mary Hardwick of Augusta, Georgia, whom he later married.

The U.S. acquisition of rights to build the Panama Canal and the initiation of steps to organize what quickly became known as "the biggest job on earth" caught the restless young officer's attention. He applied for transfer to the project and was ordered to the Isthmus in the spring of 1905.

The task of digging the "Big Ditch" involved much more than solving great problems of engineering and construction; it imposed managerial problems of unprecedented magnitude. Tens of thousands of workers had to be recruited from the United States, the West Indies, and Europe. They and their families had to be housed and fed. All supplies and equipment for the huge undertaking had to be brought in from faraway points in the United States. A government to handle the myriad details of municipal administration, including police and judicial functions, had to be provided. The lack of sufficient public health and sanitation facilities posed special problems. All the essentials of large-scale community living had to be created ad hoc and managed as part of the Canal-building enterprise.[3]

Equally dramatic was the fact that within two weeks of Wood's arrival yellow fever, historically endemic to the area and an important factor in the failure of previous efforts to dig the Canal, exploded in the "Great Scare." The death toll was heavy. In addition to yellow fever, malaria, pneumonia, tuberculosis, and intestinal diseases were rampant. There were also two cases of bubonic plague, which added a special note of terror to the prevailing mood.[4] During the summer of 1905, three-fourths of the Americans working on the Canal fled for home. Wood was warned about the hazards before leaving for Panama, but laughingly replied, "I don't intend to get sick."[5]

For Wood's purposes, the timing of his move could not have been more opportune. Work on fashioning the Canal organization and developing the various institutional and administrative systems required was still in a very early stage, and he was in a position not only to observe their evolution but also to participate in shaping them. In his words, "it was an ideal situation for a youngster. The chief engineer resigned, the assistant chief engineer resigned, most of the top echelon—it was just as if there had been a corporation office with the president and the vice president and all the first grade executives resigning, and second stringers too. For once the job was looking for the man: anyone who would stay was promoted. I was promoted three times in three months."

Thus, early during the work on the Canal, Wood was firmly positioned near the top of the organizational hierarchy. His rapid advancement, however, did not come simply by default. He arrived in Panama about the time the hitherto inept leadership of the huge project was replaced by an exceptionally able administrator, John Stevens. Young Wood was spotted early by Stevens as having the potential to play a major role in the sweeping reorganization he planned, and Wood amply justified Stevens's confidence by his handling of successively larger responsibilities. Stevens was succeeded in 1907 by Colonel (later General) George W. Goethals, who saw the task of building the Canal through to successful completion in 1915; Wood was one of his key executives throughout this entire period.

Goethals was a brilliant engineer whose whole attention was devoted to the vast earth-moving and construction phases of the giant project— a horrendous undertaking that had been the downfall of a succession of men. The tasks of recruiting, housing, feeding, and governing a work force which reached 50,000 at its peak bored him, and he was only too glad to leave them to the able and willing young Wood. Nor did Goethals want to be bothered by the onerous chore of ensuring the enormous quantities of supplies and materials required; he placed this responsibility on Wood's shoulders with the stern admonition: "The day we run out of cement, you're fired."

An uninterrupted flow of cement to the construction site was a vital requirement, but meeting it posed serious difficulties. Because of the hot, humid conditions on the Isthmus, cement could not be stored for more than a short time, so there was no practical way of building up reserve stocks; instead, the flow had to be closely geared to the pace of construction. Closed-bid procurement was too cumbersome for this kind of fine tuning. Wood therefore broke with traditional government practice and proceeded to negotiate directly with contractors selected for their reliability. They were guaranteed stated volumes of purchases at agreed upon prices provided that they met specified delivery schedules. Cement had to move from mills in Pennsylvania to the Port of New York for loading onto ships shuttling back and forth to Colon, where it was transshipped again for delivery to the construction face. The total process was carefully synchronized.

Wood learned much from his Panama Canal experience that was to serve him well throughout his career:

> Without knowing it, I was getting a wonderful education. . . . I had the whole supply system of the Canal. I was chief procurement officer. . . . I was buying steel rails, locomotives, cars and spare parts and I learned the principle of handling inventory . . . and then it gave me the business experience. I was a director of the Panama Canal Railroad [and] I was getting a magnificent preparation for my commercial career. . . . As I've often said, I made more money since but I never loved a job like that Canal.[6]

Much of the pleasure and value of the experience he owed to the excellent preceptors under whom he worked. The first of these, John Stevens, was a product of the building of the Great Northern Railroad and of railroad entrepreneur James J. Hill's system of picking good men, giving them tremendous authority, and holding them strictly accountable. Stevens brought the Hill philosophy to Panama, where it produced brilliant results and clearly left a lasting impression on young Wood as an effective means of managing large undertakings.

But it was from George Goethals that Wood undoubtedly learned the most. Goethals was a stern taskmaster whom Wood described admiringly as a man of "iron will and terrific energy." Long afterward he recalled, "I was his assistant for seven years, and I might say that everything in my life since has been comparatively easy." [7]

Few people loved or even liked Goethals, but nearly all who knew him were impressed by him. He combined an ability to see the large picture with a mastery of detail. As an observer sent to the Canal by President Theodore Roosevelt reported: "Not only did he show that he knew his business thoroughly, had absolute grasp of the work as a whole, but that he had at his tongue's end more knowledge of details than any of his immediate subordinates." [8]

One of Goethals's distinguishing traits was his sense of justice, and he went to then unusual lengths to build fairness into the workings of the organization. An especially dramatic means to that end was the open court he held every Sunday morning to give employees of all ranks and nationalities a chance to air their grievances—a practice unheard of in the labor relations of that era. The morale of the work force under his leadership was exceptionally high and remained so for the duration of the project. As Wood himself later testified, "Men reported for work early and stayed late, without overtime. . . . I really believe that every American employed would have worked that [last] year without pay, if only to see the first ship pass through the completed Canal. That spirit went down to all the laborers." [9]

The Panama Canal experience laid much of the foundation for Wood's later career. While still a very young man, he became accustomed to carrying major administrative responsibilities. He had the good fortune to work directly with superb administrators from whom he learned a great deal, not the least of which was the importance of worker morale to high levels of achievement. Significant, too, for his later work were the perceptions he gained from organizing and managing a complex supply service stretching over 2,000 miles under logistic conditions and command requirements that allowed little room for slippage or miscalculation. It was this phase of his experience which began to form in his mind the conception of a distributive system as a continuous flow process from raw materials through manufacturing to the ultimate user, a conception he was to elaborate further in his work as quartermaster general and bring to full fruition as head of Sears, Roebuck and Co. His substitution of direct negotiations with selected contractors for closed-bid procurement provided the germ from which later grew the concept of "known-cost buying," which was basic to the system of merchandising developed under his leadership at Sears. One aspect of his Canal experience in which Wood, then and later, took great pride was that in spending the vast sums for which he was responsible, "there was never a single scandal, never a penny of graft. It was a 100 per cent clean job."

On completion of the Canal in 1915, Wood and a small group of fellow officers with extended service on the Canal were permitted by special act of a grateful Congress to retire early with full benefits and advancement in rank (Wood was thirty-five and advanced to a major). In 1908 he had married Mary Hardwick, who shared his desire for a large family, and by this time four of their five children had been born. In search of a job that would be both challenging and monetarily rewarding, he applied successfully to the Du Pont Company, which was then in the process of greatly expanding its physical plant to handle huge contracts for powder which had been received from the hard-pressed French and British governments. Capitalizing on one phase of Wood's Canal experience, the Du Ponts placed him in charge of housing and feeding the very large crews that had to be hired for the construction work.[10]

His new employers were pleased with him—so much so that they raised his pay every month. Nevertheless, he was dissatisfied and before long informed Pierre Du Pont that he was resigning. "What's the matter?" asked Du Pont. "Haven't we treated you right?" "No," he replied, "you've treated me wonderfully. But this company is headed by Du Ponts. They're all able men. There's no chance for me to get to the top." Pierre and his brothers were much amused that "Major Wood is going to leave us because he wants our jobs."

Wood was strengthened in his decision by having in hand an offer from General Asphalt Company, whose president had visited him in Panama. General Asphalt was opening up large operations in Venezuela and Trinidad and was interested in Wood because of his knowledge of the trop-

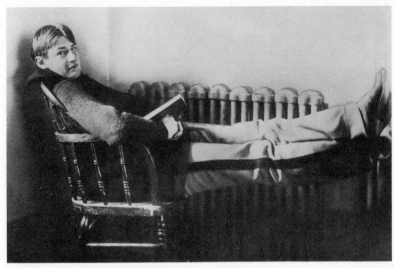

Cadet Robert E. Wood, West Point, Class of 1900.

Captain Robert E. Wood with son Robert, Panama, 1914.

Brigadier General Robert E. Wood, Acting Quartermaster General, 1918.

ics. He was made assistant to the president and placed in charge of all production, both at home and abroad, a position he held a little over a year and a half until the United States declared war on Germany on April 6, 1917.

In his retired status, Wood was under no formal obligation to volunteer for military service, and he had substantial reasons not to: a wife, five children, and a mother and sister to support. Even so, he felt he owed a debt that required payment: "I had a terrible struggle, inwardly, between my duty to my family and my duty to my country. . . . But after all, I'd gotten my education from Uncle Sam, I got it free, I got it for one purpose—and I knew if I didn't go back, I could never look anybody in the eye. [It] was tough on my wife, but I had to do it." He was assigned at once to his old boss, George Goethals, who had been promoted to general during the Canal period and who was now head of wartime shipbuilding. Goethals placed him in charge of organizing the purchasing of supplies for the program. But as Wood saw men he had known at West Point going to France on combat missions, he quickly grew restless with his stateside duties, and when General Douglas MacArthur, whom he had known at West Point, offered him a colonelcy in the newly organized Rainbow Division, he accepted with alacrity.

He led the division's advance party of officers in August of 1917. While waiting in St. Nazaire for the division's arrival, he came to the attention of General William W. Atterbury, who had been called from the presidency of the Pennsylvania Railroad to take charge of all transportation for the American Expeditionary Force in France. Atterbury had numerous railroad men to help him but no one knowledgeable in port operations. Because Wood had been responsible for, among other things, the water terminals in Panama, Atterbury asked for him and detailed him to that critical task.

At the time Wood took over, there was a great tie-up at the ports, which seriously threatened pending military operations: ships were being held in harbor as long as forty days before they could even start to be unloaded. Wood moved quickly to increase the speed of unloading once the ships had docked, but he saw at once that the root of the problem was deeper. With the personal backing of General John J. Pershing, to whom he promised results in thirty days, Colonel Wood arranged to secure in advance highly classified information on convoy arrival schedules and the content of ship cargoes. With this information, he was able to distribute the load between ports and to direct cargoes with special handling problems, such as locomotives, to ports having the necessary unloading equipment. He kept his thirty-day pledge to General Pershing.

Soon afterward he was recalled to Washington and in April of 1918, at the age of thirty-nine, Wood was promoted to brigadier general with responsibility for all services of supply to the American Expeditionary Force. His superiors (one of whom was General Goethals, now assistant chief of staff) skirted the legal requirement that the quartermaster general post be filled from the Quartermaster Corps by naming him acting quartermaster general. "I didn't care about the title," Wood said later. "All I wanted was to get the job and get it over with."

He found the Quartermaster Department in a state of utter disarray. In less than a year, it had expanded from an organization of about 300 permanent officers to something in the range of 10,000. Fiscal controls were loose and varying degrees of venality fairly common; Wood corrected both conditions promptly and decisively. Some of the officers he inherited were capable, and those who were not were replaced. He set out immediately to recruit a corps of civilians experienced in the kinds of work he needed done: packers from Chicago, merchants from Boston, heavy machinery men from Detroit. Some took commissions and were placed in command of depots, while others were dollar-a-year men who assumed the demanding task of procuring and transporting the complex range and vast tonnage of supplies needed by a modern army fighting on the far side of an ocean. It was the youthful General Wood who played a large part in building and managing the pipeline that placed the output of American industry in the hands of its fighting soldiers and those of its Allies: "The big thing was, we always kept the Army well-supplied. And the Army, of course, was the best-fed and the best-clothed, and best-equipped army in Europe. It was the overwhelming weight of our production that won the war."

There were, of course, as Wood acknowledged, "some horrible mistakes." For example, a supply clerk with a limited grasp of geography shipped by fast freight a carload of arctic overshoes to Yuma, Arizona, in summer, and a lieutenant steeped in traditional military technology shipped 300,000 horse blankets to France. But the main task was accomplished and the Allied armies had what they needed to win the war. Wood received the Distinguished Service Medal in recognition of his work.

In the process of discharging his duties, he added richly to his mounting store of experience. He learned a great deal about American industry, mass procurement, and large-scale organization. He sharpened his skill at seeing through symptoms to underlying causes. He was impressed with the kind of monumental goofs that can result from the overcentralization of decision making on operational details. He mastered logistical problems of great complexity, and he saw again at firsthand the value of finding able assistants and giving them large measures of authority. And once more he worked in close company with gifted administrators, including his old mentor General Goethals and new preceptors such as Army Chief of Staff Peyton C. March and Secretary of War Newton Baker.

As it happened, Wood's involvement in the war effort initiated the chain of circumstances that led him into his merchandising career. With the coming of the Armistice, Wood was impatient to get back to civilian life. The challenge, of course, no longer lay in Washington, and he could not support his large family on his Army pay. He was finally released in March of 1919, but only after having first settled up most of the unexpired war production contracts.

On retiring again from military service, the General, as he was always thereafter known, joined Montgomery Ward & Co., then run by five Thorne brothers and principally owned by the Thorne family. Robert Julius Thorne, president of Ward's, had been a civilian on Wood's staff and one of his great admirers. He saw in Wood a constellation of abilities and experience that could be of great value to his company. His opinion was justified; Wood probably knew more than any man then living about merchandise sources, mass buying techniques, and supply logistics. When Thorne invited Wood to become Ward's merchandising vice-president, the General accepted not only because of the challenge it represented but also because of the opportunity it afforded him to return to the Midwest, with which he felt a special affinity. He assumed his new responsibilities in March of 1919.

With Thorne's support, Wood set about introducing fundamental changes in Ward's approach to merchandise procurement by replacing what he called "top down" buying with "bottom up" buying.[11] Under the traditional "top down" approach, common to all merchandising houses of the time, the starting point in negotiations was the manufacturer's list price; the merchandise buyer sought to get the largest discount possible from list price, using all the powers of persuasion and economic pressure he could bring to bear. Each transaction stood on its own, and the buyer shifted from one source to another according to where he could drive the hardest bargain.

In the "bottom up" approach introduced by Wood, the buyer started not from the manufacturer's list price but from the cost of the raw material.

13

To this, during negotiations with the manufacturer, were added the costs of efficient conversion into finished products and a reasonable profit to determine the cost of the goods to Ward's. The General would tolerate no manufacturing frills. For example, no advertising or selling costs were to be included because Ward's bore these directly. He instructed his buyers to select as sources only those whose organizations were simple, efficient, and focused on producing goods of the desired quality at the lowest possible cost. He insisted that this be achieved through productive efficiency and not at the expense of value. The profit itself was subject to negotiation.

The "bottom up" approach was a direct outgrowth of Wood's Panama Canal and World War I experiences. In the absence of closed-bid procurement, which had proved much too cumbersome for either of these endeavors, some rational means had to be devised to determine prices, and Wood had found the most effective mechanism to be a process of negotiation based on the costs of raw material and efficient conversion. At Ward's he simply sought to apply in a normal commercial setting what he had learned earlier in the special circumstances of building the Canal and supplying the wartime Army.

He first put his theory into practice in the buying of tires and batteries. During the early 1920s, automobiles were coming rapidly into common use, and people were not getting good values on replacement tires and batteries. In seeking to determine the cost of raw material to the tire manufacturer as the first step in arriving at a satisfactory purchase price, he quickly found that the producer was compelled to set his figures high enough to cover the wide fluctuations in the market price of rubber likely to occur over a year's time. Wood's solution was to tell the manufacturer, "We'll buy the rubber so you can have a fixed price on your raw material and we'll gamble on when to buy." He made similar arrangements with battery sources for purchase of the lead they needed.

In this period, neither Ward's nor Sears enjoyed a good reputation with manufacturers, whose experience with the mail-order giants' traditional buying practices had often, from their standpoint, left much to be desired. Wood found it necessary to spend considerable time meeting with manufacturers around the country, explaining his new approach and endeavoring to secure from them the cooperation which was essential to its success. In these meetings, as well as in instructions to his buyers, he insisted that the manufacturers who could produce at low costs must realize a reasonable profit consistent with the risks run. The meetings were successful and generated favorable reactions both to the new policy and its author, and many doors of first-class sources that had been firmly shut were now open to Ward's buyers. Reflecting the impact of the new approach to buying, the values of Ward's merchandise offerings began to show significant improvement, and the company made a good recovery from the sharp recession of 1921.

The recession had caught Ward's, as well as Sears and many other merchandising houses, with excess inventories. As one means of moving these, Wood opened temporary retail stores in the company's mail-order plants and invited the public in to buy the attractively priced goods. Because these plants were in cities, the customers brought in were not Ward's traditional rural customers, a fact which confirmed a conviction already forming in Wood's mind that stores in urban areas were a way to make the most of an entirely new market. His proposals for capitalizing on these possibilities fell on deaf ears. As it happened, this was only one of a series of frustrations he experienced at Ward's.

Despite his initial sponsorship by Robert Thorne, Wood never enjoyed a secure standing within the company. Ward's was a family company and Wood an outsider. He was, moreover, openly critical of conditions which he considered evidence of poor management. He later confided to one of his early Sears associates that the people who were running the company at that time "didn't know anything about what they were doing. They were heading straight for disaster. Every decision they made was questionable." [12] Wood was not alone in his feeling on this score; J. Charles Maddison, one of the few nonfamily officers of Ward's at that time, bluntly told Robert Thorne in 1920: "For sloppy, incomplete, grossly inefficient work, we must be near the limit and I think it high time the president recognized it." [13]

Despite his excellent rapport with Robert Thorne, Wood's relationship with other members of the Thorne family soon began to show strain. Leslie Kountze, daughter of Charles Thorne, chairman of the board, later wrote: "Mr. Wood did not work well with Father. [Wood] was a spender, sometimes to excess, was highly opinionated and stubborn. Father controlled the purse strings and they were frequently at dagger's points." [14]

Wood had begun to develop an interest in retail stores well before the opening of Ward's temporary outlets. Early in his Ward career, he proposed to open an experimental automobile supply store in connection with the company's farm implement warehouse in Atlanta. Chairman Charles Thorne vetoed the idea firmly: "Frankly, our business is to promote the mail order business through the distribution of general catalogs carrying all lines. . . . [Wood's proposal] amounts to establishing a separate business and is of no value to us unless it produces sales for all the other departments. Merely selling a whole lot of goods is not our business." [15] By now, however, the Thorne family was on its way out. In a 1919 reorganization, the family had relinquished its longtime control to a New York financial group led by J. P. Morgan & Co., although active management continued for a while in the hands of the Thorne brothers. Concerned over operating problems and the severe inventory losses of the sharp recession, the New Yorkers pressured Robert Thorne to resign as president. He was replaced in January of 1921 with Theodore F. Merseles, who had been for the past eighteen years general manager of the National Cloak and Suit Company, a successful New York mail-order house.

Despite the upheavals in Ward's management, Wood's interest in retail stores had continued to grow, spurred on not only by the success of the temporary outlet stores but also by fundamental changes he saw taking place in the country. He was convinced that with the increasing mechanization of agriculture, the movement of population from farm to city would accelerate. He foresaw that the coming of good roads and the automobile would bring an end to rural isolation and a consequent erosion of Ward's traditional market. At the same time, he perceived greater merchandising opportunities in the cities and recognized the severe limitations of the catalog as a means of reaching that market. He was impressed with the rapid growth of chain stores, and in a November 1921 memorandum to Merseles he argued: "If we are so inclined, we can beat the chain stores at their own game. We can easily and profitably engage in the chain store business ourselves with a relatively small amount of capital." He cited Ward's advantages over existing chains: large and efficient distribution points in its four regional mail-order plants, a well-organized system for large-scale procurement, and "a wonderful name if we choose to take advantage of it." "I can see no reason," he added, "why we could not group 40 or 50 stores within a 100 mile radius of the four mail order houses, adding $20,000,000 of business."

Merseles, however, had other ideas. He was an experienced and able advertising man who believed that improving catalog copy and layout and increasing catalog circulation would be the most effective means of expanding sales. He maintained that the declining farm population simply meant that "the farmers who stayed home would enjoy more of the pie and be better customers." He also sought to improve service by tightening operations and by opening new branch mail-order plants closer to Ward's customers. He "was sure the mail order business would grow because many regions of the country still lacked modern shopping facilities and because farmers wanted higher quality items."

In fact, Merseles did a remarkable job of improving the catalog and mail-order operations. He had supreme confidence in the business as it was; he wanted nothing to do with retail stores and saw no particular merit in changing long-established buying practices. Wood, on the other hand, was firmly convinced that everything depended on the merchandise values offered the public and that the greatest business opportunities were to be found in the rapidly growing urban market. There were basic differences between Merseles's philosophy of advertising and Wood's philosophy of values, as well as between their conceptions of market opportunities. It gradually became apparent to both men that their differences were unbridgeable, and by the fall of 1924 the final break had become inevitable.

A contributing factor to the denouement was an unintended side effect of the meetings Wood had been holding with manufacturers. His intent in those meetings was simply to present his new ideas about buying and about relationships between Ward's and its sources. As it happened, their impact was more far-reaching: Wood soon attained greater visibility in the business world than Merseles himself. It came to be common talk in Chicago business circles, and probably elsewhere as well, that Wood would be the next president of Ward's, perhaps in the fairly near future. That Merseles grew increasingly irritated is understandable. By the fall of 1924, he had made his decision: Wood would have to go.

Merseles fired his vice president rather ungracefully; Wood received the news by telegram in late September while on a hunting trip in the West. The parting was acrimonious and left bitter feelings on both sides. In his absence, Wood's office was rifled and his files seized, over the vigorous objections of his secretary, Miss Jennie Mae Richardson.[16] Among the confiscated papers were plans Wood had drawn for a system of retail stores, along with various memoranda and data on which those plans were based.

The circumstances of his leaving Ward's were ever after a sensitive point with General Wood, and he liked to give the impression that he left of his own accord. In all probability he had decided to resign, but the facts are clear that Merseles moved first.

The General's four and a half years at Montgomery Ward were undoubtedly the most frustrating of his long career, but they were not without value. During that time he learned that his ideas for restructuring relationships with sources of supply were as applicable in normal commercial life as they had been in the special circumstances of building the Panama Canal and provisioning the American Expeditionary Force. His concept of integrating mass distribution with mass production to provide greater merchandise values to the public took explicit form, and he began to develop a sense of what consumers wanted and needed. Equally important, he saw for the first time that the mail-order business traditionally focused on rural America could be broadened through a system of retail stores to include the much larger market of the rapidly urbanizing American working and middle classes. His years at Ward's had their difficulties and defeats, but they prepared him for the opportunity he would soon have to work out his ideas in a more favorable environment.

2

Sears, Roebuck and Co.:
The Mail-Order Years

IN 1886, THE YEAR Wood was seven, twenty-three-year-old Richard
Warren Sears was station agent for the Minneapolis and St. Louis Railroad in North Redwood, Minnesota.[1] He was a farmer's son whose father
had died when Richard was sixteen, leaving him as the sole support of his
mother and sisters. Hard pressed financially, he had sought out the small-
salaried railroad post because in the hamlet of North Redwood the duties of
station agent were light and gave him an opportunity to make money on the
side, which his employer encouraged him and others like him to do. Young
Sears quickly built a thriving part-time business bringing in wood, coal,
and other products on which the railroad allowed him special rates. His
customers were local farmers and Indians from whom in turn he bought
produce to sell in other areas—again making use of his cut-rate shipping
privileges. Early in life, he developed marked skills as a trader.

One day Sears found himself with a carton of watches which had been
refused by the local jewelry store to which they were consigned. On advis-
ing the shipper that the watches were being returned, he was offered the
chance to sell them himself and keep as profit anything realized over $12 a
watch. He knew from trade catalogs he handled as station agent that this
was a good price. Intrigued with the possibility of augmenting his income,
he wrote other station agents up and down the railroad line, offering them
as many watches as they wanted at $14 each to sell for whatever over that
they could get. The shipment was disposed of in short order. After repeating
the experiment with several additional consignments of watches, which he
ordered expressly for the purpose, he quit his job on the railroad and moved

to Minneapolis where he could pursue more expeditiously what he now saw as an especially promising opportunity. There in 1886 he set up in business as the R. W. Sears Watch Company, with himself as sole owner. His success was immediate, and within a year the company had grown to a point where he felt obliged to transfer his operations to Chicago, a more central location with superior communications and shipping facilities.

By this time Sears had progressed beyond letter writing to advertising, chiefly in the numerous farm publications which were then popular and widely circulated. This greatly expanded his market beyond the station agents who had been his early customers. Ads in periodicals were soon supplemented by flyers produced to his order describing related items of merchandise he had to offer; these were mailed to prospects whose addresses were compiled from responses to earlier ads. The flyers gradually developed into catalogs. At first these were issued only intermittently as Sears acquired things to sell, and not until 1893 did they begin to come out on a regular schedule. Initially he concentrated on selling watches, but before long he added limited assortments of jewelry and silverware; even though his offerings were haphazard and conformed to no consistent pattern, the business poured in and he found himself making money faster than he had ever dreamed possible.

Since watches comprised a large part of his business, Sears found he needed a watch repairman. He hired for this job an Indiana farm boy named Alvah Roebuck, who had learned his trade through a correspondence course. The new man proved not only a skilled repairman but also an accomplished watch assembler as well. On a number of occasions, Sears was able to buy sizable quantities of surplus parts from manufacturers at a fraction of what they had cost to produce. These parts, not always from the same manufacturer, were put together by Roebuck and a few helpers and sold as finished watches at prices significantly lower than those of traditional retail merchants. The business boomed and Roebuck soon became Richard Sears's most valued employee.

But Richard Sears was a volatile entrepreneur. The readiness with which he achieved success and its very magnitude convinced him that it was too good to last. In 1889 he sold out to another Chicago company, planning to become a banker in a small town in Iowa. But the lure of trading was too much in his blood, and with Roebuck still at his side, he started a new company later in the same year under the name Warren, his own middle name. Two years later he sold the company to Roebuck, and its name was changed to Roebuck's. Within a short time, however, Sears bought back into the business with two-thirds interest. In 1892 the company was incorporated as A. C. Roebuck, Inc., and a year later reincorporated as Sears, Roebuck and Co.

Throughout this series of changes in name and ownership, few changes were made in the business itself or the way it was run. Richard Sears had a sharp nose for finding bargain merchandise he could resell at prices well under anything his competition could meet. While at first he sold only watches, he gradually added other lines. An 1889 catalog was still devoted chiefly to watches but carried limited assortments of silverware and jewelry. By 1893 offerings had grown to include firearms, sewing machines, bicycles, pianos and organs, men's and boys' clothing, and a scattered variety of athletic equipment. The 1894 catalog added shoes, women's clothing, wagons, stoves, furniture, glassware, fishing tackle, seeds, and books.

The catalog had grown in size and in the range of items carried, but these fit no particular pattern. Essentially, all that was consistent was merchandise at bargain prices. From the first, Richard Sears displayed an uncanny knack for writing folksy, down-to-earth, one-person-to-another advertising copy that appealed strongly to rural, small-town America. Customers responded to his ads by completing coupons or order forms or by simply writing letters. Orders were filled from a warehouse conveniently located near the center of the network of railroads that converged on Chicago.

As we look back today over the earliest Sears catalogs and the huge volumes of orders they generated, it is obvious that Richard Sears was one of the great promotional geniuses in American business history. He was also a poor businessman and an inept manager. He gave scant attention to the handling of the rapidly increasing number of orders his advertising and catalogs brought in, and the internal affairs of the company were chaotic. He had little interest in or understanding of business finance, and despite the success of his selling efforts—indeed, in part because of it—he found himself in financial difficulties which reached serious proportions in 1893–94.

Meanwhile, his young assistant and co-owner was growing uneasy. Roebuck disliked the long working hours (frequently sixteen a day, seven days a week) and the unremitting pressures caused by the company's haphazard internal operations. He worried about his health. Never the gambler Sears was, Roebuck was apprehensive at the extent to which the company's indebtedness exceeded its authorized limits, and he was haunted by the specter of imminent financial collapse and the personal liabilities he would

Richard W. Sears, founder of R. W. Sears
Watch Co., circa 1886.

Alvah C. Roebuck, partner with Richard
W. Sears in Sears, Roebuck and Co., circa
1890.

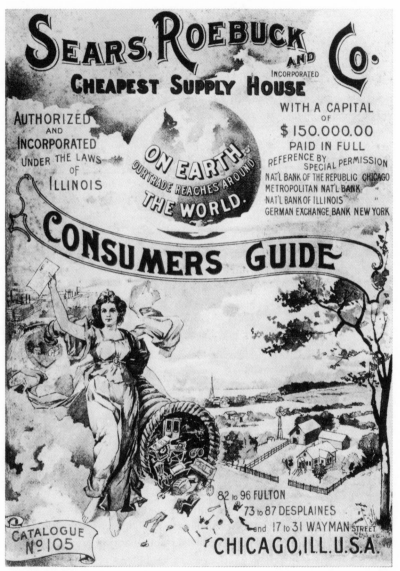

Cover of Sears, Roebuck catalog, 1897.

have to bear should it come. Finally he could stand it no longer, and in August of 1895 he walked into Sears's office and announced that he was quitting. Sears offered, and Roebuck accepted, $25,000 for his one-third interest in the business.

Sears was sorry to lose Roebuck. He liked him personally and had learned to rely on him. Moreover, he had hoped that Roebuck would develop into a man to whom he could turn over much of his management responsibility and eventually sell out most or all of his own interests; he still harbored the dream of becoming an Iowa banker. Roebuck's resignation meant that he would have to look elsewhere for support and succession.

Good luck brought a promising prospect to his attention. A Chicago businessman, Aaron Nussbaum, had used the small fortune he had amassed as a concessionaire at the 1893 World's Columbian Exposition to buy into a company that manufactured pneumatic tube systems for department stores. Shortly before Roebuck's resignation, Nussbaum had called on Sears in the hope that such a system could be adapted to a mail-order operation. While he was unsuccessful in his selling effort, he became interested in the company itself and in Richard Sears's obvious gifts as a super salesman. Richard Sears saw Aaron Nussbaum as a possible candidate for the role in which he had envisioned Alvah Roebuck.

After Roebuck's resignation, Sears offered Nussbaum a one-half interest in the business for $75,000, the equivalent of twice what he had just paid Roebuck for his one-third interest. Nussbaum found the offer attractive but beyond his readily available resources. Not wishing to pass up the opportunity entirely, he inquired among his relatives for someone who might join him in the Sears, Roebuck venture. He met with several rebuffs before reaching his brother-in-law, Julius Rosenwald, who was immediately receptive to the idea.

One reason for Rosenwald's interest was the fact that he already knew Sears and something about his business. Rosenwald was a manufacturer of men's clothing,[2] and Sears was one of his major customers. Rosenwald viewed Sears with a mixture of admiration and disapproval: while he was impressed with how easily Sears managed to sell the unusually large quantities of suits he ordered from Rosenwald's company, he was not pleased with Sears's lack of promptness in paying his bills. Rosenwald saw Nussbaum's plan as an opportunity not only to buy into a growing company but also to help solve his continuing problem with his Sears accounts receivable.

The upshot was that in late 1895 Julius Rosenwald joined Aaron

Nussbaum in buying a half interest in Sears, Roebuck and Co. For this purpose, Nussbaum put up $37,500 in cash and Rosenwald cancelled an equivalent amount of Sears indebtedness. Not long thereafter, Sears sold his new partners enough of his holdings so that each had a one-third interest in the company.

It was not a happy threesome. Rosenwald and Sears got along reasonably well, but Nussbaum was a hardheaded, heavy-handed businessman who antagonized almost everyone with whom he dealt, including his two partners. Even so, business prospered. Sears's promotional genius continued to flourish. Nussbaum, despite his rough ways—or perhaps by means of them—got the company onto a solid financial footing, and Rosenwald brought a measure of order into internal operations and laid a groundwork of the sound business policies the company sorely needed. But personal discords, particularly those between Sears and Nussbaum, were too great for the combination to endure. Finally, early in 1901, Sears gave Rosenwald an ultimatum: "Someone's got to go. Either you and Nussbaum buy me out or you and I buy him out." [3]

After thinking the matter over carefully, Rosenwald elected to go with Sears, whose superb selling abilities and intimate knowledge of farmers and farm life well outweighed familial considerations. Rosenwald offered his brother-in-law $1 million for his one-third interest, for which he had paid only $37,500 less than six years before. But Nussbaum held out for, and got, $1.25 million, thus realizing a thirty-three-fold capital gain.

With Nussbaum out of the way, Julius Rosenwald and Richard Sears were free to devote their full attention to their burgeoning company. They had already proved themselves a productive pair. Upon joining the firm in 1895, Rosenwald had brought to the enterprise something Sears had never given it: a clear definition of business purpose. This, combined with Sears's talents as a salesman, had had a tremendous impact on the direction Sears, Roebuck and Co. had subsequently taken.

As already noted, Richard Sears's merchandise offerings were limited during his first few years in business. Originally confined to watches, they were gradually augmented by new lines. But the 1889 catalog still identified the company as the "R. W. Sears Watch Company Manufacturers, Jobbers and Importers of Watches, Diamonds and Jewelry." And as late as 1894, the year before Rosenwald joined the firm, the catalog continued to refer to Sears as a "watch and jewelry house," although by this time other types of merchandise were also being carried. The 1895 catalog presented a much wider selection of offerings, but this reflected little in the way of a consistent buying pattern on Sears's part; it still represented primarily what he was able to procure on especially favorable terms. Often this consisted of manufacturers' surpluses and other distress goods. By modern standards, Richard Sears was essentially a huckster.

Rosenwald had a much more orderly, systematic mind. He watched farm income levels rise following the lean years of the early 1890s, and he saw in this a great business opportunity. Much of rural America was still dependent on a cumbersome and inefficient system of distribution built around the wholesaler, the traveling salesman, and the general store. Given Richard Sears's demonstrated ability to sell in the rural market, Rosenwald envisioned an ambitious new role for the company. By broadening its merchandise offerings and by keeping the farmer's special needs in view, Sears, Roebuck and Co. could become "buyer for the American farmer." Operating from a central location with direct access to a wide range of merchandise sources, capable aides could search out goods needed by the farmer in a way the farmer himself in his isolated position could not possibly do. It was precisely this role that Julius Rosenwald defined as the company's business purpose.

This concept was not original with Rosenwald. Over twenty years earlier, in 1872, A. Montgomery Ward had launched the company bearing his name dedicated to "furnishing farmers and mechanics throughout the Northwest with all kinds of merchandise at wholesale prices." His first "catalog," a one-page sheet, listed 163 items covering a variety of consumer needs. Subsequent catalogs identified the company as "The Original Grange Supply House" and carried the endorsement of many Grange officials, including the founder of that aggressive grass-roots organization representing agricultural interests. Pursuing his idea of supplying rural America, symbolized by but not restricted to the National Grange, Ward steadily increased both the size of his catalogs and the extent of his offerings. By 1886, the year Richard Sears first started selling watches by mail, the Ward catalog had grown to 280 pages and listed over 10,000 items.[4]

Aware of Ward's success, Rosenwald strongly encouraged Richard Sears's moves to expand the range of his own merchandise offerings while closely relating those offerings to rural needs. As a result, the 1896 catalog, the first in which Rosenwald's influence was felt, was also the company's first truly general merchandise catalog. It included work and dress clothing for the entire family, buggies, harnesses, farm tools and equipment, plumbing supplies, stoves, crockery and kitchenware, household furnishings, hunting supplies, patent medicines, dry goods, building materials, guns and traps, bicycles, organs and pianos—virtually everything a farm might require as a living household and a working enterprise.[5]

The idea of the "supply house" as implemented by Ward and then Rosenwald bore with it the implication that the "house" represented and was responsible to those whom it undertook to supply. It was therefore a natural and logical step for Rosenwald to establish the policy, "Satisfaction guaranteed or your money back"—a policy Sears, Roebuck and Co. has followed ever since. Here again, the thought was not original; Montgomery Ward's money-back guarantee had been in effect for more than two decades.[6] But Rosenwald carried the concept further than Ward had. He coupled with the new Sears, Roebuck guarantee an insistence that higher ethical standards be followed in the company's advertising and sales promotion and that the merchandise itself be of higher quality, constraints to which Richard Sears had theretofore paid little heed.

Rosenwald's merchandising creed was explicit: "Sell honest merchandise for less money and more people will buy." To which he added three supporting directives:

(1) Sell for less by buying for less. Buy for less through the instrumentality of mass buying and cash buying. *But maintain the quality.*

(2) Sell for less by cutting the cost of sales. Reduce to the absolute practical minimum the expense of moving goods from producer to consumer. *But maintain the quality.*

(3) Make less profit on each individual item and increase your aggregate profit by selling more items. *But maintain the quality.*

And a coda:

Treat people fairly and honestly and generously and their response will be fair and honest and generous.[7]

Despite his old opportunistic and freewheeling ways, Richard Sears went along with Julius Rosenwald's broadened view of the market the company would serve and the stricter ethical standards to which it would adhere. His own background had given him an intimate knowledge of rural needs, and his advertising and promotional skills, while somewhat tempered by Rosenwald's policies, had instilled in him a sure feel as to how these needs could be appealed to. Sears proved to be equally adept at selling this far more diversified range of merchandise as he had been in promoting more limited lines. But the changes Rosenwald brought to Sears, Roebuck went far beyond the contents of the catalog: while Sears had once peddled goods chosen largely on the basis of what he was able to pick up advantageously, the company would now buy according to what would most benefit its customers. In other words, its buying philosophy underwent a significant transformation. No longer would the approach be "What do I have to sell?" but rather "What does the customer want?"

This sharper and more rational definition of business purpose, coupled with volume purchasing and streamlined distribution, made it possible for the revitalized and now well-managed company to deliver goods to its rural customers at prices substantially below those of the typical general store. As "buyer for the American farmer," Sears, Roebuck served its market well and was amply rewarded. Sales jumped from three-quarters of a million dollars in 1895 to $10 million in 1900, when for the first time they surpassed those of Montgomery Ward. Ward's was never again to come close to Sears in sales.

Such rapid growth brought with it more than one unforeseen problem. By the early years of the new century, it had become apparent that drastic changes would have to be made in the company's operating methods: the sheer volume of incoming orders was threatening to drown the business. The mountains of paperwork and tons of merchandise that had to be handled taxed the capacity of the already harried staff. As Elmer Scott, a key operating executive during this period, later recalled: "The whole operation became chaotic. Long delays in shipments, a rising tide of errors leading to a flood of returned goods which in turn were badly handled, absenteeism, replacement of "quitting" employees by inexperienced people—all were combining to make the place a shambles." [8] Coordinating the movement of goods on orders which called for merchandise from more than one department proved especially troublesome. Given the continuing rapid increase in volume, the task of first breaking down incoming orders into their component parts, then routing the components to the proper departments, and finally reassembling the individual items for consolidated packing and shipping presented enormous difficulties. It seemed likely for a time that a sharp check would have to be placed on the expansion of the business; it was rapidly approaching the point of unmanageability.

The dilemma was solved by a brilliant managerial invention: the "schedule system." Largely the work of Otto Doering, plant superintendent and later operating vice president, the system required new physical facilities specially fashioned to accommodate and support it. It was time to build a new plant in any event; up until that point, the company had operated out of standard-type warehouses, and continued growth had already made it necessary to lease buildings in a number of scattered locations, thus exacerbating the problems of coordinating the rapid and complex flow of work.

Completed and placed in operation in 1906 on a forty-acre tract on Chicago's West Side, the new structure was proudly described as "the largest business building in the world." Even today, with over three million square feet of floor space, it is still one of the largest. It proved a fitting home for Doering's revolutionary schedule system.

Briefly, the system was built around the concept of reserving a specific time and place in the shipping room for the assembly of all items in each order. Upon receipt in the order entry department, an order was assigned a particular shipping room bin for a particular fifteen-minute time slot. Instructions for selecting each item in the order were then dispatched to the appropriate departments, along with information regarding the specific fifteen-minute interval during which the item was to arrive at its designated bin. Anything not arriving on time was shipped separately, and the added cost was charged back to the delinquent department. To facilitate the rapid collection of individual order items and their assembly in the shipping room, the schedule system was backed by a complex array of equipment. The 1905 Sears, Roebuck catalog carried this colorful description: "Miles of railroad tracks run through, in and around this building for the receiving, moving and forwarding of merchandise; elevators, mechanical conveyors, endless chains, moving sidewalks, gravity chutes, apparatus and conveyors, pneumatic tubes and every known mechanical appliance for reducing labor, for the working out of economy and dispatch is to be utilized here in our great Works." [9]

Otto Doering had personally overseen every detail of the design and construction of the new complex, which was literally a huge, finely tuned machine for receiving and holding merchandise and for filling and shipping orders. Goods were received in bulk from hundreds of manufacturers, stored in locations in which each item could be readily found, and drawn against by the tens of thousands of customer orders that came in on any given day. The matching of the two phases of the process—bulk merchandise in, item-by-item goods out—was a task of enormous proportions. There were no models for handling and keeping track of the enormous volume of detail: hundreds of thousands of pieces of paper and tens of thousands of items of merchandise had to end up in the same reserved piece of space at the same time with only the narrowest permissible margin of error. Yet somehow it all worked. Conceptually, the formulation was as brilliant as it was simple; operationally, it was an engineering triumph.

As operating superintendent, Otto Doering had complete responsibility for the receiving and storage of merchandise, for processing orders, and for delivering merchandise to customers. The chief merchandising executive, a position filled by several men in succession during Rosenwald's years in office, was charged with the selection, pricing, and advertising of merchandise, but it was Doering who orchestrated everything that happened to the goods from the time they were shipped from the factory until they were delivered into the customers' hands. He was an able, imaginative, hard-driving executive who produced results right up until his retirement some twenty years later.

Significantly, the new structure and the system it had been built to serve were wholly in keeping with the emerging scientific management movement. Although there is no extant record that Otto Doering or anyone else at Sears[10] ever had personal contact with Frederick W. Taylor, the so-called Father of Scientific Management, even a cursory look at the Sears schedule system reveals close affinity with many of the basic precepts Taylor espoused. There is no way now of determining whether Doering drew his basic ideas from Taylor's writings or developed them de novo, but the fact remains that the Sears system was imbued with the new ideas and spirit of scientific management. This was reflected in yet another of Doering's innovations: as part of the process of creating the schedule system, he set up a methods department responsible for the continued refinement and improvement of systems throughout the entire mail-order operation. One of the first departments of its kind in American industry, it made a substantial contribution to the high level of efficiency the organization achieved. It is likely that Doering's ideas influenced other companies as well. For whatever it may be worth, there was a persistent legend at Sears for many years that when Henry Ford was thinking through his concepts for the mass production of automobiles, he paid an extended visit to the Sears plant where he gave careful, on-the-spot study to Otto Doering's schedule system and his methods department.

A less pleasant consequence of building the vast new plant was the financial problem it precipitated. The company's working capital resources had been severely strained by its rapid growth, and the new plant required a cash outlay of over $5 million. In the spring of 1906, the need for additional capital was urgent. Rosenwald approached his longtime friend,

Henry Sachs, a principal of the New York investment house, Goldman, Sachs, for a $5 million loan to repay the bank loans incurred and to rebuild working capital. Goldman questioned the adequacy of that amount and the wisdom of this approach to meeting the company's needs. He suggested instead a public stock issue, and later in 1906 Goldman, Sachs in conjunction with Lehman Brothers, another major New York investment house, underwrote an issue of $10 million of preferred and $30 million of common stock. The issue found a ready market, and for the first time in its history Sears, Roebuck had a solid financial footing. Its great new facilities were paid for, its bank loans were repaid, and it had plenty of working capital to support its rapid increase in sales volume.[11]

When the new plant opened in 1906, the schedule system which it housed and supported was an immediate success. The system required tight discipline and autocratic control, but it had been thought through ahead of time with such thoroughness and attention to detail that after a short break-in period it worked remarkably well. Upgraded subsequently with refinements—some dictated by experience, others introduced by the then innovative methods department, and still others born of new technologies—it has continued working smoothly ever since. A company which had been on the verge of having to halt its growth suddenly found itself with a virtually unlimited capacity for continued expansion.

Sears 1900 sales volume of $10 million grew to $50 million in 1907.[12] This phenomenal increase was attributable in large part to the fortunate conjuncture of six elements: one provided by Richard Sears, two by Otto Doering, and three by Julius Rosenwald. Richard Sears's contribution was his consummate skill in advertising and sales promotion. Otto Doering's contributions were the schedule system and the tight operating procedures which accompanied it. Added to these and underlying them were Julius Rosenwald's sound concept of business purpose, superior financial acumen, and high level of business integrity based on performance guarantees that built a solid foundation of customer confidence.

While the company flourished—sales would reach $235 million in 1920—its two principals were heading for a parting of the ways. For a little over five years following Aaron Nussbaum's departure, Sears and Rosenwald were able to work together in reasonable harmony. The fact that they differed greatly in their temperaments and business philosophies was papered over by the success of their first decade together, but the downturn in sales which followed the panic of 1907 gave rise to sharp disagreements between them. Sears argued for a return to a more aggressive advertising and selling effort, with less concern for some of the niceties in promotional practices Rosenwald had imposed. Rosenwald disagreed and insisted not only on maintaining the standards he had introduced but also on tightening the organization and sharply reducing expenses, particularly sales expenses. Sears was in Europe during much of this period with his wife, who had been ailing, and most of the argument between the two men was conducted by mail. Rosenwald's presence on the scene, of course, gave him an advantage and his views prevailed. When Sears returned to Chicago in the fall of 1908, he sought to reopen the argument, but without success. Early in 1909, he submitted his resignation.

He offered to sell his stock to Rosenwald, who declined; in the words of Rosenwald's biographer, "He did not want it to be possible for anyone to say in the future that he had profited at the expense of his former partner." Sears instead sold his holdings to Goldman, Sachs for $10 million.[13] Although Rosenwald held Sears's place on the board of directors open for him until 1912, Sears never attended another meeting. After engaging in a few desultory business activities, none of any particular import, he died in 1914 at the early age of fifty, a wealthy but disappointed man.

The policies Rosenwald instituted during the panic proved wise, and the company emerged from the hard times of 1907–8 in fighting trim. Its financial condition was strong, its merchandising principles were solidly established, and its operating organization was running smoothly. Thus positioned, the company was ready to capitalize on the rising tide of farm prosperity that followed 1907–8 and would virtually explode in the face of the vast increase in demand for U.S. agricultural products generated by the war that began in 1914. Although Sears was now a public company, by far the greatest share of ownership was in Rosenwald's hands, and by the end of the war he found himself one of the richest men in America and, for that matter, the world.

Rosenwald used his years at Sears, Roebuck to good advantage, and not merely his own. He strengthened company operations by establishing two branch mail-order plants, one in Dallas[14] in 1906 and one in Seattle in 1910. In 1911 he established a testing laboratory at the company headquarters in Chicago to check on the quality of merchandise being bought by his buyers. In the same year he introduced review procedures to make sure that goods offered in the catalog measured up to the claims made for them. In 1912 he created the prototype of what soon became the county agent system to encourage better farming practices and simultaneously strengthen Sears basic markets (see Chapter 10 herein). In 1916, in a radical departure from accepted business practice and in the face of vigorous objections from many of his business friends, he inaugurated the Profit Sharing and Pension Fund of Sears, Roebuck Employees that in time became the envy of the business world and the cornerstone of the uniquely successful employee relations policies of General Robert E. Wood (see Chapter 9 herein).

As war clouds gathered in late 1916, President Woodrow Wilson appointed Rosenwald to the newly created Council of National Defense, where he was named chairman of the committee on supplies. When the work of the council was taken over by the War Industries Board, Rosenwald assumed other war-related duties. His involvement in the war effort, together with an illness and a minor physical disability, kept him away from Sears until 1919, a total of nearly three years.

During this period Rosenwald left the company in what he felt were the able hands of his subordinates. All of his key men had been with him for some years, and some were relatives by blood or marriage; all had important ownership stakes in the business, and Rosenwald thought that they could be counted on to look after their own interests as well as his. Although Sears, Roebuck was not literally a family business, it had some of the characteristics of one, especially in the sense that many of its business processes were conducted in an easygoing, familylike fashion. Internal relationships at managerial levels were notable for their high degree of informality and mutual respect. Even in Rosenwald's absence, his key people got along very well—too well, in fact, for their own good or that of the company. Rosenwald would soon learn that his confidence in them had been misplaced.

Throughout the war years and for a year thereafter, business boomed. Orders came in in unprecedented volume, and the only problem seemed to be that of keeping enough merchandise in stock to fill them. This task was easily turned over to lower-level subordinates, leaving the top merchandising executives free from worry and, for those so inclined, with plenty of time for golf and other pleasurable pursuits. The atmosphere was relaxed. The business seemed to be running itself and to require little attention. Albert Loeb, treasurer, whom Rosenwald had left in overall charge as acting president, was a good financial man but not a strong leader. Otto Doering, as head of operations, was hard put to keep abreast of the flood of orders that kept pouring in, but his dedication was a conspicuous exception to the prevailing mood.

The time of reckoning was not long in coming: the panic of 1920–21

33

caught the company's merchants completely off guard. Apparently expecting an indefinite extension of wartime agricultural prosperity, they had loaded their shelves with goods and were wholly unprepared for the sudden drying up of demand. With wheat dropping from $3.45 to $1.42 a bushel and corn from $2.17 to 59 cents a bushel, sales fell sharply. The over-expanded inventory had to be marked down drastically to move the goods at all, and then only at substantial losses. The company came within an ace of going under. It was only saved by Rosenwald seizing firm direction of company affairs and courageously pledging a sizable share of his personal fortune as a guarantee to Sears creditors.[15] During the same critical juncture, Montgomery Ward avoided bankruptcy by having previously relinquished control to the J. P. Morgan interests. When the dust settled, control of Sears remained in Sears-centered hands; control of Ward's had passed to Wall Street.

One of Rosenwald's first actions on returning to active management was to appoint a new head of merchandising. He chose his brother-in-law, Max Adler, who had held a series of senior merchandising positions since first joining the company in 1898 and who had not fallen into the carefree ways of some of his fellow executives. Under Adler's skillful leadership, surplus inventories were liquidated with reasonable dispatch while buying practices were brought under control. With Otto Doering's aid, staffs were reduced by nearly 30 percent and operating expenses were cut by more than $20 million.[16] By personal example and imperious demand, Rosenwald restored discipline to an organization that had grown lax during the lush war years. The combination of Draconian leadership and financial succor restored the company to profitability by 1922, leaving the crisis of 1920–21 safely behind.[17] But a number of problems remained to be solved in its aftermath.

Rosenwald's disappointment with the performance of those he had left in charge during his absence was a sobering experience that brought home to him vividly the need to pay greater attention to the company's organization. Under his direction, Sears, Roebuck had grown at a remarkable rate, but this growth had occurred in a loose and haphazard manner. In essence, if Rosenwald and his key associates saw an opportunity in a certain line of business, they simply hired the best man they could find, placed him in charge of the department, and gave him his head; as long as his business grew and showed a satisfactory profit, he was left virtually unsupervised. Rosenwald often referred to Sears as "a federation of independent merchants," and that was pretty much what it was.

34

However advantageous this system may have been in an earlier stage of the company's development, it had become apparent to Rosenwald by the early 1920s that a more systematic plan of organization was in order. His conviction on this score was crystallized by the experience of 1920–21; it was now clear to him that the informal, familylike relationships on which he had relied were inadequate for a company of Sears size and complexity. He had brought the business through the nightmare of the panic and had succeeded in restoring at least nominal profitability, but it was nowhere near the level it had achieved even before the unprecedented good times of the war years. Because both Sears and Ward's were public companies, their performance figures were readily available, and Rosenwald did not like what he saw when he compared the two. For that matter, he felt that neither company was doing as well as it should in the rising prosperity of the mid-twenties.

Meanwhile, he was thinking more and more about his own retirement. He was sixty years old in 1922 and wearied by the traumatic three years he had just weathered; moreover, he was becoming increasingly absorbed in his philanthropic interests and anxious to devote himself more fully to their pursuit. He decided that the time had come to find a successor.

In his methodical way, Rosenwald thought long and hard about the kind of man he wanted. Despite the loyalties he felt toward key members of his staff, he concluded reluctantly that none of them had the abilities and experience he considered essential. Adler and Doering, either of whom might have stood a chance had he been younger, were both approaching retirement age, and Rosenwald was determined to find someone who could look forward to a long tenure of office. He especially wanted someone who had proved himself in an industry which had successfully solved the problems of large-scale operations. On this score, the railroads were preeminent at that time. In casting about among railroad managements, Rosenwald's attention was drawn to Charles M. Kittle, operations vice-president of the exceptionally well-managed Illinois Central Railroad, also headquartered in Chicago. He made Kittle's acquaintance, took a strong liking to him, and offered him the presidency of Sears. Kittle accepted and assumed his new responsibilities on November 1, 1924.

Only after making the offer to Kittle did Rosenwald learn that General Robert E. Wood, merchandising vice-president of Montgomery Ward, was unexpectedly available. Wood had everything Rosenwald was looking for: a demonstrably productive career in a succession of large, complex organizations; hands-on experience with massive service of supply systems; five

35

years with a company much like Sears; and a track record of competitive performance which made Sears merchants nervous. If Rosenwald had known of Wood's coming availability thirty days earlier, he probably would have offered him the presidency instead of Kittle, but he had made a commitment and he was not a man to go back on his word. Nevertheless, he wanted Wood—wanted him badly. He could not offer him the top job, but he could and did offer him a very attractive compensation arrangement quite close to that he had presented to Kittle. More important, he could and did promise Wood the opportunity to try out certain ideas of which he was enamored, most notably that of opening retail stores to serve the burgeoning urban market. Wood accepted and reported for duty the same day as Kittle.

Doering and Adler were none too happy about being passed over, and they took a dim view of Wood and his radical notion of grafting an untried retail business onto their well-established and familiar mail-order operations. But they were loyal to Rosenwald and acceded with good grace to both of his decisions.

Rosenwald continued in his position as chairman of the board, relinquished his management duties, and turned his attention to his philanthropic interests. His carefully laid plans were rudely interrupted barely three years later by Kittle's unexpected death at the age of forty-six. Confident that he had settled for his lifetime the matter of his succession, Rosenwald overnight found himself facing the need to make the decision all over again. After a week of thought, which seemed interminable to the interested parties but was in truth admirably brief, he decided on Wood. As a consequence, Doering and Adler immediately resigned. This did not give Rosenwald cause to worry about Sears future; both men had recently indicated an intention to retire, and in any event Rosenwald was quite content to leave the responsibility for replacing them in what he by now was satisfied were Wood's capable hands. Relieved, he returned to his philanthropic concerns.

Julius Rosenwald earned a name for himself in philanthropy as great—and perhaps lastingly greater—than the one he earned as the architect of Sears, Roebuck. Significantly, his official biographer, M. R. Werner, devotes considerably more attention to Rosenwald's philanthropic endeavors than to his business activities.[18]

Rosenwald's philanthropic interests ran broad and deep, but he is best remembered for his efforts to improve Negro education in the South. In his view, this was the Negroes' greatest need. He was strongly influenced by

Booker T. Washington, whom he greatly admired and with whom he established a warm personal friendship. In large part through his efforts, over 5,000 public schools for blacks had been established in fifteen southern states by the time of his death, and over 4,000 schools had gained libraries chiefly at his insistence and partially with his aid. Tens of thousands of Negro youths received at least the rudiments of an education they would not have had otherwise. Rosenwald was a trustee and a major benefactor of Tuskegee Institute in Alabama, which Washington had founded, and was instrumental in the development of four other important centers of Negro higher education in the South. Many black American leaders in the two succeeding generations were indebted to him for the educational opportunities which provided the necessary foundations for their leadership roles. In an era when few whites were concerned with the pitiable state of American blacks, Julius Rosenwald left a lasting impact on their culture and progress.

Most of Rosenwald's philanthropic work was conducted through the medium of the Julius Rosenwald Fund, originally established in 1917 and reorganized under professional direction in 1928. A distinctive feature of the Fund's 1928 charter was a stipulation that its assets were to be spent in their entirety within twenty-five years after the founder's death. Rosenwald was vehemently opposed to setting up permanent endowments, as a number of his wealthy contemporaries had done. He did not believe in philanthropic endeavors "operated by a dead hand."

Julius Rosenwald died on January 6, 1932, at the age of sixty-nine. He left a sizable portion of his personal estate to the Fund, most of it in the form of Sears, Roebuck stock. Under General Wood's leadership, the company entered upon a prolonged period of unprecedented growth and profitability; in the twenty-five years following Rosenwald's death, the market value of a share of Sears stock increased almost elevenfold (1,082 percent) and the assets of the Fund appreciated accordingly. With the greatly enhanced resources thus available to it, the Fund was able to accomplish in the time allotted to it far more than Rosenwald had ever dreamed possible. Faithful to its charge, it completed its work and went into dissolution on December 31, 1956.

3

General Wood: The Sears Years

FOLLOWING HIS summary dismissal from Montgomery Ward's, Robert Wood did not lack for places to go. One, however, seemed both obvious and particularly attractive: Sears, Roebuck and Co., Ward's great rival mail-order house.[1]

Sears position vis-à-vis Ward's had been slipping. Between 1920 and 1924, Ward's net sales had increased by a healthy 47.5 percent while Sears had fallen by an alarming 15.9 percent. Over the same period, Sears share of the combined sales of the two companies had dropped from 71 percent to 58 percent.[2]

While the advantages of securing General Wood's services undoubtedly occurred independently to Julius Rosenwald, the intermediation of one man, Wendell Endicott, strongly influenced the course of events. Endicott had become acquainted with Wood during the war, and an especially warm and close friendship had grown up between the two men that would endure for the remainder of their lives. Endicott's business, Endicott Johnson Shoe Company, was a large supplier of shoes to both Sears and Ward's, and Endicott knew the top people within both companies. Immediately upon learning of Wood's availability, Endicott contacted Rosenwald. He pointed out that Wood, not Merseles, was the man who was making competition with Ward's so tough and advised Rosenwald to seize the chance to hire him. Simultaneously, he urged Wood to give serious consideration to Sears. In a letter dated October 6, 1924, he wrote: "I cannot get it out of my head that if Sears Roebuck today had the same intelligent policies which have been so responsible for Montgomery Ward's success, that they would forge ahead and it seems to me for an enormous institution that the opportunities to show big results that here is the logical place for you to locate." [3]

Wood had reservations about joining what he termed "a Jewish family firm," sentiments which were by no means uncommon at that time among men of his background and in the circles in which he moved. He had already expressed as much in a letter to Endicott indicating concern that he might "find myself hampered by a lot of jewish [sic] relatives, and life is too short to be surrounded by people that you do not like, no matter how much money you may be making." [4] Endicott's reply was reassuring: "I have heard it from several sources that it has been pretty generally talked that Sears Roebuck should get Gentile blood into the business." [5]

At the outset, both Endicott and Wood were thinking in terms of Wood assuming the presidency eventually if not immediately. With the Merseles experience fresh in his mind, Wood was reluctant to consider any position other than president or, as a minimum, vice president and general manager "with an absolute free hand, subject, of course, to proper financial control." Endicott concurred, but with a caveat: "Julius Rosenwald couldn't do anything better than appoint you President, and [himself] take the Chairmanship of the Board. This however, I cannot believe would take place at once. He has been the head of [Sears] for many years and now that it is going down, if he resigned, it would be an admission to a certain degree of failure, so I cannot believe that such a step as that would be taken." [6]

Endicott and Wood soon learned that Julius Rosenwald had in fact already decided to step down. But he had made plans for the presidency of his company: he had offered the post to Charles M. Kittle of the Illinois Central Railroad, and Kittle had accepted. Rosenwald still wanted Wood, however, and offered him a position created especially for him: vice-president for factories and retail stores. This combination was not as incongruous as it might appear. It united the two merchandising areas in which Wood was most interested: the development of a new basis for source relationships and the opening up of new channels of distribution.

Wood and Kittle both joined Sears on November 1, 1924. As Kittle was three years younger than Wood, there was no reasonable prospect of Wood ever succeeding him to the presidency; however, the terms of his employment were generous [7] and he was assured of Rosenwald's strong support in the pursuit of his ideas. In a lengthy letter written five days before Wood started his new job, his good friend Endicott offered some philosophical counsel:

39

The fact of being the President is, of course, a most honorary position,—brings with it a splendid standing and prominence, as well as considerable power. On the other hand, the President of a big Corporation is not the whole thing by any means. . . .

[Rosenwald] has taken you into the family, has given you a splendid proposition, and has shown you his confidence in giving you equal bonus [with Adler and Doering], which I think is tremendously fair. He has given a splendid salary and has made some confidential proposition on stock, which you admit is reasonable, so that puts you right, it seems to me, with Rosenwald.

The Railroad man [Kittle], I know nothing about. He may or may not be the right man, but in any event, he should be a man that you would naturally back up and confer with, and if this man feels from the start that your chief thought is for the welfare of Sears Roebuck, and that you are happy to play with him, the future will take care of itself. Naturally, this new man will be sensitive, especially to your feelings, because he will be wise enough to know that the thought must have come to your mind that was a job rightfully coming to you,—therefore, it seems to me that your relationship with this Railroad man must be particularly cordial . . . so if you have him with you, and you are with him, two new men coming in together, starting fresh and clean can do wonders, and can wield tremendous power, both helping the other, rather than both pulling against each other.[8]

Wood followed his wise friend's advice, and events unfolded very much as they both anticipated. Kittle and Wood worked well together. Kittle proved to be a strong financial man with a knack for absorbing masses of operating data, a useful trait in any large-scale organization, and he drew upon his background as a railroad man to make important contributions to Sears system of physical distribution. Realizing that the mail-order business was very complicated, he wisely allowed merchandising vice president Max Adler and operating vice-president Otto Doering to continue running it in much the same way as they had before his arrival.

Kittle knew as much about retail as General Wood—which was very little, since neither man had any retail experience whatsoever. It was not long before Kittle not only grasped Wood's ideas but also embraced them wholeheartedly. Much of Kittle's attention, therefore, was devoted to the developing retail business, to which he and Rosenwald gave their unstinting backing despite the sometimes reluctant cooperation of Adler and Doering. The impact of the new management team soon became apparent: over the next three years, Sears improvement in sales and profits ran well ahead of Ward's.

Wood found Sears to be a far more congenial working environment than Ward's had been. For one thing, Sears was much better run than Ward's; Wood saw little of the confusion and inefficiency which had so annoyed him in his former position. In addition, Sears was almost devoid of the personal jealousies and family cliques which characterized Ward's upper management. Wood took pains to establish good relationships with his new associates. He was deferential to Julius Rosenwald and quickly developed a genuine liking and respect for him; learning from the Ward experience, he was careful to keep his name out of the business press except in connection with the other officers.[9]

Although he often disagreed with Doering and Adler on policy matters, Wood made sure that he remained on good personal terms with them. It was not long before he was invited to accompany them to their regular Saturday afternoon lunches and card games at the Standard Club, the Jewish counterpart to the Chicago Club. They were often joined by Julius Rosenwald, and these occasions provided an opportunity to discuss business and other matters in a relaxed and friendly atmosphere.[10] Altogether, the top Sears people comprised a closely knit, smoothly running group of which Wood quickly became an integral part.

Then, on January 2, 1928, Charles Kittle died suddenly. Julius Rosenwald, who had anticipated a long tenure for his new president, now faced the task of making a fresh choice. His decision was a difficult one. His key lieutenants, Adler and Doering, had been with him for many years and had been disappointed at not receiving the nod in 1924. Lessing Rosenwald, Julius's eldest son, was about to turn thirty-seven years of age and had been a vice-president for four years. Operating out of Philadelphia, where he had located to free himself somewhat from his father's overpowering presence, Lessing had worked hard and done a creditable job; he felt he had earned the right to the presidency. As it happened, he was dissuaded from seeking it by his mother, Augusta. She urged her son to stay in Philadelphia where he had built a reputation of his own and from which he could better administer the affairs of the large family fortune.[11] Julius Rosenwald's decision thus came down to Wood, Doering, and Adler.

The week following Kittle's death was an anxious one for all the interested parties. During it, Wood wrote his close friend Endicott:

> The situation is unchanged here. Nothing has been decided and J. R. has on his best poker face. As a matter of fact, I do not think he has made up his mind. . . .
> Max [Adler] went over to see Mr. Rosenwald yesterday to propose that Doering should be made president and that the business

should be run by an executive committee consisting of Adler, Doering, and myself, this arrangement to run one or two years, at the end of which time J. R. could appoint either Lessing or myself as he saw fit. I told Max I had no objection to this arrangement, that as far as I was concerned I would be willing to serve under Lessing, Doering or himself, under the condition that it did not last over two years. Neither Adler nor Doering will serve under Lessing or myself, as they feel they were slighted three years ago and they do not feel like standing for another slight. I do not blame them the least in that respect.

While Max proposed to see Mr. Rosenwald about Doering, I think he put in a few words for himself, insinuating to Mr. Rosenwald that if he could not select Doering, he [Max] was the only other possible selection. I told Mr. Rosenwald that in view of the condition of the business, the big expansion progress we had planned . . . that it would be the wisest thing not to disrupt matters but to put Doering in, that as far as I was concerned, I would serve under either Doering, Lessing, or Adler, although I thought Doering would not want to hold it over one or two years, and I can afford to wait. Besides, I am very fond of him and of Max too and I would hate to be put in a position of hurting them.[12]

Wood had now been with Sears over three years, and he was confident of the strong position he had built for himself. His letter to Endicott continued:

I would be the real power in the company whether any of the three were selected, and it does not make much difference to me about the title if I get the money and have the power. Besides I feel that in the case of Adler and Doering, both will be very glad to retire at the end of one year or two years, in which case I would have the opportunity and if it were Lessing, I believe he would get tired of the job or on his father's death would become chairman of the board; so all in all I have nothing to lose in the selection of any one of the three, and I feel sure that with the possible exception of Max, if any one of these were put in, I would practically dictate the policies of the company.

In the end, Rosenwald chose Wood. Two factors apparently weighed against Doering and Adler: both were near retirement age and both were already wealthy men. Wood had a much more powerful incentive for business success than either of the other two and, of course, his prospects for a long term in office were much greater.

Wood was named president of Sears, Roebuck and Co. on January 11, 1928. Lessing returned to his vice presidency in Philadelphia, and both Adler and Doering retired. Doering, unlike Adler, left in anger, under the mistaken impression that he had been outmaneuvered by Wood. Although Wood and Doering had worked together for over three years in mutual cordiality and respect, if not always in agreement, Doering remained bitter for the rest of his life. He broke completely with Wood and never again came nearer than four blocks to the great mail-order plant and company headquarters whose construction he had overseen a quarter of a century before.

Thus, in his forty-ninth year, after twenty-eight years of preparation in the Philippines, the Canal Zone, the war, and at Ward's and Sears, Robert E. Wood finally achieved the position which would allow the full unfolding of his business and managerial talents.

By the time General Wood assumed the presidency of Sears, he had already made significant advances in reorienting its approach to buying and in launching the retail program. Consequently, the change in leadership involved no change in direction but rather an acceleration of processes already at work. In restructuring the top management group, Wood drew primarily on resources already available within the Sears organization. Julius Rosenwald remained as chairman of the board. Lessing Rosenwald was named vice president of operations to succeed Doering, but in deference to his personal wishes was allowed to continue to make Philadelphia his headquarters. Donald Nelson, assistant to Max Adler, was moved into Adler's old position as vice president for merchandising. E. J. Pollock, who had long been the elder Rosenwald's and then Kittle's good right financial arm, was retained in the critical role of comptroller. Thus, Kittle's death and the departure of Doering and Adler created no sharp organizational break and the transition to new leadership was accomplished smoothly.

At the same time, men brought into Sears by General Wood began to move into positions of prominence. A number of these were men Wood had worked with at Ward's, and some of them he had originally hired there. Men who were considered Wood supporters had found things uncomfortable at Ward's after he left; some had been fired and others had departed of their own accord. Several had found their way to Sears in a series of select, individual moves over about a two-year period. Despite the great rivalry and lack of goodwill between the two companies, there was a gentlemen's agreement of long standing that neither would hire directly from the other. In keeping with the letter if not the spirit of this understanding, those who left Ward's for Sears had to wait a month before going on Sears payroll. They were never identified within Sears as a "Ward's group." [13]

Former Ward's men brought over to Sears included T. V. Houser, a brilliant merchandising strategist; E. P. Brooks, a skilled organizer and administrator who played a key role in the early retail development and then moved on to other important posts; and C. E. Humm, a keen figure man on whom Wood relied for objective operational and financial analyses. Others were Arthur Barrows, who would later become president of Sears for a short time; Frank Judson, who played an important part in shaping the new buying strategy; and Colonel Gilbert E. Humphrey, who succeeded Wood at Sears as vice-president for factories.

J. M. Barker, who became one of Wood's key lieutenants, was originally hired by Julius and Lessing Rosenwald in Philadelphia in 1928. Barker was a Boston banker with Latin American experience who emerged as a central figure in the retail program, succeeded Pollock as Wood's financial alter ego, and ultimately became chairman of Allstate Insurance Company.

It was altogether a diverse and remarkably able group of men, each supplying an important element of strength and all contributing significantly to the emerging enterprise. With the exception of Barker, the members of the new top management team were all on board at the time of Wood's succession, accustomed to working together, and ready to be moved into the positions from which they were to exercise decisive influence in the years ahead.

The General was expert at bringing out the special talents of the people with whom he worked. He knew almost instinctively how to mediate the conflicts which inevitably arose between them, and he was adept at molding their widely dissimilar personalities into a cohesive partnership. He was especially sensitive in his relationships with the two Rosenwalds, father and son. He consulted with the senior Rosenwald on all major personnel and policy matters and took pains to maintain cordial relations with the younger man. When the separation of operating headquarters in Philadelphia from corporate and merchandising headquarters in Chicago proved too cumbersome, Wood proposed a solution that evidenced his respect for Lessing and his willingness to accommodate him.

Specifically, Lessing would be advanced to a new position above that of the other vice-presidents while T. J. Carney, Lessing's protégé, would be appointed operating vice-president. Carney and operating headquarters would be moved to Chicago, while Lessing would be free to remain in Philadelphia and devote more time to his home and family. Carney would still report to Lessing, and Lessing would continue in full charge of operating policies. This was not exactly the neatest of organizational arrangements, but it suited the circumstances. Wood outlined the details of his proposal in a letter to Lessing dated July 3, 1929: "Under this plan, you will be left in Philadelphia as Senior or Executive Vice President as free lance, free to investigate any feature of the Company—mail order, retail or factories—that you see fit." [14] He would furnish Lessing with whatever staff he needed and see to it that he received frequent reports of the business. In addition, Wood stated his intent to create a new executive committee that would meet monthly, sometimes in Chicago and sometimes, for Lessing's convenience, in Philadelphia, and encouraged Lessing to attend all of the meetings.

Wood stressed in his letter that this arrangement would enable Lessing to "be of even more value to the business than at present." Before putting his plan into effect, he awaited Lessing's response: "I would like you to think this over and discuss the matter with me on your next trip to Chicago. If there are any features of the arrangement that I have suggested which you want modified or changed, we can consider them then." Significantly, Wood did not commit in advance to accept any changes Lessing might wish to make. Nevertheless, Wood's proposal proved acceptable to Lessing, who was named vice-president on March 4, 1930. He was also at that time appointed vice chairman of the board, a position he held until his father's death in January of 1932 elevated him to the chairmanship.

Throughout the years until Lessing's retirement in 1939, he and Wood remained on the most amicable of terms. The files are replete with lengthy exchanges of correspondence between the two men, and they often met. Rosenwald had a deep interest in all aspects of the company and its affairs, and kept up a lively flow of information and suggestions; Wood consulted with him on all major issues as well as on many of minor import. While he did not always agree with Lessing and firmly rejected some of his ideas, he was invariably respectful and considerate in his dealings with him.

Thus General Wood began his tenure as president of Sears, Roebuck and Co. with a staff he could trust and with whom he enjoyed excellent working relationships. Having accomplished what he had set out to do in 1924—namely, to become the head of the organization—he could now devote his efforts to shaping it according to ideas he had been formulating for many years.

But even a company the size of Sears could not command his full attention. Wood was a man who had long been aware of and concerned with what was happening in the world around him. He was especially alert to external conditions and trends likely to have an impact on Sears business; he therefore followed closely developments in politics and government and sought in various ways to influence their course. Although a lifelong Republican, he supported Franklin Delano Roosevelt for president in 1932 because "I knew that certain reforms were needed in the capitalistic system and the old Republican Party wouldn't make them." [15] As he later recalled: "In 1932 I had the idea that the Republican Party . . . had gotten into the hands of New York and New England, and a pretty cold and selfish set of men, and that they didn't see that there were certain reforms that had to be made." [16]

He was in touch with the newly elected president even before his inauguration. In a letter to Roosevelt dated January 27, 1933, he urged a policy of inflation through devaluation of the dollar as the only means for arresting the disastrous downward spiral of commodity prices. He began by establishing his own credentials:

I know that you are overwhelmed by unsolicited advice from all classes of people. . . . I thought, however, that you might be interested in the viewpoint of an executive of a national corporation which deals directly with the consumer all over the United States—the farmer in the rural districts and the wage earner in the cities. We have, probably better than anyone else, an opportunity to observe the conditions of the masses, and we, probably better than any other one business concern in the United States, see the conditions of the masses steadily getting worse. [17]

The new administration had not been long in office when Wood became sufficiently acquainted with Secretary of Agriculture Henry A. Wallace to write to him as well, stating his views as to what the administration's priorities should be. In a letter dated March 26, 1933, Wood listed three recommendations: "1. Devaluation of the dollar. . . . 2. The application of the farm bill to restrict production to a point where the price can be maintained or increased. 3. [The] industry control bill, bringing better wages and reducing unemployment." [18]

Wood supported the greater part of the New Deal, including the Agricultural Adjustment Act, the Soil Conservation Act, the rural electrification program, the Securities and Exchange Act, the Federal Deposit Insurance Corporation, the Utility Holding Company Act, the Tennessee Valley Authority, the Civilian Conservation Corps, the Social Security Act, and the reciprocal trade program. He also approved the wage and hour and child labor provisions of the National Industrial Recovery Act, although he disagreed sharply with its price-fixing features and curbs on competition. And he was most unhappy with the administration's labor policies, which he saw as badly skewed in favor of organized labor and against business.[19]

A series of consistent themes runs through Wood's positions on these important issues of public policy. He was strongly in favor of measures which would improve consumer income, curb the power of eastern moneyed interests (which he conceived of as inimicable to the general good), and foster trade and competition. From the early days of his business career, he had seen clearly that a broadly based company such as Sears had a deep and abiding interest in the well-being of the American "masses." The impact that the Great Depression had on Sears business further convinced him that his company could prosper only as the American people prospered. He therefore threw his support fully behind measures which he conceived would promote the best interests of the majority of Americans. His lucid perception of the direct relationship between Sears business and certain New Deal programs is illustrated by a letter he wrote to Secretary of Agriculture Wallace in the late spring of 1938. In it, he pointed out that "according to the division of my office which checks with your department's payments," agriculture payments for the first half of 1938 would run about $1 million behind those of the first half of 1937. "It seems to me particulary important," he chided, "that the payments be expedited this summer."[20] After all, the new Fall and Winter Catalog would soon be in the customers' hands.

Wood was one of the few big businessmen who supported Roosevelt and most of his early policies, and a warm friendship quickly developed between the two men. Wood was a guest at the White House on more than one occasion and was one of the original members of the Business Advisory Council, established by the secretary of commerce at the president's behest in an effort to build a bridge between the administration and the business community. Wood supported Roosevelt for reelection in 1936, but relations between the two men began to cool early in the second term. This was chiefly due to Wood's dissatisfaction with the administration's labor policies and spending on federal relief projects as well as with the undistributed profits tax.[21] He was particularly concerned with what he perceived as the anti-business rhetoric of some of those in Roosevelt's cabinet; he found some of the pronouncements of Harold Ickes and Rexford Guy Tugwell especially disturbing.[22] Relations were further strained when Wood spoke out against the president's effort to increase the size of the

Supreme Court. The final break came with the onset of war in Europe and Roosevelt's moves toward intervention, which Wood strongly and publicly opposed.

Wood was deeply concerned about America's drift toward involvement in the European conflict. He believed that capitalism could survive a Hitler-dominated Europe but not American participation in the war. In the fall of 1940, in a major address before the Chicago Council on Foreign Relations, he spelled out his apprehensions:

> Victorious or not, we will be faced at the conclusion of such a war with great economic dislocations—the rich would face a capital levy, the middle classes impoverishment, and the masses a lowered standard of living and the loss of most of the social gains so far secured. Competent observers believe that if the war is prolonged in Europe over one or two years, it will result in communism in all Europe, and a species of national socialism in England. If we are involved, it probably spells the end of capitalism all over the world.[23]

Wood found others whose views were similar to his in the America First Committee, an influential and vocal political pressure group. Although he was not one of its original organizers, he was offered and accepted its chairmanship and became one of the Americans who were most prominently identified with opposition to President Roosevelt's foreign policy. There was considerable anti-interventionist sentiment in the country at the time (the Draft Act of 1940 passed by a single vote), and the America First movement attracted wide support, some of which had pronounced anti-Semitic and other extremist overtones.

America First quickly became the target of attack, much of which was focused personally on General Wood because of his public stature and the leadership role he had assumed within the group. Harold Ickes, secretary of the interior and Roosevelt's hatchet man, called Wood a "Nazi fellow-traveler," a sentiment echoed by many other Roosevelt supporters. Especially strong attacks came from a number of Jewish leaders and spokesmen for Jewish organizations, who were gravely concerned by the overt anti-Semitism of some of the more rabble-rousing elements which crowded together under the America First banner. One of the most visible of those identified with America First was Colonel Charles A. Lindbergh.

In 1940 Lindbergh visited Germany, where he was the personal guest of Air Marshal Hermann Goering, who went to great pains to give him a firsthand view of Germany's military might, especially in the air. Lindbergh was a close personal friend of General Wood, and on his return to the

States he reported to Wood in some detail what he had seen and sounded his conviction that Germany was invincible.[24] Not long afterward, Lindbergh delivered an address in Des Moines, Iowa, in which he not only dwelt on Germany's might but also charged that American Jews were among the principal forces leading America toward war.

The speech confirmed the direst apprehensions of leaders within the Jewish community and raised a violent storm of protest, much of it directed at Wood personally. Wood was angered and deeply resentful; he himself had never expressed the views voiced by Lindbergh, and he felt it unfair that those views were attributed to him. The fact that many of the attacks originated in the East from quarters which Wood identified as "Eastern financial interests" did not help matters. This only increased his bitterness and reinforced the dislike and distrust he had felt for the eastern financial community since his days at Montgomery Ward and perhaps even since his youth.

Wood took pains to reassure his personal Jewish friends and business associates of the true state of his feelings, and most of these accepted his explanation at face value. A notable exception was Lessing Rosenwald, who was not content with a private reassurance but demanded that Wood publicly disavow the Lindbergh allegations. When Wood failed to do so, Lessing broke with him completely and the long-standing personal relationship between the two men was never afterward restored. Max Adler, who after his retirement as Julius Rosenwald's merchandising vice-president had become an important Chicago civic figure, shared Lessing's views. Adler's son Robert vividly recalled his father's feelings many years later: "I know that [my father] was . . . greatly distressed at the General's attitude. Notwithstanding General Wood's protestations that he was not in any way or manner anti-Semitic, he simply wouldn't do anything to prove he wasn't. He wouldn't openly come out and say publicly that he wasn't." [25]

Here, probably, lies the key to understanding Wood's attitude. He was a proud man who resented the implication that he was guilty unless he proved otherwise. The episode left an aftermath of rancor on both sides that lasted for the remainder of Wood's life and persists to this day in the minds of many influential members of the Jewish community. The alleged anti-Semitism which in some quarters mars Wood's reputation rests largely on this unhappy chapter in his long and active life.

Wood's relationship with America First was more complex than it appeared on the surface. He was opposed to American intervention in the war, but he was not a pacifist. Nor was he unaware of the ragtag character of some of the groups attracted by America First who had little in common except their attitude about the war and their antagonism toward Roosevelt. As Wood explained at the time to one of his younger Sears associates:

> When the America First Committee was formed, it was formed by good people and had good, high ideals. But some very undesirable people got involved in it. The easy thing for me to do, with all this criticism, was to just drop it and walk away. But I want to tell you something. There's going to be a war in this country, and the day war is declared I'm going to disband it. If I walked away, somebody would take over who wouldn't disband it and it would make a lot of trouble for America and the American people. So I'll just take the criticism. The day war is declared, I'll disband it.[26]

He was as good as his word. Immediately after the bombing of Pearl Harbor, Wood called an emergency meeting of the America First board and declared the organization dissolved forthwith. He told the board: "Listen, we formed this committee to prevent our country from going to war, but it is in war, so our function is done. Now let's all go out and do what we can to help our country."[27]

Although he was by now sixty-two years of age, Wood volunteered for military service. When he was turned down, his good friend General H. H. ("Hap") Arnold intervened by asking Roosevelt to put him back on the active list; Arnold's reason was that he needed Wood's help in improving the Air Force service of supply. But Roosevelt vetoed this proposal and, according to Wood, told Arnold that "while he had no objections to my doing this work for the Air Corps he would never allow me to wear the uniform."[28]

Undaunted, Wood agreed to assist Arnold as a civilian. During the war years, he visited every air base in every theater of war and made two complete circuits of the globe—altogether over 200,000 miles by air.[29] Knowledgeable Sears people came to realize that when Wood was not seen about for a longer time than usual, it probably meant he was off on assignment for General Arnold, checking the service of supply backup for a major up-coming military campaign. Bringing to bear all his rich experience in supply operations,[30] he was able to make an important contribution to the success of General Arnold's undertakings and was awarded the Legion of Merit for his efforts. Wood later estimated that during the war years he had devoted about 40 percent of his time to the military.[31]

Despite the demands of the military and his continued responsibilities in the management of Sears, General Wood in 1944 found time to promote the presidential candidacy of General Douglas MacArthur. In 1948 he himself conducted and won a vigorous campaign to be elected delegate to the Republican National Convention, where he again endeavored to secure the nomination of MacArthur. He devoted considerable time to international affairs, including U.S. military strategy in Korea and the rebuilding of Western Europe. In a reversal more apparent than real of his earlier espousal of major portions of the New Deal, he lent the weight of his prestige and influence to efforts to reorient the Republican party along lines other than those represented by Wendell Wilkie and Thomas Dewey, which he equated with "Eastern financial interests." He strongly supported Robert Taft for the 1952 Republican nomination and was bitter over Taft's defeat by Dwight Eisenhower.

Wood was also a strong supporter of American Action, a short-lived organization which sought to revive some of the elements of America First, and of the American Security Council, which was concerned with the threats of Soviet Communism. What with one thing and another, time certainly did not weigh heavily on him.

That he stayed on to head Sears over these many years was due in part to a deft sleight of hand. At General Wood's behest, the Sears board of directors in 1934 had established mandatory retirement ages for all employees, a practice not yet widespread. While he set age sixty-five as the age of retirement for most employees, he fixed that of officers and executives at sixty to accelerate the replacement of older key personnel with younger, more vigorous talent. This proved to be a wise policy that was of material aid in building organizational strength.

However, when he himself approached the designated age of sixty in 1939, Wood was far from ready to relinquish control. He encouraged Lessing Rosenwald to retire as board chairman, a position he had held since his father's death in 1932, to devote full time to his many philanthropic and cultural interests and the management of the Rosenwald family's financial affairs. (The personal break between the two men had not yet occurred.) Wood had himself elected chairman in Lessing's stead and had the board adopt a minute stating that for purposes of the retirement policy the chairman was not an employee and the policy did not apply to him.

In selecting his successor as president, Wood had chosen between his operating and merchandising vice-presidents, both able men who had given Sears long years of service and were qualified for the higher position. His choice fell to T. J. Carney, his chief operating officer. Donald M. Nelson, chief merchandising officer, received as consolation prize the newly created post of executive vice-president. T. V. Houser succeeded Nelson as merchandising vice-president, and Gordon V. Hattersley succeeded Carney as operating vice-president. The changing of the guard was accomplished smoothly and without a break in organizational continuity, echoing the events of more than a decade before.

At the time of his move from president to board chairman, Wood had announced his intention to relinquish active management of company affairs and devote more time to his family, civic, and recreational interests, and there is little doubt that this is what he genuinely meant to do. But two events intervened to change his course. The first was Pearl Harbor and the subsequent plunge of the company into the wrenching dislocations of a war economy; the company faced critical problems of adjustment which commanded his personal attention. The second was the untimely death of the man he had chosen to succeed him as president, T. J. Carney.

Carney fell ill early in 1942 and died in June of that year. Had Donald M. Nelson still been at Sears, Wood might have awarded the position to him, but Nelson had been called to Washington to head the War Production Board. Wood turned to Arthur Barrows, who had followed him from Ward's and had headed the Sears Pacific Coast territory since its creation in 1940. This proved to be an unfortunate choice; Barrows soon mounted a cabal to depose Wood. Barrows's efforts, however, were rather maladroit, and Wood neutralized them by moving Barrows out of the presidency and into the newly recreated but essentially dutiless post of vice-chairman of the board.

Choosing a successor to Barrows was difficult because Wood could not be sure how far the intrigue had reached; he needed someone whose personal loyalty he could trust and who had close connections with the field organization, where Wood felt it necessary to assure his strength. He found the man he wanted in Fowler B. McConnell, about whom he had no doubts whatsoever and who as vice-president for personnel and retail administration had the solid field relationships Wood considered important. McConnell was something less than a brilliant leader and he was certainly no innovator, but he did possess a manifest quality of personal integrity which aided in the rapid restoration of internal harmony. Moreover, he was a capable administrator on whom Wood could rely to execute his wishes competently and keep company affairs on an even keel during his extended absences. McConnell suited his purposes well.

Considering the circumstances of the company presidency and the uncertainties of the wartime situation, Wood understandably felt constrained to keep his hand in more closely than he might otherwise have done; as he observed in a 1945 memorandum: "Up until 1939 practically all power was vested in the president of the company and ever since 1939 administrative and executive power had been technically vested in the president though I have been able as chairman to guide decisions when necessary." [32] In Wood's mind, "when necessary" and "fairly often" were synonymous.

General Wood accurately foresaw the tremendous economic expansion which would follow the end of hostilities. His estimate of the shape of things to come differed sharply from that of Sewell Avery, who had by this time long been head of Montgomery Ward (see Chapter 11 herein). Convinced that there would be a severe and extended postwar business slump, Avery rigorously husbanded his resources, building up large financial reserves to bolster liquidity. Wood, to the contrary, saw the time as one of unparalleled opportunity and plowed every dollar he could lay his hands on into new, expanded, and more efficient facilities. In the eight years following the war, Sears opened 134 new retail stores, relocated 83, and enlarged 149. More millions of dollars were poured into larger parking lots, warehouses, mail-order plants, and other facilities.[33] During this same period, Wood embarked on the building of a great system of retail stores in Latin America and moved into Canada in a joint venture with Simpsons Ltd. (see Chapter 11 herein). Planning and overseeing this vast hemisphere-wide expansion placed demands on Wood, and these years were among the busiest and most productive of his entire career. He had the added satisfaction of seeing Sears sales almost double while Ward's dropped by nearly a tenth.[34]

But time was running out on him. As he approached his seventy-fifth birthday in June of 1954, he was finally prevailed upon by his outside directors, led by his longtime friend and financial confidant, Sidney Weinberg, to retire. This he did with reluctance but good grace. He continued, however, as an active member of the board of directors for another fourteen years; during the first half-dozen of these he still exercised considerable influence on the course of company affairs, especially in the selection of senior officers. Thereafter, his level of involvement gradually diminished, and he finally relinquished even his director's post to become honorary board chairman in May of 1968. He died on November 6, 1969, at the age of ninety.

When General Wood joined Sears in 1924, the company was engaged exclusively in the mail-order business and served only the rural American market. That year it had sales of $206 million, made a profit of $14 million, and employed 23,000 people—a sizable business for its day. When Wood laid down his duties as chief executive officer thirty years later, Sears was the world's largest merchandising organization with sales of $3 billion, profits of $141 million, and 200,000 employees.

In 1924 the company's entire business was conducted through four mail-order plants. In 1954 there were eleven plants, 694 retail stores, and 570 catalog sales offices; there were Sears units in every state of the Union, as well as the seven most populous provinces of Canada and six Latin American countries. The wholly Sears-owned Allstate Insurance group of companies was a giant in its field, and fifty-nine manufacturing enterprises in which Sears had ownership interests supplied over a quarter of the company's sales volume. In 1953, Wood's last full year in office, well before the introduction of revolving charge accounts and credit cards, over six and a half million American families were paying on Sears current time payment accounts, and more than one out of every twenty dollars spent by Americans for general merchandise was spent at Sears.[35]

Even more significant than figures such as these was the place Sears had achieved in the minds of the American public and in the culture of the country. Under the leadership of Robert E. Wood, it had become far more than merely a successful economic enterprise; it had taken its place as an American institution and remains one until this day.

Julius Rosenwald, center, welcomes General Wood to Sears; Charles M. Kittle stands at Rosenwald's right. November 1, 1924.

General Wood, vice-president of Sears, circa 1926.

General Wood, left, and Julius Rosenwald with the ten millionth Allstate tire, circa
1928.

General Wood, right, with President Franklin D. Roosevelt, at the American Retail Federation banquet, Washington, D.C., July 18, 1939.

General Wood, right, and Colonel Charles A. Lindbergh, America First rally, 1941.

General Wood in his office, January 1948.

General Wood, left, and Sewell Avery, chairman and chief executive of Montgomery Ward & Co., circa 1955 (Calvin Potts).

William Wallace, executive director of the Profit Sharing Plan, General Wood, and the author reviewing employee questions at "Big Board" meeting, April 1950.

PART II

THE STRATEGIES

4

The Business Purpose

THE SHARP IF BRIEF panic of 1920–21 left both Sears, Roebuck and Montgomery Ward bloodied but alive. Both companies subsequently underwent extensive reorganization and refinancing; both trimmed away excess accumulations of staff and overhead; and both were again operating profitably within a couple of years. However, neither regained the vigorous and exuberant vitality that had characterized it earlier in the century. Growth resumed, but at modest rates; profitability was restored but was harder to sustain. As it turned out, the problems of both companies were more deep-seated and intractable than anyone realized at the time. In short, neither company recognized the far-reaching changes which were taking place in its basic market. And neither, at least initially, perceived the need to redefine its strategic goals or basic business purpose.

Richard Sears was an ad hoc businessman. His concept of market opportunity was simply to sell what he was able to buy advantageously, and this he did with remarkable skill. His concept of business purpose was simply to make money, and this, too, he did very well. To him, his market—the rural, small-town America he knew and understood so thoroughly—was something to exploit rather than serve.

Upon joining Sears, Roebuck in 1895, Julius Rosenwald introduced a radically different and far broader concept of business purpose: to serve that same market by systematically identifying its needs for goods and finding means for satisfying those needs at prices it could afford. Under him, the company evolved from "seller *to* the American farmer" to "buyer *for* the American farmer." If in the process the firm made money—which it certainly did, and in figures far greater than Richard Sears had ever dreamed of—the reward was for service rendered. Rendering service became the primary objective of the business; reaping profits was derivative.

Montgomery Ward had long conceived its business mission in similar terms, and once Rosenwald established the concept at Sears both companies proved fabulously successful. The American farmer was better served than he had ever been served before, and the two companies prospered as few firms before them had.

By the early 1920s, however, the "buyer for the American farmer" concept had begun to lose its relevance to economic and social realities. With the coming of the automobile and good roads, rural America rapidly became less isolated, and the kinds of merchandise of interest to the farm family came more and more to be the kinds of merchandise of interest to city dwellers as well. In this process, radio advertising also played a significant role. There was no longer a separately definable rural market with its own unique characteristics and needs; that market, and the previously distinct urban market, were homogenizing into a general American mass market.

The then managements of Sears and Ward's alike failed to grasp the significance of these new developments. They knew that their companies had problems; sales were increasingly difficult to get and profits were slipping. Alarmed, they sought to improve matters by doing better what they were already doing. They drove harder bargains with their merchandise sources, stepped up their advertising, opened new plants to be closer to their customers, streamlined operations, and eliminated unnecessary costs. They failed to understand that the root of their difficulties lay in the fact that their market had undergone far-reaching changes and that they had failed to change with it.

Sears found the answer first—fortuitously. By bringing General Wood into the company in November of 1924, Julius Rosenwald acquired much more than the higher order of managerial skills he was seeking. He acquired a man who was capable of introducing a new entrepreneurial concept as fully responsive to the needs and opportunities of the times as Rosenwald's own had been to the needs and opportunities of a quarter-century earlier.

Wood, lately and briefly of Ward's, came to Sears unfettered by notions of either company's proper role. Because he was not steeped in the traditions of an established and hitherto highly successful business, he was able to see the problem clearly and conceive means for dealing with it. Years later, thinking back on the positive value of lack of previous experience in a business, he noted: "You can see things that men who are very close to the business don't see. It's the old story of the forest and trees." [1] What General Wood saw was the "forest" of demographic and cultural movements that were irrevocably altering the structure and character of American society.

One of Wood's interesting personal traits was a fascination with census data. This had its origins during his years on the Canal, where good reading material—or, for that matter, any reading material—was scarce. The story is told that once, while confined to the infirmary with a minor ailment, the only thing Wood could find to read was the *Statistical Abstract of the United States*, which he began perusing simply to pass the time but soon came to study avidly. Whether or not the infirmary story is apocryphal, it is clear that in his Canal experience he acquired a taste for and an understanding of demographic and economic statistics that stayed with him for the rest of his life. During his mature years, there was a widely circulated myth (probably grounded in fact) that the *Statistical Abstract* was his favorite bedside reading. In any event, his keen grasp of major trends in American life was evident in his business planning and even ordinary conversation. He was frequently consulted by the Bureau of the Census and other governmental generators and users of statistics who valued his insights into the social realities reflected in their data.

He was a student not only of the census but also of the American scene as a whole. In his own words, he had "always been a reader," [2] and while his chief recreational reading was history [3] a sizable part of his attention was devoted to what was going on in the contemporary world at large. In the 1920s America was in a state of ferment, and Wood observed it closely. There was the mass movement of people—especially younger people—from the farms and small towns to the cities, impelled in part by the allure of high wages, dramatized by Henry Ford's $5 a day, and in part by the revolution in agriculture which greatly increased farm productivity and brought about a surplus of farm workers. There were the vast transformations generated by the automobile and radio which created an atmosphere of rising expectations and expanded the range and diversity of consumer wants. In that prosperous decade, goods that had once been luxuries reserved for the select few became objects of broader aspiration; as more and more people moved from the lower class to the working class (whose income was rising) and many to the middle class, the basic structure of American society was forever changed.

Wood not only recognized that the business would have to change with the times but also that the times brought with them an array of unprecedented opportunities. Looking back on this era many years later, he observed: "Merchandising is not merely the shrewd buying or selling of goods . . . it is the perception of the underlying trends of our country by those in control of a company, and the adoption of policies conforming to those trends, the understanding and execution of those policies by the employees of the Company and their adaptability in changing from a policy or course of business, wise in the past but disastrous in the future."[4]

In response to what he perceived to be "the underlying trends of our country," he reformulated Sears business purpose. Instead of serving as buyer for the American farmer, the corporate role that Julius Rosenwald had outlined some thirty years before, Sears would now provide a service of supply for the American mass market. This was a far broader concept than Rosenwald's had been, and it included within it a significant social purpose as well. In comparison with the traditional needs of rural America, the emerging needs of the new working and middle classes were much more diversified and demanding. What Wood intended to do by meeting these needs was to improve the American standard of living, a theme he reiterated on numerous occasions.

General Wood defined marketing as the "study of needs and wants of the customer, and the fulfilling of those needs and wants with a superior product or service at the very lowest possible prices."[5] This was a far cry from Richard Sears's earlier notion that marketing was simply selling what one could buy for whatever one could get. Future scholars and writers would view Wood's ideas as pivotal. In *Management Tasks, Responsibilities, Practices*, for example, Peter Drucker examines the Sears, Roebuck that Wood fashioned and observes: "True marketing starts out the way [Sears, Roebuck] starts out—with the customer, his demographics, his realities, his needs, his values. It does not ask, 'What do we want to sell?' It asks, 'What does the customer want to buy?' It does not say, 'This is what our product or service does.' It says, 'These are the satisfactions the customer looks for, values and needs.'"[6]

Improving American living standards by serving customer needs was not the only social goal Wood envisioned in his concept of business purpose. He saw the company itself as an agent of social change. In a memorandum to the Sears Board of Directors dated August 3, 1940, he wrote: "We are also giving the opportunities of employment under liberal conditions to an increasing number of employees, [and] we are providing promotion and greater opportunities to our key men and our younger executives." [7] Important as these concerns for the people in his organization may have been, they were ancillary to what in his mind was the primary reason for Sears existence: the furnishing of value to the customer. Wood often reminded his buyers that it was the customer, not he, who was their boss, and that their future and that of the company depended on giving the customer the best value for the dollar. In 1936, for example, he told them: "The business has grown great because it has given the American people values. The moment it ceases to give values, that moment it will begin to decline." [8] The buyers took his words to heart. Years later, Wood would admit that they sometimes made mistakes, but he would stress in almost the same breath that "they've never departed from the original principle that their business is gained from giving value to customers." [9]

This did not mean that all Sears merchandise had to be low in cost. Wood had no objection to higher-priced items as long as they met certain definite criteria. As E. P. Brooks recalls: "When it came to merchandise, the General was interested in value. It could be a high priced thing, but for that price there must be more value offered than by any competitor. The price could be the same, but there had to be more value." [10]

One of the things that Wood set out to do was to develop a mass market for goods that previously had been confined to a class market. What Sears accomplished with refrigerators serves as a case in point. Until the 1930s, electric refrigerators were available but not widely affordable. An article in the September 1925 issue of *Scientific American* contained this passage: "You have seen the electric refrigerator advertised for a number of years, yet you do not find them in universal use, nor are they yet even commonplace. Although the initial cost of these home units is no higher than that of a flivver [the least expensive contemporary automobile], and the upkeep less, they have not yet reached the stage in their evolution where operation is near enough to perfection to bring the wide market that their many good points warrant." [11] In the year in which the article appeared, the Model T Ford sold for about $350. By 1931, six short years later, the Sears catalog was offering electric refrigerators for $139.50 and the appliance was well on its way to common use. Today an electric refrigerator is regarded as a necessity, not a luxury, which would not be the case if it still cost the same as an inexpensive automobile—in 1983 terms, about $5,000. This example, which could be multiplied many times over, suggests something of the revolutionary impact that Sears merchandising methods had on the American standard of living. Other forces were also at work, of course, including technical innovation and the response of competitors to the challenge presented by Sears, but Wood's concept of business purpose and the brilliance of its execution played a leading role in reshaping the daily lives of the American people.

Throughout his long business career, General Wood's primary goal was always that of serving the customer. This orientation may have traced back to his Canal and World War I experiences. In each instance, his work focused on meeting urgent needs—first the needs of engineers and workers at the Canal construction face, and then of officers and men in battle—rather than making a profit. He learned to look on goods and their distribution from the perspective of the user, not the manufacturer or the merchant. This habit of thinking, deeply ingrained by the time he arrived at Sears, translated readily and perhaps unconsciously into a genuine concern for the needs of customers.

Wood was as interested as anyone else in making money for himself, his associates, and his shareholders. But, like Julius Rosenwald before him, he viewed profits as rewards for services rendered. He also viewed them as the means by which Sears could continue rendering those services. With this in mind, he kept a watchful eye on the internal operations of the company; his subordinates were keenly aware of his commitment to the efficient allocation of resources, of which operating profits were the measure. This, too, was essentially a social and not a narrowly economic concern.

More than once, Wood was willing to sacrifice profit maximization to his larger goal of meeting the needs of the growing Sears market. The inside front cover of the Fall 1934 catalog—delivered while the country was still in the depths of the Great Depression—carried this letter signed by him:

> When it came to setting prices for this Fall 1934 Catalog, we felt it was only fair and right, under the circumstances, for us to think first of our customers' present ability to pay, to disregard wholesale costs and to make, if need be, a real sacrifice in our profit.
>
> This has been done.
>
> You will note that prices in this book, despite advances in raw materials, wage rates and increased expense in practically every direction, are in most cases below those of our Spring Catalog and in many cases lower than a year ago.
>
> As this is being written, drought conditions in large crop-producing areas are most serious. The income of our customers in these regions is thus adversely affected. To do our part in relieving this condition,

we have priced articles of real need—underwear, hosiery, shoes, utility apparel, textiles—close to actual cost of production.[12]

With his pride plainly showing, Wood sent a copy of this letter, together with a table of comparative prices, to Henry A. Wallace, then secretary of agriculture. He included a personal note to Wallace: "The message is not just 'hokum'; it states the facts. We are making dangerously low pricing. If we get a large volume, we will come out all right, but if we do not it will raise the devil with our profits. This is, of course, confidential. However, I believe we will continue to maintain the good will of our customers and that the lower prices will not do us any harm in the long run." [13] Wallace replied promptly: "You have adopted a policy which I think is admirable, and I trust that your clientele will respond to it. If more businessmen would follow your example . . . I am sure we would have a larger volume of consumption and, therefore, a higher level of industrial improvement." [14]

Two years later, in 1936, Wood delivered a talk to his buyers that encapsulated what by that time had become a well-defined line of policy and action. Regarding the Sears philosophy on customer needs and company profits, he stated emphatically: "The trouble with most businesses is that they put the cart before the horse—they look at the profits first and the customer afterwards. It should be just the reverse." [15] Although the country was better off then than it had been when the Fall 1934 catalog came out, Wood admonished his audience to continue doing their utmost to keep prices down: "I believe we could easily increase our present gross profit, but I do not believe it good policy to do so. We must do our part in holding down the increase in the cost of living to the American people. If we do so, we justify our existence and contribute to the economic prosperity of the country. Not only must we, as merchants, price moderately, but as buyers we must fight hard all but the most moderate and justified increases from our manufacturers." He also listed in order of their priority what he considered to be "the three great interests in the business—the customer, the employee and the stockholder." He added important dimensions to Rosenwald's earlier concept of business purpose by acknowledging that to serve the customer a business must serve other interests as well. Arguing against the widely held belief that generating dividends for stockholders was a business's first duty, he said: "The stockholder comes last, not because he is least important, but because, in the larger sense, he cannot obtain his full measure of reward unless he has satisfied customers and satisfied employees."

Many years later, at the very height of his career, he would elaborate on this philosophy by including a fourth business "interest": the community. In a 1950 address before the Association of Cotton Textile Merchants of New York, he outlined in explicit terms how a business should regard each:

> There are four parties to any business—the customer, the employee, the community and the stockholder and the management of every business should preserve the balance of the interests of each. I have named them in what I regard as the order of their importance.
>
> The customer comes first, for unless he gets good values, courteous and fair treatment, is satisfied in every respect, he will not continue as a customer, and the business eventually decays and dies.
>
> The employee comes next. Every head of a business should consider himself a trustee for his employees as well as his stockholders. If the business is well-established and prosperous, he should try to do his utmost for his employees without their having to exert pressure on him to get their proper rights. He should regard as one of his objectives the constant raising of the standard of living of his employees. If employees have confidence in the fairness and sense of justice of their employer, and feel that he is truly interested in their welfare, that his feeling for them springs from his heart as well as his head, the employees will respond, and there is a vast difference in the quality and quantity of the work performed and of the amount of supervision required between such employees and those who feel just the opposite to their employer.
>
> Then comes the community in which are located the factories, the stores, offices or headquarters of a business. Due to the changes in the tax laws, it is more and more difficult for the wealthy individual to support the charities and the welfare enterprises of the community. A portion of that burden must shift to the corporation and I believe it the part of wisdom for every prosperous corporation to respond to the needs of the community, willingly and generously.
>
> Last comes the stockholder. All I can say is that if the other three parties above named are properly taken care of, the stockholder will benefit in the long pull.[16]

History has shown that Sears stockholders did in fact "benefit in the long pull"—quite handsomely. So, of course, did its customers and employees, as well as the communities into which the company ventured.

That Wood took pride in his company's accomplishments was no secret. But, as he told an audience of Sears executives in 1950, "I could not have this feeling of pride if Sears had simply made good profits and sales. Sears has been a clean business, an honest business, it has performed a real service to the American people, it has sincerely tried to guard the welfare of its employees, it has performed its obligations to the communities of our country. In short, it is not merely a business—it is a great American institution." [17] Wood's concept of business purpose was revolutionary for his era, and it established standards which kept Sears in the vanguard of business practice for many years thereafter. The current concern of leading businessmen for corporate social responsibility owes much to the example set by Sears and General Wood.

5

The Buying Strategy

EARLY IN HIS BUSINESS career, General Wood became deeply committed to the idea of integrating mass distribution with mass production. He saw this as the only way to effectively provide better quality goods at lower prices to a vast new market: rapidly growing and increasingly complex urban America. In keeping with this entrepreneurial concept, he fashioned a dual strategy. As he envisioned it, the buying part of this strategy would consist of developing partnerlike arrangements with sources of supply; the selling part would consist of grafting a far-flung chain of retail stores onto an existing system of mail-order marketing.

As a practical matter, there were only two places where Wood could work out his ideas: Montgomery Ward and Sears, Roebuck. He believed for a time that Ward's would prove to be his testing ground. In a talk delivered before Ward's buyers in March of 1924, nine months before his unceremonious firing, Wood noted that he hoped to "do for distribution what Henry Ford had done for manufacturing" through "linking up with progressive and efficient manufacturers" and plotting out "the most economical route . . . between raw materials and all classes of manufactured products and the consumer." [1]

Like his fascination for demographic statistics, this concept probably had its inception during Wood's years on the Panama Canal. To meet George Goethals's imperious demand for an uninterrupted supply of materials and equipment under difficult logistical conditions, he had to enter into long-term contracts with mills in Pennsylvania and arrange for the orderly movement of their output through the Port of New York and down to Colon by a fleet of ships shuttling back and forth over a 2,000-mile course. Subsequently, the experience he gained from keeping the American Expeditionary Force supplied during World War I gave him further insight into the potentials of organizing the movement of merchandise as a continuous flow from producer to ultimate user. By the time he joined Montgomery Ward in 1919, he was ready to develop the idea in a civilian setting; although he was able to make some progress, his tenure at Ward's proved too short and the atmosphere too inhibiting to allow for significant accomplishment there.

Both mass production and mass distribution were well-established features of the American economy by the mid-1920s. Manufacturers were turning out goods on a large scale, and merchandising organizations such as Sears, Ward's, Penney's, and Woolworth's were mass distributors by any definition. Until Wood came on the scene, however, little or no effort had been made to integrate production and distribution in a single, continuous process. The break in continuity came at the interface between producer and distributor.

In the traditional buyer-seller relationship, the origins of which were solidly grounded in classical economic theory, each party to a transaction was expected to be concerned solely with his own interests. This worked so long as all parties were at least roughly equivalent in terms of their economic clout. But the emergence of enormously powerful mass merchandisers resulted in a situation in which the benign consequences envisaged by classical theory were grossly distorted in practice. The stronger party, whether buyer or seller, drove the hardest bargain possible as a matter of course, with no regard for its effects on the other.

One of his young lieutenants described the typical buying procedure Wood found at both Ward's and Sears: "Bargaining would start from the manufacturer's list price. The buyer would work the manufacturer down, discount after discount. After he had hammered him down as far as he could, he'd take the source into the [merchandising vice president's] office and [he] would try to get another 2–3 percent discount for cash."[2] A star Sears buyer of the time had "the reputation of being able to bargain with the Sears source to the point where the source had nothing in the way of profit left. It was doing business with Sears for the fun of doing business with Sears."[3]

Even when a manufacturer built up his facilities in the hope of not only snaring one large order but also of being awarded repeat business, he had no assurance that this was the way things would turn out. In fact, the only guarantee he did have was that the buyer would put him through the same arduous bargaining process again and again—and place the order wherever he could get the best price. Loyalty between buyer and seller was unknown.

"When I came into the business," Wood later recalled, "these merchants [of Ward's and Sears] had a very bad reputation with manufacturers." He introduced a sharply different approach, but not without some difficulty: "[What I] tried to do . . . was to link up this mass distribution with the mass production. To do it, you had to have continuity. For these buyers to realize that the manufacturers had to make a profit as well as they. . . . But to do that you had to have confidence in each other and deal fairly with them. Our buyers . . . weren't dealing fairly. . . . I finally got the concept established but I had to fire several at Ward's and, after I became president, I had to fire several at Sears." [4]

General Wood was fortunate in having as one of his key lieutenants Theodore V. Houser, who had worked for him first at Montgomery Ward and joined him at Sears in 1928. Houser had been educated as an engineer, a fact which had an important bearing on the way he helped shape Sears buying policies and methods. A man of intellectual brilliance, he immediately grasped the implications inherent in the concept of integrating production and distribution; the idea appealed to his engineering mind. Soon after joining Sears, Houser became Wood's right-hand man in applying the concept to the broad range of Sears merchandising interests. [5] Over time, Houser built up around himself a corps of exceptionally able merchants who competently executed the new buying strategy. Outstanding among these was Edward Gudeman, who joined Sears as a trainee fresh from Harvard in 1927 and served as Houser's principal assistant until 1952, when he succeeded his mentor in the top Sears merchandising post.

The cornerstone of Wood's buying strategy was the development of sources on which Sears could rely for quality merchandise at low cost. But low cost was not to be achieved merely by wielding Sears great bargaining power; nor would it be sought on a transaction-by-transaction basis. Instead, Wood wanted sources who could supply not only today's needs but also tomorrow's and on into an indefinite future. His objective was to build stable, partnerlike relationships in which both parties would have a significant stake and which would be in the interests of both to strengthen and maintain. This meant that the source as well as Sears would have to be able to count on a reasonable profit. The tremendous volume in which Sears bought was not to be used as a club to beat down the source's prices but as a foundation on which the source as well as Sears could build a prosperous business.

Achieving this goal became the primary responsibility of every Sears buyer. Wood urged them to seek out sources who were good manufacturers, had low overhead, and knew how to control their costs. Sources that met these criteria were to be cultivated, and every effort was to be made to award them enough business that Sears would become their most important customer and command the first attention of their owners and managers.

Under Wood's overall direction and with Houser's and Gudeman's brilliant implementation, the Sears buying organization developed a series of means by which producer and distributor could work together for their mutual advantage and, ultimately, the benefit of the consumer. These means fell into three broad categories: design specification, manufacturing economics, and straight-line distribution.

Traditionally, manufacturers designed and developed products, and buyers from merchandising organizations made their selections from whatever was available. Wood's strategy converted the design and development of goods into a joint undertaking between Sears and its sources. In a sense, he reintroduced the practice—which predated the industrial revolution—whereby "merchants" farmed out the fabrication of goods and later assembled them for transport and resale. Thus Sears was able to realize the advantages of vertical integration without having to assume the rigidities and capital requirements of corporate ownership. Rather than purchasing factories outright, buyers worked with sources to determine what should be made and when and to find ways of reducing costs at all stages, from the acquisition of materials through manufacturing, distribution, and final delivery to the customer.

This posited an entirely new role for Sears buyers. About this role, Wood made his expectations abundantly clear in his 1936 "Talk to Buyers": "There is no longer any room in the [Sears] buying force for mediocrities, for routine buyers or order placers. . . . [We] must have men and women in our merchandising force who study and think, who know the most intimate details of the manufacture of their line, who are quick to recognize trends, who are keen judges of style, who are good pickers of the right kind of manufacturer, in the right location. That type will be rewarded, the other type must go." [6] A little over two years later, in an address to a meeting of all parent and field executives, Houser further defined the buyer's responsibilities: "[The buyer must know] what makes [an article or particular feature] of value to the customer . . . and strive to incorporate in product specifications those qualities that will add to the serviceability, convenience, appearance or life of such articles." [7] In other words, the buyer not only had to choose the most appropriate manufacturers but also had to understand what customers wanted (or, given the opportunity, would want) and develop a "feel" for the features customers would appreciate and the prices they would be willing to pay for them.

This process, which Houser labeled "specification buying" (a term which became deeply imbedded in the Sears vocabulary), allowed for the incorporation of sales features not found in competitive merchandise, or found only in goods bearing higher price tags. It also afforded opportunities for the redesign of merchandise in the interests of aesthetics as well as utility. It became a vital characteristic of the buyer's job to balance the added attractiveness of new features against the added cost of providing them; how effectively this was accomplished was seen as a prime measure of the buyer's knowledge and skill. In Houser's words: "The buyer must visualize the materials out of which his goods are made, must know where such materials come from, must know what processes these materials go through, by whom and at what cost, in order to reach the form in which you see such goods. The more a buyer can know about these matters, and at the same time be imaginative as to knowing the qualities in the finished article that the public really want [sic], the better job he can do in this way of 'specification buying.'" Houser went on to cite a specific example: the decision in 1933 to market a six-cubic-foot refrigerator (offered first in 1934) rather than remaining committed to the four-cubic-foot appliance that had theretofore been the industry standard. Six-foot boxes were being offered by some competitors, but only at a sizable price differential. The Sears buying department found that the larger size required only forty-five pounds more steel, which added less than $5 to the manufacturing cost. The head of the buying department, as Houser noted, wrote "a new chapter in the electric refrigerator business. . . . He priced and promoted the six foot size on the basis of its true production cost. In other words, he reached from the factory and a knowledge of factory costs to the consumer with an imaginative grasp of what the customer really wanted." The customer response was immediate and immense, and both the manufacturer and Sears were hard pressed to meet the demand. Profits to both parties were eminently satisfactory, and the buying public enjoyed the benefits of a merchandise value that had not previously been available.

Sears buyers became something of a phenomenon in the merchandising world. They were expected to be—and usually were—among the best informed people in the country on their particular industries. Gudeman, in a 1947 presentation to a group of merchandising executives, went so far as to claim that they should not be called "buyers" at all: "Our company is attempting to buy in a way that is entirely different from any other concern, and frankly, the name 'buyer' is incorrect. Our men are not buyers. Rather, you might almost say they are sales representatives of the factory." [8]

The story of how Sears came to be involved with the company which developed into its refrigerator source is particularly interesting. Louis C. Pfeiffle, a Sears veteran who was closely associated with Wood during Wood's early years there, recalled it many years later.[9] Apparently Wood read one day in a newspaper that not a single steam locomotive had been bought by a U.S. railroad in over a year. He knew of a company in Evansville, Indiana, that specialized in making driving rods and other parts for steam locomotives. Acting on a hunch, he picked up the telephone and called the head of the company.

"What are you going to do?" Wood asked him, "You haven't got any work coming in from the railroads. You've got a big plant and you've had to lay off a lot of people who are probably still out of work. What are you going to do?"

"I don't know," the man at the other end of the line replied. "I'm at my wits' end."

"I've got a suggestion for you," Wood continued. "You make refrigerators for us. We'll make an investment with you so you can take your whole plant, rip out the machinery you have, put in the machinery we need, and together we'll make refrigerators."

This signaled the beginning of a long and mutually profitable relationship. With Sears help, the locomotive parts company became a skillful refrigerator manufacturer. In time, it merged with yet another manufacturer of Sears appliances, and together they eventually metamorphosed into Whirlpool, Inc., which today occupies a place well up in the "Fortune 500" list of major U.S. corporations.

Specification buying gradually evolved into a highly sophisticated system. In a typical procedure, a buyer would conceive an item of merchandise he wished to develop that embodied features he felt customers would value and could be offered at prices he believed customers would find attractive. Significantly, this was almost never a *new* item of merchandise, previously unknown to the public. Sears became a great mass merchandising organization not by introducing goods with which customers were unfamiliar but by finding ways to upgrade existing lines and offering the resulting products at prices lower than those of its competitors.

So far as merchandise per se was concerned, the Sears innovative spirit was confined to improving quality and price rather than introducing the wholly new.

To aid the buyers in their task, Wood and Houser expanded the scope of the merchandise testing laboratory that had been established during Julius Rosenwald's regime. Its original purpose had been to ensure that merchandise brought in from manufacturers measured up to the claims made for it; it would now provide direct assistance in the preparation of specifications for better lines of merchandise. Renamed the Merchandise Testing and Development Laboratory, it was staffed by specialists in design and by technicians who were not only experts on various materials—such as metals, wood, plastics, fabrics, and the like—but who also had a thorough understanding of manufacturing processes and their costs.

The development of improved merchandise that would represent attractive values to the consumer was in fact a three-way partnership. The buyer was the leader, responsible for satisfactory volume and profit. The Merchandise Testing and Development Laboratory worked out the optimum design features that could be incorporated within a desired range of manufacturing cost and selling price. The manufacturer, who was usually brought into the process well before the specifications had been finalized, contributed his own expertise and made sure that the specifications could be met on terms that were satisfactory to him. Toward the end of the process, all three cooperated in outlining methods of fabrication, production schedules, and projected costs. The partnership proved to be a highly effective one; both Sears and the source prospered. In the long run, however, it was the customer who benefited most.

At each step in the procedure, the primary emphasis was on customer value. As Wood frequently admonished his buyers, "We should be known for our values, not our low prices." E. P. Brooks tells of a conversation he once had with Wood regarding a new line of hosiery that had been developed by the Sears buying department with the aid of the Laboratory and in cooperation with the source.[10] "It was a remarkable stocking," Brooks recalls, "but it had to be sold at a pretty high price." Brooks himself thought the price was too high and that the goods would meet with too much customer resistance. His talk with Wood went something like this:

"Is this the *best* hose we know how to make?" Wood inquired.

"Yes, apparently it is," Brooks replied. "There's nothing on the market like it, but we have to sell it at such-and-such a price."

"But then, it's a great value?" Wood wanted to know. On Brooks assuring him that it was, Wood closed the discussion with, "That's all right, then. Go ahead with it."

"It wasn't cheap," Brooks adds, "but at that price it was more than you could get anywhere else. This is what [Wood] meant by value."

The buyer's special relationship with the source enabled him to contribute importantly to improving the efficiency of manufacturing operations. With his own knowledge of materials and processes and the ongoing support of laboratory technicians on whom he could call, he could often make suggestions for lowering costs or upgrading quality.

There were two additional means by which the buyer could help the source to achieve major efficiencies. First, he could place orders in such a way that the source could keep its workers and machines operating at a steady pace over long periods of time. This effectively smoothed out the peaks and valleys in the yearly production cycle and allowed the source to realize dramatic cuts in production costs. True, the source had to pile up sizable inventories during slow selling seasons (lawn mowers in January, blankets in July), but the great savings outweighed the risks.

Second, the buyer—since he was buying for Sears—could order enough of the items Sears was interested in to allow the source to produce only those instead of the larger number of items necessary to serve the general trade. This, too, had the end result of evening out production runs; it was far more efficient for the source to keep its machines and workers turning out what Sears wanted than to shift them frequently from one item to another.

In his 1936 "Talk to Buyers," General Wood outlined these two principles and stressed Sears role in their implementation: "If a factory . . . manufactures consistently day in and day out, and manufactures a few numbers only, it will achieve efficiency. Sears is the only big concern that recognizes that production problem. A number of companies who could take advantage of this information do not, while others are not able to, since they do not have a volume that is large enough to run a factory the whole year long." [11]

Other elements in Wood's buying tactics helped widen the Sears competitive margin even more. He had learned at Montgomery Ward the advantage, in certain lines of goods, of having the distributor take responsibility for raw material procurement; this relieved the manufacturer of having to speculate in the volatile commodities markets and assured the distributor of predictable cost prices. At Sears, he was able to take this practice much further. By 1939, the raw material content of important

Sears lines ran into substantial figures: 107 million pounds of cotton, 47 million pounds of rubber, 40 million pounds of hides, 15 million pounds of copper, one million pounds of silk.[12] Because no single source could use more than a fraction of raw material quantities such as these, the fact that Sears assumed responsibility for their procurement yielded cost advantages in lines where even small differences in cost could make large differences in the price of finished products. Furthermore, it enabled Sears to engage in hedging operations with added cost advantages.[13]

In his 1939 address to Sears executives, T. V. Houser noted still another benefit inherent in Sears buying practices: " 'Specification buying' permits the use of a number of factories throughout the country located properly from the standpoint of transportation costs on incoming raw materials and outgoing finished goods. . . . In other words, a uniform product is possible in Sears stores, built to a common specification and with costs based on a common raw material." [14]

Buyers were expected to be thoroughly versed in the economics of the industries with which they dealt; it was not enough merely to know their technologies of production. For example, when the costs of tools and dies and other capital facilities were too great to permit duplication, the manufacture of certain items—such as refrigerators—was concentrated at one location. The production of mattresses, on the other hand, required far less of an investment, and because the product was bulky and expensive to ship it was best to manufacture it at plants located at strategic points around the country. A relatively small capital investment, however, did not always point to the need for decentralized production. The manufacture of women's apparel did not require a large outlay of capital, but there were advantages to concentrating production in a few style centers, and this could be done without difficulty because shipping costs were not an important element of the final cost. In other words, the economic characteristics of industries varied widely, and it was an essential part of the buyer's job to know those characteristics and design his procurement strategies accordingly.

Under Wood's concept of integrating production and distribution into a single, continuous process, the source was provided with yet another major advantage: the economies of what Wood liked to call "straight-line distribution." Sears relieved the source of virtually all the costs and managerial problems of moving its output from the end of its production line to the hands of the ultimate consumer. To Wood, Houser, and other senior officers, this was in keeping with the buyers' role as "sales representatives of the factory." In one of his discussions of that role and its implications,

Gudeman described the typical experience of a factory which sold to Sears as well as to independent department stores:

> That factory will have a sales manager who contacts the independent department stores and tries to keep them happy. But, in selling to Sears, that factory deals with a buyer, who provides the same thing that a factory's own sales department provides for the independent department store trade. Our buyers tell the factory what they need. They work out with the production men the best methods of manufacturing what they want most efficiently. They arrive at a just price. They provide the manufacturer with a profit that reflects the savings that can be made by operating efficiently. Then the buyer, through his merchandise list and through his catalogs, fans out his merchandise for nationwide distribution through the retail stores and mail order plants.[15]

This nationwide distribution service was one of the most important things the buyer had to offer. As Gudeman went on to say: "There is no selling expense in our cost because the manufacturer doesn't have to sell us. Our buyer goes to the factory. There is no credit risk because we pay our bills; there is no sustained advertising." The rule of thumb at the time held that a manufacturer had to get 15 to 20 percent more when selling in the usual way to realize the same profit he enjoyed when selling to Sears. "[Generally], I believe," Gudeman concluded, "the manufacturer makes more selling Sears, and we want him to."

During all the years of General Wood's active involvement in the management of Sears, these buying methods produced cost advantages in major Sears lines that the competition was simply unable to match. This competitive margin enabled Sears to offer merchandise values which played a significant part in the company's phenomenal growth under Wood's leadership.

A considerable share of Sears merchandising success was due to the skill with which savings in cost were used. Gudeman outlined the several options open to the buyer: "One, he can take the item into Sears line at a higher gross profit and sell at the same price as competition so stores can make a higher gross. Two, he can take that cost saving, and he can put it into sales promotion. . . . Three, (and this is what we really want to do) he can take that cost saving, put it back into the quality of the product and still maintain a competitive price."

While the establishment of stable, long-term relationships with efficient, dependable sources was the basic element of Wood's buying strategy, he made it clear that he did not want to take the source's entire output.

For one thing, he believed that the source should remain subject to the general market, not just Sears. He wanted to take a substantial part of the source's output and to be its most important customer, but he felt that the source should also have to fight for enough non-Sears business to realize a satisfactory overall corporate profit. Wood feared that the source would grow soft and lose competitive vitality if it had an assured taker for all its output; similarly, he was reluctant for Sears to grow wholly dependent on the source. Wood was keenly aware of the dangers in store for both Sears and the source should this type of situation arise: "If Sears were to withdraw, it would ruin them. On the other hand, it works the other way too. Sears has these big lines, and if the supplier decided he was through, it would take two years for us to get [back] into the business." [16]

For certain lines, however, it proved necessary to have single-source procurement. These were lines whose manufacture required large tool-and-die expenses, such as refrigerators and other major appliances. Here it was more economical to place all the company's eggs in one basket and to rely on other means for keeping the source on its toes and assuring its continuing dependability; the most effective of these means was for Sears to acquire a share in the ownership of the source. Usually this was accompanied by Sears representation on the source's board of directors.

This route was followed only under special circumstances, however. Wood held unswervingly to the view that Sears proper role was that of distributor, not producer. He wanted his people to focus on their merchandising problems and not be distracted by the technical, labor, and financial problems of running factories. He knew full well that they could spread their efforts to encompass these areas when necessary, but in the absence of compelling reasons to the contrary, he cautioned them to "concentrate on distribution because distribution is our field." [17]

Sears, of course, was a prosperous—even wealthy—company, but its treasury was not unlimited, as Wood was often reminded by the urgent entreaties of his officers for additional facilities to accommodate their rapidly growing markets. Throughout his entire Sears career, he had to husband his capital resources carefully; for example, he knew from experience that he could generate a better return on money invested in new and enlarged stores and wareouses than in factories, and he structured his capital budget accordingly. Moreover, his keen political instincts warned him that the American public would be sensitive to excessive concentrations of economic power, as large-scale vertical integration might easily be perceived to represent.

Despite these solid reasons for adopting a general policy of eschewing ownership in sources, Sears found in a number of instances that partial ownership was essential to the achievement of its merchandising goals, and Wood was quite ready to invest in a key source when it was clear that doing so would serve a useful merchandising purpose. One such purpose was to protect Sears interests where the source was Sears sole supplier of a particular item or items. Another was to strengthen the capacity of a supplier who had proved reliable. Sears buying relationships were often first established while sources were still relatively small; as their business volumes grew under the stimulus of Sears burgeoning demand, many found themselves hard pressed for capital. Sears provided financial assistance to such sources in a number of ways, including loans, payments for merchandise in advance, and the like. In cases where the need was substantial, as for major capital expenditures, and sufficient funds were not readily available on reasonable terms through customary financial channels, Sears sometimes found it expedient to make an equity investment. Finally, there were times when it was apparent that a capital expenditure would result in lower costs to Sears; as E. P. Brooks recalls, he never had any problem getting Wood to agree on a capital investment provided it met this criterion: "Our job in the factory office was to see that we had low cost facilities. [Wood] never held back on capital expenditures if I had good reason to think they would contribute to low costs." [18]

Where for good and sufficient merchandising reasons Sears made such investments, it was careful in all but the rarest instances to restrict itself to a minority ownership position. One such instance involved a farm implement manufacturing company which Julius Rosenwald had acquired many years before as a means for penetrating the market then firmly under the control of the farm machinery trust; while the trust had long since been dissolved, Sears found it convenient for a variety of reasons to maintain ownership of the factory. Another special case was an electronics firm where a number of financial, managerial, and technical circumstances made it logical for Sears to assume full ownership. Examples such as these were few and far between and represented conspicuous departures from firmly held policy. Wood's reasons for holding to this policy were simple: minority ownership, whether or not it included representation on the source's board, was sufficient to protect Sears interests while simultaneously keeping prime responsibility for satisfactory performance where it belonged—in the hands of the manufacturing partner.

Significantly, Wood and his lieutenants did not try to fit Sears buying practices into rigid patterns. They were pragmatic men who had clear notions of what they wanted to accomplish and the end results they wanted to achieve, but they also knew how to adapt methods to practical circumstances. "Specification buying" was not appropriate for all industries; the fact that a manufacturer of silverware with a well-established trade name was scarcely likely to modify his product or forgo the use of his name did not discourage the buyer from dealing with him or Sears from carrying his merchandise. While Sears was reluctant to shoulder even minority ownership responsibility, it did so without hesitation where ownership served a valid merchandising purpose. While it tried in general to avoid becoming wholly dependent on a single source or allowing a source to become wholly dependent on it, both types of dependency were by no means unknown, although steps were usually taken to provide a measure of protection to the partner—whether Sears or source—to whom the weight of dependency ran. And so on through the incredibly complex array of hundreds of industries, thousands of factories, and endless numbers of special circumstances with which buyers and their suppliers worked.

Obviously, a degree of mutual dependency was inherent in the very concept of partnership. If for no other reason than that Sears bought in huge volume, in the great majority of cases the source was more dependent on Sears than Sears was on the source. Although the buyer tried to avoid becoming the manufacturer's sole outlet, the "most important customer" status he sought to establish carried with it a degree of dependency. This tended to make some people nervous. It is of interest that those who seemed to worry most were usually not themselves Sears sources. Often they were independent manufacturers who cherished the sense of freedom they associated with having a multiplicity of customers, no one of which was critical to their survival; others were scholars or social critics who were apprehensive over inequalities of economic power in the marketplace. Both the independents and the critics may well have had some justification for their feelings, but the fact remains that under General Wood's leadership a pattern of Sears-source relationships developed which was remarkable for its stability and mutually satisfactory results.

Sears set great store on the quality of its relationships with its suppliers and took pains to keep them in good order. Shared trust and confidence were absolutely essential to the system Wood and his lieutenants built. From the outset of his work with Sears—and earlier during his years at Ward's—Wood insisted that his buyers be men of integrity, a theme he was to reiterate throughout his professional life. In an address delivered in

1950, for example, he told a major meeting of executives from all branches of the business what he expected his buyers to be: "They must be men of character, who in their relations with their sources must always be fair, and when their word is given to a source that word must be kept regardless of cost. . . . I want Sears buyers to be marked men, marked as men of ability, character and fair dealing. I want them to stand head and shoulders above other buyers of the country." [19]

Documentary evidence exists to support the assumption that, by and large, Sears buyers lived up to this charge. In 1948 Houser commissioned an independent research firm to interview a random sample of sources for the purpose of learning about the experiences they had had with Sears and their attitudes toward the company. One source replied: "Sears buyers do business the way we like to do business. They know what we want, and when they place orders they take the merchandise they order. They make mistakes—all buyers make mistakes—but we don't have to pay for those mistakes. If they overbuy, they take what they ordered and take their loss." [20] And another: "One reason I like to do business with Sears is because of the informal manner in which I can operate with the buyer. He may call me on the phone, or he may come down here and sit across the table, and when he says he wants a particular quantity, I know I can begin production immediately, without waiting for confirmation of that order." This manufacturer went on to add that for other customers with whom he dealt, "I will not turn a wheel until I get a confirmed order."

There were other sure signs that Sears buying practices were generally approved by its sources. One was the length of time manufacturers continued to do business with Sears. Although no hard data for the General Wood era are now extant, it was a matter of pride for many buyers and their supervisors of the period that they had little turnover among their sources, many of whom they dealt with for years. Typically, sources prospered from doing business with Sears, many of them handsomely. It was not uncommon for manufacturers who had begun their involvement with Sears as men of relatively modest means to retire as millionaires many times over.

In general, Sears sources felt that they were part of the Sears team; typically, they tended to talk and act as though they were part of Sears, as in attitudinal and operational fact they were. And their feelings were reciprocated. Years after his retirement, General Wood noted wryly, "I made our sources our partners, and they have stuck by us. In fact, they work a lot harder for us than lots of people on the payroll." [21]

Following his retirement, Sears maintained an office for General Wood in its corporate headquarters on Chicago's West Side. When former associates stopped by, as they often did, Wood sometimes liked to sit back and philosophize. On one such occasion he commented, "The greatest contribution I ever made to this company has never been recognized: the development of sources." [22]

But Wood's accomplishment was far more than that alone. The development of sources was only one aspect of the integration of mass distribution with mass production, the challenging objective he had set for himself so many years before and brought to brilliant conclusion.

6

The Selling Strategy

ALTHOUGH MAIL ORDER had proved to be a highly efficient means for serving the rural and small-town market, its usefulness was severely limited when it came to serving the newer, broader mass market of rapidly urbanizing America. As early as 1920, General Wood saw clearly that the only way to reach this much larger market was through a system of retail stores. Practically speaking, there were only two places where the opportunity existed to develop his concept of integrating mass distribution with mass production: Montgomery Ward and Sears, Roebuck. When Ward's was closed to him, his only alternative was Sears.

There is little doubt that Julius Rosenwald's willingness to support at least a trial retail program was a key factor in the General's deciding to join Sears with something less than the "absolute free hand" he desired. Rosenwald was not fully sold on the retail idea, but he was greatly impressed with Wood and wanted him badly for Sears; if Wood's price was a chance to give retail a try, Rosenwald was willing to pay that price.

Wood lost no time in putting his ideas to work. On February 2, 1925, just three months after joining Sears, he opened his first retail store on the first floor of the Chicago mail-order plant. Before the year was out, he opened seven more stores and began testing the viability of different types of locations. Five of the stores were on mail-order plant premises, logical places to start since space, personnel, and backup stocks for store inventories were all readily available. The other three stores presented considerably greater risks. Two were in Chicago, but distant from the central Sears plant; the third was in Evansville, Indiana, a city far removed from any other Sears presence.

Rosenwald questioned the necessity for opening two detached stores in Chicago. Why wouldn't one do? Recognizing that the success of his stores would depend on two things—management and location—Wood answered: "I'll tell you why I want two stores. If I chose the wrong location or a poor manager, retail will get a black eye. I want to divide my risk." [1] His foresight was wise. Both locations, Lawrence Avenue and 79th Street, proved good, and Sears stores are still operating on each site. But while the 79th Street store was ably managed, the man picked to run the Lawrence Avenue store left something to be desired; had Lawrence Avenue been the only detached store opened that year, the General's retail experiment might have suffered. Wood could have used the same argument for establishing two retail outlets in a non-Sears city, but he knew when to stop pressing and was content to let the Evansville store stand on its own. Fortunately, in Evansville he had both a good location and a good manager, and the store was a success from the start.

Because the two detached Chicago stores and the Evansville store were opened late in the year, it was decided to give them time to prove themselves before venturing further with more stores posing similar risks. Thus only one additional store was opened in 1926, and that was safely located in the mail-order plant built that same year in Atlanta. By the end of 1926 the soundness of the retail idea had been securely established, and thirteen new stores were subsequently opened in 1927: two in the new Memphis and Los Angeles mail-order plants, three in detached locations in mail-order cities (Chicago, Los Angeles, and Philadelphia), and eight in cities with no previous Sears presence (Camden, New Jersey; Chattanooga and Nashville, Tennessee; Denver, Colorado; Green Bay and Milwaukee, Wisconsin; Jacksonville, Florida; and Tacoma, Washington). These, combined with the nine stores opened previously, yielded a grand total of twenty-two Sears retail outlets that had been made fully operational in less than three years. [2]

In keeping with Wood's conviction that the greatest opportunities lay in the larger urban centers, all stores except for Green Bay were in major cities. And all (again except for Green Bay) were situated outside of established downtown shopping areas. In a retrospective talk delivered before the Boston Conference on Distribution in 1937, Wood clearly stated his reasons for formulating such a strategy:

> The automobile has revolutionized American business, yet the great body of retailers were long oblivious to its eventual effect on retailing.
> In most American cities of over 100,000 people, transportation

was first by street car—first horse, then electric—by elevated, by sub-way. The avenues of transportation usually converged in a central dis-trict—the so-called business and shopping district. The large depart-ment stores of the average large American city were usually grouped closely together in this central shopping district. The outlying stores were limited to a clientele within walking distance or within range of a street car line. With these limits they were small and could offer no effective competition to the larger stores of the central shopping district.

With a larger and larger proportion of the population possessing automobiles, the problem of parking space, traffic congestion and re-sulting inconvenience to downtown shoppers became more and more serious. The automobile made shopping mobile, and this mobility now created an opportunity for the outlying store, which with lower land values, could give parking space; with lower overhead, rents and taxes, could lower operating costs, and could with its enlarged clien-tele created by the automobile offer effective competition to the down-town store.[3]

Unlike most of his peers, Wood foresaw that the advent of personal trans-portation would profoundly change traffic patterns and that the downtown districts would gradually lose their drawing power. He put his stores where they could be easily reached via major traffic arteries—directly in the path of the newly mobile American public.

At around the same time, retail stirrings were being felt in the most unlikely place: Montgomery Ward.[4] Considering how adamantly its presi-dent, Theodore Merseles, had resisted Wood's attempts to involve Ward's in the retail business—a factor which had led to the final break between the two men—it must have come as a surprise to the General when Ward's began making tentative moves in that direction. Admittedly, its initial approach was oblique, and Wood's surprise was probably mingled with amusement. Rather than simply opening stores where people could come in and shop, Ward's in 1926 established what it termed "display stores" in three small towns that had thus far been solid mail-order markets: Little Falls, Minnesota; Marysville, Kentucky; and Plymouth, Indiana. The pur-pose of these stores was not to sell merchandise but to exhibit goods carried in the catalog so "visitors could see what the catalog described and compare quality and price." As it turned out, however, the "visitors" were not content with merely looking and soon began to insist on buying and carrying away the samples on display rather than waiting for mail-order delivery. When the resulting sales proved profitable, Merseles—still deeply skeptical of the whole retail store idea—authorized a modest trial

83

program for a limited period, and by May of 1927 the company had eight display stores in operation in towns with populations ranging from 4,000 to 14,000.

While this cautious experiment was in process, Ward's was following Sears retail activities closely and could not help but be impressed by its competitor's apparent success. New management under George B. Everitt, who took over from Merseles in 1927, determined not only to follow Sears example but to outdo Sears at its own retail game. Late that year, Ward's announced plans to have 1,500 retail stores in operation by 1929. This unrealistic goal was later scaled down to 500 stores, but even that was a highly ambitious figure.*

---

*Montgomery Ward launched its ambitious retail program with remarkable confidence and decisiveness. Announcing its intention to open hundreds of stores in a little over two years suggests that Ward's management had a very clear idea of what it wanted to do and the direction it wanted to go. It is difficult to imagine an undertaking of this magnitude with no or little staff work behind it; at the same time, it is difficult to visualize when this might have been done. Merseles's skeptical attitude toward retail stores and his very limited experimental program do not suggest any extensive analysis and preparation under his regime, and Everitt had been in office only a few months before making his sweeping announcement. What led Ward's management, with the backing of its board, to make such an audacious commitment on what appears to be so little spadework?

An interesting possibility suggests itself. It will be recalled that Wood's files were seized by order of Merseles when the General was fired while absent on a hunting trip. It is quite likely that included in these files were plans for opening retail stores which Wood had been unable to sell Merseles. There is some reason to think that initially Wood viewed the stores not only as a way of tapping the new urban market but also as a means for shoring up a threatened rural and small-town market. It is clear, however, that by the time he joined Sears he was confident that mail order could hold its own in its traditional areas of strength while the stores could be used as a vehicle to move into entirely new areas.

If this line of speculation is correct, it is possible that Wood's files contained plans for a retail program which included small towns as well as large; if so, the small-town element may have struck a responsive chord with Ward's established patterns of thinking. Perhaps when Ward's new management under Everitt saw the success Sears was achieving in its retail venture, Wood's old plans were brought out and those parts with which Ward's was most comfortable used as the basis for its new retail program. If this is what happened, it is unfortunate for Ward's purposes that Everitt and his colleagues failed to realize that Wood's thinking had changed in important respects between the time he drafted his original plans for Ward's and the time he actually launched Sears on its retail course.

We will probably never know how much the difference in the retail orientation of the two companies owes to the use and perhaps misreading of outdated plans found in the files of a dismissed executive. But there is no doubt that Sears obvious success under the leadership of that executive was the proximate reason for Ward's abandoning its old stance and adopting a retail strategy. And it may well be that Everitt launched his dramatic new program with such boldness and so little apparent preparation because he felt he was following a course Wood himself had already laid out. Sheer speculation. But intriguing.

The very magnitude of the proposed undertaking was clear evidence that Ward's was pursuing a strategy quite different from that of Sears. In fact, the reasoning of both managements started from the same two premises: that the coming of the automobile and roads would profoundly change the buying habits of the American people, and that the increased productivity of the American farm would lead to a drop in farm population as people moved from rural areas to cities. But each came up with widely disparate conclusions based on these premises. Merseles and Everitt were convinced that a smaller, more productive farm population would be a more prosperous one. They did not foresee the rural market withering away, but Everitt at least feared that the greater mobility provided by the automobile and improved roads would free farmers of their long-standing dependency on mail order. The success of the "display stores" had shown that actual merchandise was more attractive to customers than catalog descriptions. Anticipating a steady decline in the mail-order business as a whole, Ward's saw its new retail system as taking up the resulting slack and, in essence, conceived this as its primary function. Accordingly, Ward's set about locating its stores in smaller and medium-size communities— cities of from 4,000 to 75,000—where they would be more accessible to its traditional customers.

General Wood, on the other hand, was confident that catalog merchandising would continue to occupy an important place and that the true aim of retail stores should be the penetration of an entirely different market: rapidly urbanizing America. His original intent was to concentrate Sears stores in cities of 100,000 and over. With the unveiling of Ward's grandiose plans, however—which were announced with considerable fanfare in the fall of 1927—Wood found himself having to modify his strategy. He knew that if Ward's stores succeeded they would not only pick up Ward's mail-order customers but those of Sears as well, a loss which Sears could ill afford.

Wood moved with characteristic decisiveness. Calling a meeting of his key executives, he analyzed the threat and outlined the countermeasures he felt it necessary to take.[5] These included greatly accelerating the rate at which new stores were opened and broadening the scope of retail objectives to encompass smaller cities. During the meeting Wood stressed that both these moves would require a sharp increase in executive workloads. E. P. Brooks recalls, "The General asked for and got the complete support of those old warhorses, the supervisors of the various departments."

Table 1. Number of New Retail Stores Opened by Sears and Ward's, 1925–29

Year	Sears	Ward's
1925	8	1[a]
1926	1	3[b]
1927	13	27
1928	138	213
1929	108	288
Total	268	532

[a] Located in new Baltimore mail-order plant.
[b] "Display stores."
SOURCES: Sears data from Sears Archives. Ward's data courtesy Public Relations Department, Montgomery Ward & Co.

The pace of Sears store openings was stepped up dramatically. While only twenty-two stores had been opened in the three-year period from 1925 to 1927, 138 were opened in 1928—an average of more than one new store every other working day. But Ward's moved even faster (Table 1). Having entered the retail market later than Sears, it nevertheless ended 1928 doing business in 244 locations as compared to Sears with 161. In the following year Sears slowed down somewhat and added "only" 108 new stores; Ward's, in contrast, raced ahead with an incredible 288, more than reaching its scaled-down goal of 500 stores "by 1929."

Although they proliferated in far greater numbers, Ward's stores were much smaller than Sears. As against average 1928 sales of $558,000 per Sears store, the Ward's average was $197,000, not much more than a third that of Sears.[6] In accordance with its chosen strategy, Ward's tended to locate its stores in smaller cities (Table 2). Well over half the cities in which Ward's opened stores during these years had populations under 25,000, and 142 had populations under 10,000; of this latter group, twenty-seven had populations under 5,000.

In the contest, Sears had the definitely larger-size cities more or less to itself, as Ward's had the definitely smaller-size cities. The field of confrontation was the broad spectrum of cities between these two extremes. Here again, Wood moved decisively; as he later wrote, "I raced for the big[ger] cities first. I thought the greatest opportunity was there. Ward's put their stores in the smaller towns."[7] Of the nineteen stores Sears had opened in the three years leading up to 1928, all except one were located in very large cities: Chicago, Dallas, Los Angeles, Atlanta, Philadelphia, and the like. In several of these cities, more than one store was opened. Under

Table 2. Population of Sears and Ward's Store Cities, 1925–29

Population	Number of Cities		
	Sears Only	Sears & Ward's	Ward's Only
Under 25,000	18	20	320
25,000–99,999	52	84	47
100,000–499,999	47	10	6
500,000 and Over	11	1	—
Total	128	115	382
Median Population	82,682	43,573	11,647

SOURCES: Sears from Sears Archives. Ward's data courtesy Public Relations Department, Montgomery Ward & Co. Population data from 1930 *Census of Population*.

Wood's revised strategy, 121 of the 138 stores begun in 1928 were either in middle-size cities—such as Battle Creek, Michigan; Erie, Pennsylvania; Knoxville, Tennessee; and Peoria, Illinois—or in more outlying areas of the great urban centers.

Although it was inevitable that the two companies would overlap to some extent, the centers of gravity of their retail systems were markedly different. The median size of cities having only Ward's stores was under 12,000; the median size of cities having only Sears stores was over 80,000. By early 1930 Sears had definitely established a larger-city and Ward's a smaller-city orientation, an important distinction that prevails to this day.

Throughout this period of accelerated growth, Sears moved somewhat more slowly than Ward's, but the pace was nevertheless hectic; in 1928–29, 200 stores were added. This meant that 200 suitable new locations had to be found, most of them in cities strange to Sears. Land had to be purchased. Stores had to be built from the ground up or installed in existing space that was either leased or bought. Managers had to be recruited and store staffs hired and trained. Meanwhile, everyone involved was faced with having to learn how to organize and manage an entirely new enterprise, about which no one had knowledge or experience on which to draw.

Those entrusted with the task of opening new stores—often new recruits themelves—lived for weeks at a stretch out of suitcases, working all day and traveling much of the night to reach the next location on time. Store managers were moved frequently and on short notice to keep abreast of the frantic opening schedule. One recalled, years later, how he was

87

called at his home one evening and told to report at 8:00 the following morning in a city several hundred miles away; he had been with Sears for less than a month. His experience was not uncommon.[8]

Hastily acquired store space often proved unsatisfactory and difficult to work with. Heating, lighting, and ventilation were inadequate or temperamental. Floors were not always level, and when two adjoining properties were thrown together to create one store of sufficient size, ramps sometimes had to be built between them because of discrepancies in floor heights. It was altogether a difficult and far from orderly period—and one in which General Wood participated fully with his staff. He was in the prime of his life, drove himself as hard as anyone, and enjoyed every moment of it.

Changing Sears retail strategy in response to Ward's challenge posed even more problems for Wood and his team. The original plan had called for the opening of primarily full-line department stores and a few small specialty stores. Located in outlying areas of large cities, the former would serve markets of sufficient size to permit them to carry the company's entire range of retail merchandise offerings; the latter would specialize in tires and automotive supplies, with limited lines of hardware, paint, and major appliances. The merchandising characteristics of both full-line stores and specialty stores were clearly conceived. Those of stores midway between, however, were annoyingly ambiguous. Medium-size cities—those into which Sears was now forced to move—could not support the larger full-line stores, yet they required more than the scaled-down selection found in the smaller ones. If they were to carry merchandise representative of all departments, the assortments would be too sparse to make the stores attractive places to shop. Not all departments could be represented. But which should be retained, and which dropped? Which departmental lines should be carried, and how many items from each line should always be on hand?

At first there was little in the way of coherent policy. Many stores tried to carry too wide a range of merchandise and ended up spreading themselves too thin. Attempts to hold inventories to manageable levels resulted in incomplete departments and spotty stocks. Customers had no assurance of what they might find in a given department, and the stores as a whole often presented a nondescript, ragtag public image. Sears own senior executives spoke scornfully of "bobtail departments" and "orphan lines" as they worked to formulate guidelines the stores could follow.

It took years to resolve these problems in stores for the middle-size cities, but out of the confusion there gradually emerged a classification system applicable to all stores based on the ranges of merchandise carried. At the apex were the "A" stores—full-line department stores of the type originally envisioned by Wood as comprising the bulk of the Sears retail establishment. At the other extreme were the small, specialized automotive and hard-line stores, or "C" stores. Between them were the "B" stores, which were further divided into three subcategories: "B-1," "B-2," and "B-3," to provide an orderly gradation between the broadly based "A" stores and the narrowly specialized "C" stores. How a particular "B" store was classified depended on the range of departments represented: the "B-1" stores were modified department stores, while the "B-3" stores approached the narrow departmental specialization of the "C" stores. Within individual departments in different store classes, a rational structure of merchandise assortments was established to ensure that offerings could still be logical even though limited in breadth and depth. This made it possible to provide a reasonable balance of merchandise offerings that could be easily adjusted in response to customer demands.

The process of working this out was fraught with false starts and errors, but the end result was a system of stores with soundly conceived merchandising characteristics and a clearly defined public image. The overall structure of store types and the internal structure of departmental merchandise assortments provided a flexible means for adapting to a wide range of circumstances and to changing local market opportunities. As populations and market potentials grew, levels of service could be upgraded in an orderly fashion; many "B-1"s moved up to become "A"s, "B-2"s to become "B-1"s, and so on. By the time the many fine-tuned arrangements were in place, the Sears retail system had reached a degree of maturity and sophistication far beyond that which prevailed in the late 1920s.

The need to open stores in mid-size cities—and to do it quickly—also meant that Wood had to modify temporarily his concept of locating all stores in outlying areas. The company could still follow this policy in the larger cities, which were and remained the General's primary focus of interest; usually this required that stores be custom-built for Sears, since existing accommodations suitable for its "A" stores were seldom available in the locations desired. In medium-size cities, Sears initially followed Ward's example by seeking out buildings alongside established retail merchants. These were usually acquired on a lease basis and converted to suit the new occupant. Later, many such stores were built to the company's specifications by local landlords on leaseback arrangements in which a sliding scale of rent was geared to sales volume.

As the typically twenty-year leases on the first generation of Sears stores in downtown shopping districts expired, however, Wood was able to return to his original goal of siting stores in outlying areas accessible to principal traffic arteries with ample parking facilities. This in turn had a major impact on the structure of the American city. Other retail organizations—including many of the large department stores around which the downtown shopping areas had originally been built—rushed to establish outlying branches of their own; Montgomery Ward was for years a notable exception. In the period following World War II, the rapid development of great shopping centers in what had hitherto been wide-open spaces radically changed the economic geography of urban America.

In his drive to expand the Sears system, General Wood gave special attention to the South, the Southwest, and the West. The census figures with which he was so familiar told him that the greatest increases in population were occurring in those parts of the country, and also that growth had leveled off or was actually declining in New England, the Mid-Atlantic states, and the Upper Midwest. Louis Pfeiffle, who worked closely with him during the early retail years, later recalled: "The General had a great knowledge about America and a sense of excitement about the country's growth. . . . He knew the drift of population. . . . He wanted to go where the country was growing, and that was westward and southward."[9] Sears had a marked tendency to enter cities of smaller size that were expected to grow, anticipating that the stores would grow along with them. Consequently, there was at the outset a somewhat disproportionate representation of Sears stores in the West and Southwest. Montgomery Ward, on the other hand, appears to have located its stores with little regard for projected increases in population and is therefore underrepresented today in those parts of the country which have grown the most in the past half century. Here again, Wood's grasp of changing trends gave him a significant competitive edge.

While shaping Sears, Roebuck into a major retailer, General Wood introduced an innovation that was to have far-reaching ramifications. In essence, he thoroughly revamped previous notions of what lines of merchandise retail stores should carry and for whom the stores should be designed. Up until that time, stores had typically handled such things as food, clothing, household necessities, and luxuries intended for a fortunate few—

lines of merchandise for which women were the chief customers. But Sears (and Ward's) catalog business had long been concerned with the entire farm family—men, women, and children—as well as with the needs of the farm itself and its household. Wood determined that his new stores would serve the needs of whole families, and concerted efforts were made to promote shopping as a family affair.

With more families buying their own homes, the interest in home maintenance and repair increased, and this in turn generated needs for paint, hardware, building materials, electrical goods, and other types of merchandise which were seldom found in department stores—items for which men rather than women were the usual customers. As the automobile became a prominent feature of American life, backyard mechanics, mostly men, needed tools, accessories, and tires. In other words, it was no longer enough for stores to cater to women; Wood recognized this fact and acted on it.

The new urban market which Sears targeted as its own was to a large extent a young market: the young men and women who were moving from farm to city, and those, often of immigrant stock, who were rising into the mainstream of American life. Many couples in both groups were forming households—a trend the General followed closely in the census data—and had need for all the varied lines of merchandise pertinent to that purpose. With developments such as these in mind, Wood deliberately fashioned Sears into an agent of social change. The country was moving in directions of which he approved, and he wanted to lend the formidable support his company could provide. Specifically, with the aid of his buyers and working through his rapidly expanding network of strategically located stores, he would bring the necessities of life more nearly within the reach of the general run of American families, and he would bring to the mass market goods which had previously been confined to the class market alone.

At first Wood determined to appeal to this burgeoning market by means of "no-frills" stores—stores that got down to the business of selling people what they really needed with none of the attendant hoopla usually associated with retailing. Falling back on his Canal and wartime experiences, he conceived of Sears serving as the "commissary" (his term) of the nation, supplying merchandise of such values that fancy and expensive surroundings would not be necessary to bring people into his stores. He conceived this philosophy even before coming to Sears. E. P. Brooks recalls a conversation he had with Wood in the interim between the General's leaving Ward's and starting his new career: "I don't think the public wants to pay for frills [Wood said]. I don't think we have to have expensive fixtures. If we have values, people will come in and buy. And we're not going to have sales [where we drop prices and then move them back up]. If we have to reduce the price, it will be reduced and stay there. We're going to offer values to the great middle class buying public of American citizens." [10]

In keeping with this spirit, the early Sears stores were austere at best. The story is told—and it apparently has some basis in fact—that at least some of the "display tables" in the first store, which was opened in warehouse space taken over from the Chicago mail-order plant, were nothing more than the upended wooden crates in which merchandise had originally been received. There is no doubt that fixtures bought for the stores during the first few years were the least expensive available, and many were picked up locally at secondhand. There were no merchandise displays in the modern sense of the term; goods were simply stacked on wooden tables and customers rummaged through them to find what they wanted. Because men were expected to be a large part of store clientele and were presumed to be less finicky than women, housekeeping suffered. There were no elevators or escalators; customers used the stairs. Functional but rather drab, the early Sears stores bore a strong resemblance to warehouses, which in fact they were: warehouses open to the public.

With the strong emphasis on economy, salespeople were used sparingly; their function was not so much to "sell" as to ring up sales of merchandise customers had found on their own. Business was done for cash, and there were no free deliveries. Relying almost wholly on the drawing power of merchandise values, the stores engaged in little sales promotion. They advertised, but they did not conduct "sales" with prices reduced only for the event. Not until 1933 did the company conduct its first "Anniversary" and "Sears Value Days" sales, [11] both of which subsequently became prominent features on its merchandising calendar.

It soon became evident that this Spartan approach was a mistake, and Wood gradually changed his thinking on fixtures, store appearance, sales promotion, and selling service. While he was a man of strong convictions not easily diverted from a chosen course of action, he was willing and able to learn from experience and to alter his course accordingly. Two men made major contributions to his learning process: L. S. Janes, who developed a flair for store design and merchandise display, and M. C. Penticoff, who brought with him to Sears solid prior experience in store management and sales promotion.

Janes became manager of store planning and display and in that capacity not only improved Sears performance in these areas but also revolutionized the retail industry's concepts of store construction, customer traffic flow, the internal logistics of store backup stocks, and display fixture design. Impressed by Janes's work, Wood began to allow more money for store and merchandise appearance than he originally deemed necessary. In time, he came to employ local architects to help give his new structures a local flavor, and ultimately he even allowed escalators, but few elevators. E. P. Brooks remembers this time well: "[Wood] made tremendous changes in what he would accept [in the way of physical facilities and amenities] as he learned what worked and what didn't. The commissary idea didn't work. The value idea always worked." [12]

M. C. Penticoff, who had been the original manager of the 79th Street store in Chicago—Wood's first successful detached retail operation—became in due course manager of the entire Chicago group of stores and from that vantage point helped move the company toward more effective store management and sales promotional practices. Under the influence of Janes and Penticoff, supported by that of other experienced merchants recruited during the early retail years, Sears stores in time became models of attractiveness in appearance and efficiency of design, and Sears promotional practices evolved into some of the most aggressive in an already aggressive industry. Clearly, people liked to shop in pleasant, convenient surroundings and have merchants actively solicit their patronage; as Wood came to see, good values looked even better when they were agreeably presented.

There were many more things Sears and General Wood had to learn about running a successful retail business, and there were skeptics who predicted that they would never make it. J. M. Barker, at one time Wood's senior field lieutenant, had close connections with the New York financial community, and later recalled the views some of them took of Sears new direction: "The mail order was a going concern. The mail order had reached a stage of refinement so that the financial people in New York used to say, Sears was a master of the mail order business but it knew very little about the retail, and they went so far as to say it was doubtful whether Sears would ever master the retail end of it . . . retail was considered a pretty unfortunate offspring for Sears to put time on." [13]

Large retail store chain organizations were, of course, nothing new. F. W. Woolworth had been founded in 1879, J. C. Penney in 1902, and W. T. Grant in 1906; by the latter part of the 1920s these and many other less well-known chains had worked out the problems of multi-unit operations and established themselves as eminently successful enterprises. A widely read trade magazine, *Chain Store Age*, offered a convenient forum for the exchange of ideas and experiences between knowledgeable chain-store operators. But the fledgling Sears retail system, like that of Montgomery Ward, presented two sets of problems for which the experience of other chains offered little guidance. One involved the difficulties of running stores offering far wider ranges of merchandise than any chain store enterprise had previously carried. Barker stated the problem succinctly: "The company was not running a chain of specialty stores, carrying for example a few restricted and allied lines of merchandise, but instead was endeavoring, even in its smallest stores, to present to the purchasing public a collection of varied lines of merchandise." [14] With no models to consult, Wood and his colleagues had to find their way on their own.

A second set of problems unique to what Wood was seeking to accomplish had to do with integrating a new and untried retail system with a well-established mail-order system. What Wood (and very few others) saw clearly at the time was that merging the two systems would open up operating economies and market opportunities that neither could possibly achieve on its own. Retail stores strengthened the mail-order market, and the catalog encouraged buying in the stores. Combining the merchandise needs of the two systems greatly enhanced the company's buying power. And the ten (later eleven) mail-order plants comprised a ready-made infrastructure of strategically located warehouses and the basis for an efficient jobbing service which created operating economies of scale for the plants and were important elements in the success of the new retail venture. These were assets vital to the success of Wood's selling strategy. But integrating the two quite different systems presented difficulties.

For one thing, relationships between the highly organized, smoothly functioning mail-order system and the burgeoning, catch-as-catch-can, upstart retail system were characterized by considerable friction and mutual distrust. The mail-order buyers and their supervisors were generally unsympathetic to the retail development, an attitude in which they were encouraged by the well-known feelings of their longtime mentors, Max Adler and Otto Doering. Old-time mail-order men saw retail as spelling the ruin of their cherished mail-order business; moreover, with the great emphasis on retail expansion, they resented what they viewed as the favoritism being shown retail. In the early retail days, buyers' bonuses still depended on mail order; while there were well-established procedures for recording the sales of buyers through mail order, it took time to work out comparable means for tracking sales figures by buying departments in the mushrooming retail system. According to E. P. Brooks, it was understandable that buyers and supervisors "loved the mail order and hated the extra work they were put to by retail." [15]

A memorandum dated September 20, 1925, from Adler's General Merchandise Office instructed all buying departments to use the stores as dumping grounds for unwanted goods: "We want to make every effort to clean up our surplus and discontinued merchandise through the retail stores." [16] For some years, it continued to be common practice for buying departments to unload their excess inventories on the stores at the end of each selling season; just as they received no credit for sales of their goods through retail, they suffered no penalty for unsold goods left to languish on retail shelves. The reactions of retail executives were predictable.

Viewed objectively, the integration of the new retail system with the established mail-order system involved the working out of orderly and mutually supportive relationships among three essential processes: central buying, regional jobbing, and local selling.

In the pristine days of mail order, organizational relationships were relatively simple. The heads of the various buying (or merchandising) departments worked with a high degree of autonomy, deciding on their own authority what items to carry, what quantities to purchase, and what prices to charge. So long as their departments produced a satisfactory volume and profit, they were left largely on their own. Supporting the work of the merchandisers was an operating organization responsible for the physical receiving and warehousing of goods and for the processing of customer orders. Over time, the complementary merchandising and operating functions had been honed to a smooth and highly efficient routine. Even the introduction of branch mail-order plants presented no great difficulty because these were concerned chiefly with the physical side of the overall process; the merchandising functions in which they did become involved consisted primarily of local inventory control conducted under the close surveillance of the central merchandise departments.

The mail-order merchants had trouble learning the special requirements and opportunities of retail. They had long experience in procuring merchandise for farms and for farm and small-town families, but the needs of customers served by the new retail stores differed in many important respects, and retail store managers often had difficulty convincing buyers at the distant central buying offices to furnish them with the kinds of goods their customers wanted. To further complicate matters, customers' needs varied much more widely in retail than in mail order. The mail-order business was highly standardized, and while the catalog offerings of the several branch plants differed somewhat from region to region the differences fell within well-ordered limits. The buyers were simply unaccustomed to the kinds of variations they found in retail.

They were also unaccustomed to the more exacting demands of retail customers and had to learn to give more attention to style and detail; goods sold in stores were subject to closer inspection and comparison than goods sold through catalogs. Also, merchants brought up in a strictly mail-order tradition were used to going their own way with little thought for what their fellow mail-order merchants were doing. So long as his total sales and profits were acceptable to his superiors, the buyer of men's hats did not have to concern himself with coordinating with the buyer of men's suits on matters of color and style; so, too, with buyers of hosiery and lingerie, of furniture and rugs, of bedspreads and draperies. But in the retail store, where related lines of merchandise were displayed under the same roof and often in adjoining departments, some at least elementary coordination soon became imperative, and this further complicated the work of the central buying organization.

Meanwhile, the retail organization was acutely unhappy over the buying services it was receiving, and particularly over the practice of buyers unloading their mistakes on the stores. Pressures developed within the retail system for establishing its own buying and merchandising organization independent of mail order. This, however, Wood firmly resisted; only through a single buying organization could the great advantages of mass purchasing power be realized, and only through using the mail-order plants to perform jobbing and warehousing services could the economies of mass distribution be achieved. At the same time, he was not unaware of the problems faced by the retail stores which were so dear to his heart. E. P. Brooks, then a senior district manager, went to him one day and related a series of particularly flagrant examples illustrating how the stores were being victimized by the merchandising executives. Wood listened closely before replying: "All right . . . I know. And I know what you're up against. Now, the good ones will learn. The bad ones we'll retire. But the strength of these men is such that I can't throw it away. I know how strong they are. They know the basics of their industries. But we'll get rid of those that don't see the light, those that do this kind of thing to you. They'll work or we'll retire them. Just have patience. Work with them." [17]

It was clear to Wood, if not always to his subordinates, that Sears enjoyed a tremendous advantage by having in place a buying organization staffed with experienced people who were deeply knowledgeable in their particular lines; it would have taken years to build up a specialized retail buying staff with comparable expertise. At the same time, there was a limit to his patience, and over succeeding years a number of changes in key buying posts were quietly made. Gradually, the buying organization learned to work effectively with a retail organization that was itself growing in competence and assurance. Above all, General Wood understood that once the problems of integrating the mail-order and retail systems were solved, each would add strength to the other and the resulting unified enterprise would be far stronger than one permanently divided.

Not only did the relationships between the retail stores and the central buying organization have to be worked out; there were additional difficulties inherent in adapting the branch mail-order houses to the jobbing function newly required of them. From the outset of the retail venture, it was obvious that these branches should be used to provide a jobbing service to the stores: receiving bulk merchandise shipments from manufacturers and distributing goods to local retail units in quantities suitable to their needs.[18] In the early days, the branch mail-order houses transcended the jobbing function and tried to run the stores in their service areas virtually as detached departments of the plants themselves. The results were not happy.

Mail order was traditionally a highly routinized business operating on a basis of manuals and detailed written instructions. The new stores were deluged with memos and bulletins and procedures covering every conceivable contingency. These were sometimes contradictory, often confusing, and always in too great bulk to be read carefully by harried people many miles removed trying to do business face-to-face with a clamorous public. Understandably, relationships between the mail-order and retail systems were strained and often antagonistic.

The branch plants had become very proficient in serving the needs of mail-order customers in large geographic areas. They had learned how to keep close control of their inventories and to order in quantities which ordinarily would not result in serious out-of-stocks or overstocks. But while it was one thing to estimate the sales of a particular item for a large number of widely scattered customers, it was quite another to predict the needs of a retail unit serving a limited area with demographic and economic characteristics that were to some extent peculiar to itself. The law of large numbers, useful for mail-order merchandising, had sharply limited applicability to individual retail stores. Mail-order merchants based in distant regional plants proved less than skillful at judging the requirements of the stores for which they were responsible, and overstocks and shortages at the point of sale were chronic. Stores often found themselves with more of certain kinds of goods than they could possibly sell while at the same time they were pleading for and unable to get goods which were in urgent demand. The difficulty was compounded by the frequency with which merchants at central buying headquarters made arbitrary shipments to the stores. Horror stories were many and became folk legends remembered long after: cowboy boots were shipped to Maine and skis to Texas; heavy underwear to Florida and summer sportswear to Minnesota in the dead of winter; earmuffs to San Diego. These were often honest mistakes but sometime deliberate efforts to shift cost burdens from mail-order to retail shoulders.

It was clear that more autonomy would have to be vested in retail stores, if only because local managers and department heads were better positioned than central or regional staffs to know their own needs. But in the early days of retail, store personnel were ill-equipped to make certain types of decisions. For one thing, there was no adequate system for recording items and quantities of merchandise sold and hence no historical facts on which to make informed judgments on bringing in new merchandise. Knowledge derived from direct contacts with local markets was useful, but it was not enough; some form of historical documentation was also needed. In response, a unit control system was gradually developed by means of which accurate records could be kept concerning items and quantities of merchandise ordered and sold. These records could then be used in making reorder decisions and future merchandising plans. J. M. Barker, head of retailing in the East in the early years, considered this system to be "one of the most vitally important tools for improving the merchandising of the stores for which I was responsible,"[19] and he aggressively promoted its refinement and use. This was, of course, long before the time of computers. But even though the system was wholly manual and cumbersome by today's standards, it served its purpose well for many years and was a key factor in making possible the unusually high degree of local autonomy which became the heart of General Wood's managerial philosophy.

Of interest, the manual unit control system was refined to such a high degree of effectiveness that in later years it proved to be a serious obstacle to progress. Because Sears entire service of supply organization was built around manual record-keeping and control techniques, extensive modifications had to be made before computers, when they became available, could be utilized. Other retail chains which had not developed their manual systems and supporting organizations to a comparable level of perfection found it much easier to enter the computer age.

A more complex and intransigent problem surfaced in determining the qualifications of key store personnel. Policy on providing management staffs for the new stores moved through several stages. In the beginning, it was assumed that the stores would be headed by department managers transferred from mail order; while expedient, this method of selection quickly proved unsatisfactory. Experience in the orderly, controlled environment of a mail-order plant was poor preparation for effective performance in a location far removed from comfortable organizational surroundings and involving direct customer contact. Retail work was psychologically different from mail order and required a quite dissimilar mindset. Moreover, mail-order experience involved no exposure to the principles of store layout or merchandise display, and while it involved a considerable amount of reorder work to maintain balanced stocks, keeping on top of the unfamiliar, idiosyncratic requirements of a local retail clientele was a wholly different matter.

When it became obvious that mail-order personnel were not suited to the retail setting, Sears began recruiting large numbers of experienced executives from other chain department store organizations. Ever pragmatic, Wood realized that this was the only way to keep up with the rapid retail expansion beginning in 1928. The times proved auspicious for this purpose; although it was well before the Great Depression, many retail organizations were already beginning to experience difficulties and to reduce their executive staffs. One source proved particularly valuable to Sears: J. C. Penney. This well-established chain had built up a considerable surplus of promotable people for whom Penney's by the latter 1920s offered few prospects for advancement. Some of the men who played important roles in building the new Sears retail system and in time rose to high positions in Sears came from Penney's. Sears found Penney's sizable reservoir of well-trained manpower, together with its strength in soft-line merchandising, so attractive that in 1929 the idea of a merger between the two organizations was seriously discussed. While nothing in the way of a merger materialized, Sears managed to tap into Penney's manpower pool by more informal means.

Although managerial personnel recruited from Penney's and other retail establishments were in general far superior for retail purposes to per-

sonnel transferred internally from mail order, the policy fell short of consistent success. Executives who were released by other retailers or who were discouraged by prospects for promotion elsewhere were not always of top caliber and were sometimes distinctly second-rate. J. M. Barker often referred to them disdainfully as "cast-offs":[20] "What we had done was staff these stores as far as management was concerned by taking managers from Woolworth's, from Penney, anybody that wanted a job. We were opening stores so rapidly that they had to take pretty much anything they could get. . . . There was no attempt, really, to judge their competence. It was a question of try them out and see if they can produce a few dollars of profit and if they couldn't you got rid of them."[21] Even the best of those who were recruited in this fashion had difficulty adjusting to Sears if only because their experience had been in retail organizations quite different from that which Sears was in the process of building. If they came from chain stores, including Penney's, they were accustomed to stores that carried much more restricted lines of merchandise. If they came from department stores, they had no knowledge of the hard lines which formed the backbone of Sears retail business. And no one, of course, had had any experience working within a system which had at its heart the integration of the dissimilar systems of retail and mail order.

Gradually it became apparent that Sears would have to "grow its own" managers. Since Sears was building a new kind of retail system, and that system was still amorphous, the only experience that really counted was the sort of experience that could be gained only at Sears itself. In due course, an executive personnel department was established and charged with overseeing an ambitious executive development program and implementing a policy of promotion from within, moves which were to influence profoundly the character of the company and its subsequent evolution (see Chapter 8 herein). It would be some years before the new approach could begin to take hold and provide the reserves of manage , d talent required. Meanwhile, Wood and his staff worked with the res̩urces available to them and concentrated on learning how to operate their innovative enterprise.

It is interesting to note that the men who were most responsible for fashioning the new retail order—including the General himself—were wholly innocent of retail experience. J. M. Barker had been an international banker; E. P. Brooks was an engineer; T. J. Carney and F. B. McConnell, both of whom would later become presidents of the company, had reached high levels in the mail-order structure before assuming retail responsibilities. Only two men with retail backgrounds played significant roles in framing the new structure of policy and practice: H. F. Murphy and C. H. Kellstadt. It seemed as if prior knowledge of retailing was more of a hindrance than a help.

Everyone, in other words, had much to learn. In his "Reminiscences," J. M. Barker tells a revealing story about one particularly productive learning experience. Concerned with the poor performance of many of the stores in the eastern territory, for which he was at the time responsible, he conceived the notion of singling out one department and using it as an example of how departments could and should be run:

> I picked the hardware department to be the guinea pig for this experiment. It was then headed by Mr. Arthur S. Barrows.
> When I went to him and told him of my idea that if we could get the hardware department right in these stores of mine, it would be a great thing for his hardware sales, and at the same time it would increase the standards of store operations, and hence eventually sales all over the country, he as always was ready to cooperate. We agreed that the thing to do was to get a thoroughly competent hardware man as an inspector and teacher. I commissioned him to get such a man for me, and he eventually sent me Herbert F. Murphy who had learned the business with the Simmons Hardware Co.
> Murphy's job was to travel among the stores, work with each manager and hardware division head and show them how to set it up and how to run the department successfully. He kept in constant touch with me.[22]

The experiment was eminently successful. It resulted not only in a quantum improvement in the operation of the hardware departments but served as a model for other store departments to emulate. Although Barker makes no mention of the fact, store personnel were not alone in profiting from this venture. Murphy kept in touch with Barrows as well as Barker, and Barrows learned from Murphy what was needed at both the buying and the store levels to build a profitable hardware business. And as other store departments learned from hardware, other buying department supervisors learned from Barrows. A salient characteristic of the Sears organization at this stage of its internal evolution was an openness to learning in the light of experience unhampered by too many preconceptions of how things "ought" to be done.

General Wood himself did much to set this learning mode. He did not leave the learning to subordinates. Much of the most useful learning was his own, acquired in direct contact with the men and women at the scene of

101

action. During the early retail years, a large part of his time was spent in the stores working with store managers, department heads, salespeople, unit control clerks—in short, anyone in a position to tell him how things were actually working and what needed to be done to make them work better. A common question to a department head was: "If this were your business, what changes would you make?" He took voluminous notes, and on his return to Chicago issued streams of memos of inquiry or direction to persons in positions to correct problems he had found. Frequently he did not bother to dictate memos but called people into his office. His usual practice was to go directly to action points rather than through a chain of command; if something needed correction by a buyer, Wood did not want to be bothered with going through his supervisor, let alone the vice president for merchandising. By this policy of direct contact with problem points and action points the General not only learned a great deal himself about how to integrate the multifold elements of the interlocking buying, mail-order, and retail structures; he also fostered extensive learning on the part of many others in his organization.

Throughout this crucial startup period, the Evansville, Indiana, store played a particularly important part. Evansville was the first store opened in other than a mail-order city, and it had been opened precisely to provide Sears with experience in operating a store far removed from the central buying organization and the protective proximity of a mail-order plant. Knowledge gained in Evansville, therefore, was especially valuable. For this reason, Wood followed the figures on the performance of that store with particular care and for the first two or three years spent a great deal of time there. He insisted that his staff do likewise. Louis Pfeiffle, who as a young man worked directly with Wood, recalled a typical exchange between them:

Wood: When were you last in Evansville?
Pfeiffle: Last week.
Wood: Well, go back down tonight. That store's not doing well on something.[23]

Although no record exists to document the time spent by Sears men on railroad sleeping cars between Evansville and Chicago during this period, the recollections of old-timers suggest it was considerable. Quite clearly, the travel was productive; much of the learning how to run a retail store within the overall Sears structure took place through the close attention given Evansville.

Sears retail store, located on the premises of the Seattle, Washington, mail-order plant, 1925.

First of two stores in a mail-order city located at a distance from the mail-order plant, Lawrence Avenue, Chicago, 1925.

First store located outside a Sears mail-order city, Evansville, Indiana, 1925.

Store at Battle Creek, Michigan, 1928.

Interior of first Sears retail store, located on the premises of the Chicago mail-order plant, 1925.

Sears retail store, circa 1926.

Typical postwar store, Dayton, Ohio, 1948.

Sears first Mexico City store, Avenida Insurgentes, 1947.

Radio and television department, typical postwar store.

Men's furnishings department, typical postwar store.

Women's wear department, typical postwar store.

The intensive education Wood and his staff received in those early years, whether it took place in Evansville or at other points in the new retail system, did not come easily. Most of it was trial and error, and, as General Wood noted on more than one occasion, there were plenty of errors to look back on and benefit from: "The management, the supervision, the rank and file were absolutely green. In the early days of our stores I often remarked to my associates that we had a 100% record of mistakes—that we hadn't overlooked a single mistake—we had made them all." [24]

Despite the mistakes, and despite the need to learn a new business quite literally from the ground up, the retail venture was successful from the start. Retail sales and profits moved ahead rapidly as the new stores were opened, and by 1929 sales reached $175 million, 40 percent of the company's total business. Growth slowed but did not halt as the Great Depression fastened its grip on the country, and in 1931 retail moved ahead of mail order for the first time. Only once during that troublesome era—in 1932—did retail volume suffer a year-to-year drop, but with the far greater drop of mail-order sales during that dismal year retail still accounted for 50 percent of Sears business. As the country moved out of the Depression, Sears retail continued its steady advance until by 1939 the company was two-thirds retail and one-third mail order. [25]

In retrospect, Wood and Sears were fortunate that the Depression occurred neither sooner nor later than it did. While the chief reason for the company's early retail success was unquestionably the soundness of the General's strategic concepts, the prevailing prosperity made it easier than it otherwise would have been to surmount the many inevitable mistakes.

Wood accurately sensed the temper of the period. It was a time of great mobility, geographic and social. Moving from farm to city, from one part of the country to another, moving up the social scale; rising personal incomes, increased leisure, more rapid new household formation—all these created new needs and demands. Consumer tastes were broadening and becoming more diversified. Greater speed in the transmission of new ideas and the newly pervasive national advertising were generating new consumer preferences. As the editorial content of newspapers and magazines—indeed, whole magazines—came to be directed more and more toward the home and better ways of living, customers were growing more knowledgeable and sophisticated. The new Sears retail system was in tune with these far-reaching changes in the structure and spirit of American society.

By concentrating on the rapidly growing urban markets, by siting stores to tap the rising tide of personal transportation, by broadening traditional retail offers to embrace a much wider spectrum of consumer interest, and, above all, by providing values that gave it a sharp cutting edge with its competition, Sears was able to cater directly to the needs and tastes of the newly emerging American middle class. These were strategic advantages which swallowed up one mistake after another and gave Sears the maneuvering room to learn an untried and complicated way of doing business.

But sound strategy must eventually be supported by sound tactics. By coming when it did, the Depression forced a slowdown in the rapid pace of new store openings and compelled a review and assessment of policies and practices. Also, the slackening pace of sales increases focused attention on troublesome problems that the ebullient times had theretofore obscured. J. M. Barker, who was certainly in a position to judge, later recalled: "It was a very fortunate thing that Sears, Roebuck started [its] retail expansion on the eve of the Great Depression. If that had not been the case, we would not have been forced to face the fundamental facts, recognition of which has made us great. We would have made substantial profits in spite of the deficiencies in service, but those profits would have been founded on a much weaker base than is now the fact. As it was, every officer had to use every ounce of ability that was in him." [26]

During the straitened years of the Depression, unprofitable and poorly located stores were closed. Less competent personnel were eliminated, and costs—especially overhead costs—were cut to the bone. Store classifications were clarified, merchandise assortments were given logical order, and store appearance and customer service were markedly improved. Sears retail identity, which differed from the old mail-order identity, became clearly defined in the public mind. Stores acquired greater control over merchandising and pricing decisions, store managers became better merchants, buyers learned to serve retail needs more effectively, and the mail-order plants sharply upgraded the efficiency of their jobbing and service-of-supply functions. Methods and practices at all levels were simplified and improved. The foundations were laid for a comprehensive body of personnel policies, and the company became more self-sufficient in meeting its own executive needs. Above all, the relationships between stores, mail-order plants, and central buying offices were clarified and a logical, workable organization was set in place.

By 1935, the Sears retail system was solidly established. Its mission was clear, its leadership confident, and its machinery running smoothly. It had taken ten years to reach this state. They had been ten hard years, but they had also been years of achievement during which Wood and the men around him were able to forge a new and highly effective means for serving the changing needs of a changing America.

PART III

THE POLICIES

7

Organizational Policies

A T THE OUTSET of Sears retail period, General Wood did not anticipate the need for any important organizational changes: he simply
assumed that the new retail stores would be administered within the existing organizational structure.[1] That structure was highly centralized on a
functional basis. Under the president were three vice-presidents in charge,
respectively, of merchandising, operating, and accounting and finance.
The merchandising vice-president handled all buying and sales promotion;
the operating vice-president was responsible for the physical management
of goods as they moved from the sources through the mail-order plants and
ultimately to the customers; and the vice-president for accounting and finance was charged with supervising control and finance functions. The
general manager of the mail-order plants executed the instructions of the
president and the three functional vice-presidents.

These organizational arrangements were securely in place and working well, and the introduction of a few retail stores did not appear to call
for any significant modifications. The venture into retail meant that the
merchandising vice-president and the buying departments under him would
now have to utilize advertising media other than the catalog alone, and that
the operating vice-president and his staff would have to oversee the movement of goods through stores as well as mail-order plants, but the finance
and accounting functions would continue to be performed in much the
same manner as before. The only changes that seemed necessary—and
these did not appear too important early on—were to make the general
manager of each mail-order plant responsible for the retail stores in his
region, and to provide him with help in the form of a regional retail mana-

ger. Overall direction of the retail program was vested in Wood himself, assisted by a staff of four young men to do some of his legwork.[2]

This centralized structure proved adequate while the number of stores was still small. With the tenfold increase in the rate of new store openings in 1928, however, grave weaknesses quickly developed and the old mail-order system nearly buckled under the strain. Improvisation became the order of the day as harried executives, many of them newly hired and none of them seasoned in the emerging way of doing business, sought to deal ad hoc with emergency piled on emergency and crisis heaped on crisis. E. P. Brooks, who lived through the period, later wrote: "Every problem associated with growth presented itself. Management was in a constant state of flux. Ideas changed from month to month."[3]

Wood may not have foreseen these problems, but when they arose he acted resolutely to deal with them. He began by slowing the frantic pace of new store openings, cutting back from 138 in 1928 to 108 in 1929 and to only nineteen in 1930. Early in 1929, in an effort to inject a measure of retail experience into the system, he hired Alvin Dodd, a recognized authority on retail marketing and management. Wood gave Dodd general instructions to "get things straightened out" but neglected to define with any precision what duties he was to perform and how much authority he was to exercise.

Later that same year, in a far more important move, he retained George E. Frazer, a pioneer in the field of professional management consulting, to aid in designing a new and more effective organization structure. By this time it was clear that the old structure was no longer sufficient and that more systematic arrangements were necessary, not only for administering the now sizable number of retail stores but also for coordinating the flow of supplies from the mail-order plants to the stores and for enabling the parent merchandising organization to better serve the combined mail-order/retail distribution system. On September 3, Wood wrote to Lessing Rosenwald explaining that he had retained Frazer for the purposes of "the building up of an organization chart and the examination of our organization by an organization expert. I consider George Frazer the best man in the country in this line."[4] Wood appointed a five-man committee of senior executives to work with Frazer. Frazer and his committee worked diligently, and in January of 1930 they produced a report which strongly influenced the future evolution of the organization.[5]

At the heart of the report were recommendations calling for a combined geographic and functional organization. The stores were to be grouped into thirty-three districts, each under a district manager. The districts, in turn, were to be divided among four (later five) territories, each headed by an officer who would also supervise the mail-order plants in his geographical jurisdiction. The line of "executive authority" was to run from the president through the territorial officers and from there to the mail-order managers, the retail district managers, and finally the store managers.

The new geographic structure was superimposed on the old functional structure. This structure—which consisted of merchandising, operating, and accounting and finance, each headed as before by a vice-president— was replicated at the territorial, district, and local levels, creating, in effect, two parallel organizations, one line and one functional, each with its own chain of command and communications channel. An officers' board was given responsibility for coordinating the complex functional and territorial activities and for making policy recommendations to the president. Frazer was explicit on how the dual system was to work:

> The plan of organization provides for immediate and constant direct communication between the head of each function . . . and the functional officers and employees of the business wherever located throughout the country. . . . It is expected that each employee of the business will receive and obey instructions communicated to him on the functional line of authority and will be entirely free to report to his superior officer in his functional line. . . .
>
> The territorial organization, including the general managers of mail order houses and the district retail manager, is likewise authorized and directed to give orders and instructions to the members of their respective units. . . .
>
> In order that both the functional organizations and the territorial organizations may operate to the fullest efficiency, it is required that all instructions given by a functional officer to his functional subordinates in a territorial unit shall be given directly and at the same time that a copy of such instructions shall be given to the territorial officer in charge of the unit affected. . . .
>
> Territorial officers are on the executive line of authority reporting directly to the senior vice president [Lessing Rosenwald] and president. Such officers are authorized and instructed to stop or change any or all orders affecting their territories if, in their judgment, the best interests of the Company are thereby served. . . . If agreement cannot be had between the functional officer and the regional officer, the matter will be at once referred to the senior vice president and/or the president for final executive determination.[6]

The new organizational structure was in important respects an outgrowth of the old. It preserved the three traditional functions and reas-

111

serted their jurisdiction over the field. The most significant innovation of the Frazer Report—other than the fact that it spelled out clearly the responsibilities and authorities of key positions throughout the system—was the realignment of the field organization. The retail stores were removed from the supervision of the mail-order general managers and placed in districts under retail district managers, a far more congenial arrangement. Territories were established, each under its own officer, and each officer was put in charge of both the retail districts and mail-order houses in his geographic area. For the first time since the initiation of the retail venture, there was a clear line of executive authority running from the president to the territorial officer to the district manager to the store.

Although the new plan, which was placed in full operation in February of 1930, was a major improvement over the chaotic state of affairs that had come to prevail, problems began to surface almost at once. The responsibilities and points of view of the two sets of officers differed widely. The functional officers were charged with overseeing the performance of their respective specialties, not total operations. In contrast, the Frazer Report specified that "the two principal duties of the [territorial] officer [lay] in recommendations on matters of personnel and in the coordination of merchandise supplied between the mail order houses and the retail stores in the territory"; at the same time, the territorial officer was to be "responsible . . . for the activities of the Company in the territory, including assets, profits, expenses, inventories, sales, warehousing, personnel, and the goodwill of the Company." [7] Compared to the relatively narrow charter of the functional officers, this charter was very broad indeed. And since the two sets of offices had to deal with the same organizational units, disagreements and tensions were inevitable.

From the beginning, the territorial officers labored under distinct handicaps, the most noticeable being their inherently conflictual relationships with their functional counterparts. It did not help matters that the functional officers were all vice-presidents while only one of the territorial officers enjoyed that status. The vice-presidents sat on the officers' board, which played a key role in setting major policies, and the fact that the territorial officers were underrepresented on this board put them at a distinct disadvantage. This was exacerbated by the circumstance that the functional officers were all based at the central point of corporate authority in Chicago, while the territorial officers were widely dispersed. Moreover, the functional officers, whose positions were solidly in place long before the Frazer Report, were well supplied with staff support. Both Wood and

Frazer had strong aversions to overhead and at the outset specified that the new territorial officers were to be limited to three assistants each: a traveling auditor, a merchandising inspector, and an operating inspector, all answerable to their respective functional officers as well as to their territorial superior. In the inevitable power struggles between the functional and territorial officers, the latter often fared poorly.

On the other hand, the territorial officers had certain advantages going for them. They were nearer to the scene of the action and could speak with greater knowledge and confidence on the practical problems of running the stores. And they enjoyed closer and more supportive relationships with their district and local managers, whom they were likely to consider as "their own."

The territorial officers did not long remain short of staff. Opposed as he was to overhead, Wood was forced to recognize, within limits, the merits of his territorial executives' pleas for additional help. A territorial officer with only three assistants could at most perform policing functions, but the fledgling retail organization needed much more. The "B" stores in particular presented special problems.

The "A" stores by and large had the strongest managers and the best-defined merchandising characteristics. The "C" stores likewise had a clear mission as limited hard-line stores, and most of them were located in larger cities where they could be supervised by nearby "A" stores. But the situation of the medium-size "B" stores differed markedly. There were many more of them and they were widely separated geographically. It was harder to find competent managers for them and, once found, these proved more difficult to supervise. Because the "B" stores' merchandising mission was ambiguous, they needed many kinds of help: with merchandise assortments, sales planning, advertising and sales promotion, store layout and display, inventory control, expense control, and personnel selection and training—the gamut.

Pressures were felt for enlarging both territorial and district staffs, and a modest buildup ensued. As it turned out, there was greater buildup at the district than at the territorial level. In midsummer 1930, one member of the officers' board wrote a memorandum to General Wood in which he argued convincingly that "[each district manager should have] a staff of merchandise men, each in charge of related lines, whose duty it would be to supervise the Heads-of-Stock in the stores in that district, to keep the buying organization . . . informed as to conditions in the field and to see the policies and plans of the parent organization are carefully carried out in detail in the field."⁸ This recommendation was strongly supported by the territorial officers and reluctantly approved by Wood.

Actually, the augmentation of district staffs was probably greater than it appeared on the surface. Most district managers were also managers of "A" stores, and most of their staff members were store personnel assigned part-time to district duties. Because people in their stores were under their command and it was easy to bury their costs in store costs, the district managers were able to deploy larger staffs than their books disclosed. Thus, both openly and covertly, the district staffs soon became significantly larger than had originally been intended. To General Wood, who was also monitoring the increase in territorial staffs, this represented a worrisome growth of overhead.

At first, this side effect of the new organization plan was accepted, if reluctantly, because it greatly improved service of supply to the stores and materially strengthened the quality of their merchandising performance. But as the iron grip of the Great Depression progressively tightened, Wood was forced to reappraise the situation and soon began questioning the wisdom of the whole territorial setup. He grew increasingly concerned about the organizational strains resulting from the division of authority and responsibility between the functional and territorial structures, strains which might have been inconsequential if business had been good but were becoming intolerable as conditions worsened.

In truth, Wood was none too happy with the performance of his territorial officers. When they were first appointed, he was sufficiently uncertain about them as a group that he made only one of them a full vice-president; the others had to be content with the new lesser status until, presumably, they proved themselves. More than one was slow in doing so. The new plan had been in operation only a little over a year when Wood wrote to Lessing Rosenwald: "I feel, Lessing, that from now on we must be a little hard-boiled about some of our top personnel. We cannot delay indefinitely for results. I believe in patience but sometimes patience is over-done. If ―――― and ―――― cannot build up their territories within the next six months, they will have to be removed."⁹ And six months later:

>―――― is such a fine fellow, so conscientious, so hardworking and so loyal to the company that it is hard to appraise him without prejudice. The fact remains that he has made a virtual failure. Everything that has been accomplished so far has been done under pressure. He has either not the ability or the insight to solve his problems unaided. However, I feel we should let him remain and, in line with your

suggestion, I did not mention to him the possibility of his ultimate removal. I sincerely hope that he will have the territory in such shape by the end of the year that it will not be necessary to remove him.[10]

General Wood was particularly displeased with what he perceived as the tendency of his territorial officers to spread themselves too thin and go about problem solving in the wrong way. In a memorandum dated December 21, 1931, he urged them again—as he had often done before—to concentrate on personnel, which he viewed as their primary responsibility. He concluded with this strong admonition:

> Again, I want to impress you with the vital selection of personnel. Our whole future depends on the proper selection, proper reward and proper elimination of personnel. You cannot personally remedy matters in any unit under your control. You haven't got the time. But you can remedy matters by getting the right man in the right place and I have not seen a single instance of any Territory, Mail Order House, District, or Store where the selection of the right man did not almost immediately bring results. Put your personnel work first because it is most important.[11]

Unfortunately, ambiguities in the Frazer Report and the actual trend of administrative practice were working inexorably toward broadening the role of the territorial officers beyond the confines Wood envisaged. In a memorandum to the General dated December 16, 1931, T. J. Carney pointed out that "it has been our practice to expect a territorial officer to be in a position to correct merchandising, operating, and even accounting, as well as sales promotion weaknesses that exist in a particular district or store."[12] As operating vice-president and a firm supporter of Wood's personnel-centered concept, Carney argued against this practice, but the fact that he felt compelled to do so is evidence of its prevalence. J. M. Barker, the strongest of the territorial officers and the only one with vice-presidential status, responded to Wood's memorandum by reminding him that the functional officers did not have direct responsibility for sales and profits, that as a practical matter this was vested in the "line of executive authority," and that "[in] any case, the Territorial Officer, responsible for personnel, but not for profits, would undoubtedly find it difficult to fit personnel into a scheme unless his choice of individuals would be judged by profit results over which he had no control."[13]

In a two-day meeting between the functional and territorial officers held in January of 1932, an abortive attempt was made to clarify the role of the territorial officers.[14] It soon became apparent that there were only three viable alternatives: to give them real autonomy, which would have meant a considerable increase in staff; to reduce them to little more than field arms of a central personnel department; or to do away with them altogether. The following May, Wood chose the latter course. Clearly his decision was influenced in large part by his concern for costs and overhead.[15]

To replace the territories, Wood established a much simplified structure. The mail-order plants reported to Carney as operating vice-president; the retail stores, now numbering well over 300 from coast to coast, reported to a new office of retail administration in Chicago. Headed by J. M. Barker with F. B. McConnell as his assistant—the two strongest of the former territorial officers—the new office was responsible for personnel, for appraising store results, and for taking necessary action to correct problems. Significantly, this "necessary action" was assumed to be personnel action. The retail stores continued to be organized in districts as before, and the functional officers retained their direct relationships with the district managers and the stores. To facilitate coordination and cooperation, a retail committee was established with Barker as its chairman. Barker also took over and strengthened the small central personnel staff which Wood had first created during the previous year and began to set up systematic procedures for recruiting, training, and promoting competent managerial and trainee personnel for the stores.[16]

The new arrangements were a definite improvement over the old. Under Barker's firm hand, the work of the functional officers was effectively coordinated. The retail committee proved to be a useful administrative tool. Problems of store classification and merchandise assortments which had so vexed the "B" stores were attacked systematically and were soon on their way to resolution. The more orderly attention being paid to the selection, training, and placement of store executives began to show positive results. And as economic conditions got better, the atmosphere became increasingly relaxed and optimistic.

By the latter part of 1934 it appeared that the rough years were over. The integrated mail-order/retail system Wood had envisioned from the outset was a reality. The central merchandising organization had learned to buy for the new urban markets, and the service-of-supply mechanisms were for the most part fine-tuned to the not always uniform needs of the individual stores' trading areas. The store managers were becoming more adept at controlling inventories and expenses, and their skills in personnel selection and sales promotion were improving. As a group, the "A" store managers had evolved into competent merchants and operators, and the "B" store managers were making encouraging progress.

Wood felt that the time had come for the managers to stand on their own feet, freed from the close supervision which he had come to view as "interference." Significantly, he felt that the managers would gain in competence and confidence more rapidly if they were allowed greater autonomy.

Accordingly, at the start of 1935, over the strenuous and unanimous objections of his subordinates, he wiped out at one fell swoop both the office of retail administration and all the districts. Stores located in the same metropolitan areas and using the same advertising media remained under group managers and group merchandising staffs for the purpose of coordinating local sales promotions, but otherwise all store managers— now numbering over 400—were to report directly to him. The district managers, most of whom were also "A" store managers, were readily absorbed into this new scaled-down structure. Barker was moved to the position of senior financial officer of the company, and McConnell became Wood's assistant to help him carry the added workload he had assumed.

As it turned out, the abolition of the retail office was short-lived. It was not long before McConnell, still carrying the "assistant to" title, was functioning in very much the same way as Barker had when the latter had officially headed that office. The retail committee was reconstituted under McConnell to include the functional officers' retail assistants rather than the officers themselves. In keeping with General Wood's emphasis on "the proper selection, proper reward and proper elimination of personnel," the central personnel function was greatly strengthened by the appointment of Clarence B. Caldwell as director of retail personnel, reporting to McConnell. In 1939, with the office of retail administration firmly reestablished, McConnell was promoted to vice-president for retail administration and personnel and as such became one of the most powerful officers of the company. Five years later he succeeded to the Sears presidency and in due course was named chairman of the board.

Abolition of the districts was a much more drastic move than the transient discontinuance of the office of retail administration. The district structure based on the recommendations of the Frazer Report was never revived in its old form during Wood's remaining years in office. Stores clustered in the same metropolitan areas reported to group managers. Group managers and all store managers who were not members of groups

117

reported directly to Chicago. A new position, zone officer, was created in 1935 to assist McConnell in his task of appraising store performance. The zone officers, originally numbering four, were assigned to geographic areas and dealt only with the unattached "B" stores in those areas; their role was simply to serve as "the eyes and ears of the officers in the field," and they exercised no managerial functions. The number of zones was gradually increased until by 1939 there were eight.

Considering that the Sears organization now comprised over 600 retail stores and mail-order plants, the field structure was remarkably unsophisticated. The mail-order general managers reported to the operating vice-president, Carney, while the retail group managers and the independent "A" store managers reported to McConnell. The unattached "B" stores likewise reported directly to McConnell. He had a small cadre of personal representatives in the field—the zone officers—who facilitated his relationships with the "B" stores, but these were not intended to be "managers" in the chain of command as the district managers had once been and the group managers still were.

What had begun as a highly centralized organization was in this way converted into a highly decentralized one. The functional officers still exercised their functional authority, but they no longer had counterparts at the territorial and district levels and their connections with the stores were tenuous. Only the accounting and credit organizations remained centralized, and these continued to report up administrative channels of their own which were parallel to but independent of the remainder of the field structure.

During the transitional period between these two distinct forms of organizational structure, Wood learned a great deal. In his first ten years at Sears, he had tried a number of organizational expedients, some of which had worked and some of which had not. At one point he had even agreed to the formation of merchandising staffs in the district offices; this decision had been based at least partly on the argument, put bluntly by one of his close associates, that the hiring of capable merchants at the district level would permit "the use of mediocre men" at the store level.[17] But Wood had learned that he needed *good* men, not mediocre men. He had learned that what could be accomplished by organizational contrivance and administrative fiat was strictly limited but that good men, given broad direction and encouragement, could work wonders. He wanted his managers to have enough freedom to succeed or fail on the basis of their individual merits

118

without relying on district staffs for guidance; he had confidence that they would develop into stronger men if they were not held up by crutches.

Abolishing the entire district structure took courage. Prior to 1935, supervision of the individual stores was close and detailed; decisions of even minor import had to be cleared by the district office. With dramatic suddenness, managers who had been accustomed to looking to higher authorities were forced to act on their own and to take full responsibility for whatever happened as a result of their actions. It was sink or swim, and some sank. But the high proportion who survived developed into a corps of exceptionally able executives from whose ranks emerged a generation of senior administrators and officers who carried the company to new and previously undreamed of levels of achievement.

Toward the end of the sharp 1937–38 recession, when sales and profits were down and the top officers were voicing concern, General Wood appointed a special committee to study the situation. The committee did its work thoroughly and brought in a series of recommendations, some of which called for closer checks on the stores to keep them from making the kinds of mistakes the committee had uncovered. In responding to these recommendations, Wood came as close as he ever came to a definitive statement of his managerial philosophy.

> I want members of the [committee] to constantly bear in mind certain principles from which we must not deviate. We can make modifications in detail, but we must never change the principles themselves.
>
> To begin with, we have a decentralized system for our stores, of which the manager is the key point. While our retail stores have developed certain weaknesses during the past year, which have been brought out by the depression, I do not regard them as serious weaknesses. The best proof that the system has worked has been the record of sales and profits. I want this system to endure. . . .
>
> To make their stores successful in a decentralized system, it is essential that the responsibility be placed on the manager. He must decide just what merchandise he must select from the offerings made to him, and just what price he must put on this merchandise. If his initiative in this regard is removed and if he is visited constantly by supervisors and inspectors and representatives of the parent organization, it is only a matter of time before his morale will break down. . . .
>
> Having spent the greater part of my adult life in large organizations, I think I know their besetting weaknesses and the reason for the decay of most of them. No organization is perfect, even the most efficient one. The easiest thing in the world is to find weaknesses in a

119

large organization. The natural human tendency for the men at the top and for the bright young members of their staff, if they discover a weakness is to set up a system of checks and inspection that will obviate that weakness, forgetting that in most cases the remedy finally turns out to be worse than the disease. While systems are important, our main reliance must always be put on *men* rather than systems. If we devise too elaborate a system of checks and balances, and have too many inspectors going out as representatives of the parent organization, it will be only a matter of time before the self-reliance and initiative of our managers will be destroyed and our organization will be gradually converted into a huge bureaucracy. . . .

I have faith in the great majority of our managers. I believe they will work out their own salvation with a relatively small amount of supervision from the officers and the staff. While system is important, I repeat that our main reliance must be on men rather than on systems, and the proper selection and training of managers is the most important work of the officers and the retail staff.[18]

Wood was convinced that no matter how wise and capable corporate or district staffs might be, they could never do as good a job of running the stores from a distance as competent management could do on the spot. He wanted his local managers to have enough autonomy to adapt and respond to local conditions, both problems and opportunities. In a 1939 address to an assembly that included all the store managers, he stated his thinking clearly: "You are all familiar with our policy of decentralization. We have deliberately tried to treat you as independent merchants and men. We have tried to give you the widest possible authority and scope. We have tried to free you from a horde of bureaucrats, functionaries, [and] inspectors who might nag and harass you. We have endeavored in a chain store system to have a cooperative democracy. I think the system has succeeded beyond our best hopes." [19] Some years later, when the Sears organization structure had more than proved itself, he told an audience of leaders of the retail industry: "The greatest weakness of a large organization is its tendency to centralize controls, to establish rigid rules of procedure, to build up staffs which arrogate all thinking, to treat the great mass of employees as robots. Our aim has been in the opposite direction, to decentralize authority and responsibility, to have very loose controls, and to minimize staffs." [20]

Fundamental to Wood's approach was a deep-seated reliance on the capacity of his managers to prove equal to the challenges they faced, provided they were well selected in the first place. He did not want them subjected to too close supervision and direction. He did not want them hemmed in by organizational supports on which they could easily become

120

dependent. He wanted them to have freedom to develop and grow, and he wanted an organizational structure and style of management that would support and not inhibit growth.

For a military man, General Wood had a curious distrust of formal organization. During his tenure at Sears, few organization charts were drawn and few job descriptions written. A chart of the overall company organization was included in the 1940 *Annual Report*, but this served an essentially cosmetic rather than operative purpose: not many Sears people had ever seen it before and not many ever saw it again. For several years after entering the retail business, the company had no retail store organization charts, which students of management and other outsiders found hard to believe. It was sometime after World War II that Wood permitted the personnel department to publish store charts and then only with the strict understanding that they would be limited to external use only. I was then assistant to the director of personnel, and I still recall the General's stern instructions: "I don't want any charts distributed within Sears, because if you do some managers will think that's the way we want them to do it. I want each manager to figure out what's best in his particular situation and set up his organization accordingly." [21]

The duties and responsibilities of the various segments of the company were set forth in the broadest, most general terms, and there were no precise definitions of departmental or functional jurisdiction. People whose tasks intermeshed were expected to work out between themselves where one's responsibilities ended and the other's began and to collaborate harmoniously in a common effort. In most cases, the results were more than satisfactory. For example, no explicit definition of the respective spheres of the organizationally coequal merchandising and factory vice-presidencies was ever stated, but these two offices maintained a long record of cordial and mutually supportive relationships under a succession of officers. [22] There was a similar lack of precision in the jurisdictions of the operating and merchandising departments and in that of the personnel department vis-à-vis all the other departments with which and through which they worked. The ability to work well with peers without the imposition of external constraints or the intervention of superiors was an implicit requirement of all persons in key positions in the company. Wood felt that he had more important things to do than to try to define in other than the broadest terms the areas of responsibility of his key people, and he felt equally strongly that they had more important things to do than squabble over the details of who did what.

Wood himself paid little heed to formal lines of organizational structure. For those who were not accustomed to his mode of operation, his habit of ignoring lines of reporting and authority was at first disconcerting. If he wanted to find out about a problem, he would go directly to the person who was most knowledgeable about it; if he wanted to solve a problem, he would call in the person who was in the best position to do something about it. In both cases, he often bypassed intermediate levels of responsibility. Subordinates learned that part of their job involved keeping their superiors informed of contacts Wood had made with them, and their superiors learned that being bypassed implied no lack of respect for their positions but was simply the way the General worked.

Wood's distrust of formal organization—and his propensity to ignore it when it got in his way—grew from a conviction that it is the people in the structure, not the structure, that get things done, and that unless care is taken in designing organizations the structure itself can impede accomplishment. Some of his associates developed a mistaken belief that "Wood doesn't know anything about organization," [23] or that he "paid no attention to management principles." [24] In fact, he understood far better than they the real meaning of organization. To Wood, organization was not merely a means for mobilizing and coordinating human effort; equally important, it represented an opportunity to foster human growth. He conceived the task of building a business as essentially that of developing people. He had no use for "mediocre men"; he meant for Sears to be the kind of company that would put a premium on finding good men and then provide them with a working environment that would bring out their best.

The structure he designed for this purpose has been characterized as "broad" or "flat" in contrast to the more "vertical" or "tall" structures having many organizational levels between top and bottom. [25] In formulating and implementing this structure, Wood ran directly counter to "span of control" (now more commonly termed "span of management") theories, which hold that the number of subordinate executives reporting to a single superior should be strictly limited to enable that superior to exercise the detailed direction and control usually considered necessary. At Sears, key executives in both the field organization and the parent merchandising organization were deliberately spread thin and given more subordinates than they could possibly control closely. This effectively compelled the maximum decentralization of authority and relegated responsibility to successively lower levels within the organization.

The purpose of maximum decentralization, in turn, was to build strength at all levels. Since Sears offered little in the way of structure on which people could lean, they had to rely largely on themselves. Their superiors could give them only limited help, but by the same token they could not severely restrict, through too-detailed supervision, the unfolding of the potentialities of their subordinates. Not all individuals could perform effectively in this kind of organization; it required large measures of self-reliance, self-confidence, and personal capacity. The system placed a premium on finding people with these qualities and tended to weed out those who lacked them. It was certainly no place for "mediocre men."

The "broad" or "flat" design of the overall Sears structure was duplicated to a considerable extent in subordinate segments. In the parent merchandising organization, the heads of the forty-odd buying departments reported directly to the merchandising vice-president. Although this vice-president had four staff assistants—one each for buying, retail sales, mail-order sales, and inventory control—none was in the line of authority. The typical retail store was organized under a comparably broad span of control, with thirty or forty heads of selling departments reporting directly to the store manager or, in some cases, to a merchandise manager.

This structure had several advantages for the parent buying organization and the stores.[26] Because the amount of time a superior executive could devote to his subordinates was, on the average, severely limited, the only way for him to accomplish his own job was to have people in key positions who could function well with only general direction and occasional help. The result was an overall quality of personnel and organizational effectiveness which was in many ways unique in the annals of enterprise.

For these and other reasons, the period following 1935 was an exceptionally exciting one at Sears. Most of the people in the organization were young. They felt that they and the company were going places. They worked long and hard; their jobs and the company were seldom out of their minds, and their social lives, from choice, were largely confined to other Sears families. Sears wives—commonly described as "Sears widows"—often found themselves stranded at parties while their husbands withdrew to talk shop. Recurrent efforts on the part of Clarence B. Caldwell, the retail personnel director, to discourage store executives from putting in excessively long hours fell mostly on deaf ears. On more than one occasion, a physician whose practice included many Sears people warned Caldwell that too many of them were driving themselves too hard, not because of pressures from above but rather compulsions from within. These, the physician took pains to point out, were much more difficult for people to deal with.

Without question, Sears was a highly motivated organization during those years, and the results showed it. Net sales nearly trebled from $337 to $969 million in the seven-year period following 1934. Two hundred new stores were added, and many existing stores were relocated and enlarged.[27] The 44,000 employees of 1934 grew to 73,000 in 1939 and 130,000 in 1941.[28] It was a time of great movement and great opportunity; the élan in the organization was almost palpable. The sustained burst of energy was comparable to that which accompanied the opening up of free economic institutions in the larger economy. Wood had, in effect, created within the body of a corporate structure a system of organizational arrangements which approximated a free society.

And yet by the late 1930s the company had begun to feel the strains caused by the rapid expansion in its scale of operations. Worried about the administrative consequences this entailed, Wood wrote a memorandum to his directors in which he noted:

> We must face the fact that our present and future size brings many problems. With the expanding number of stores, plants and the increasing ramifications of our business, it becomes humanly impossible for the President and his officers, no matter how able they are, to know personally or to deal personally with more than a small portion of even the key personnel. The element of personal knowledge and acquaintanceship between officers, managers and merchants which has always been such a vital element in the strength of Sears will gradually disappear, important decisions will eventually be made, not from first-hand knowledge, but primarily from reports from subordinates; in short, the business, in spite of the efforts of its officers, will tend to become a bureaucracy.[29]

In truth, the development of a suprastore structure, if not a bureaucracy, was already well underway. Despite the elimination of territorial staffs in 1932 and district staffs in 1935, the size of staffs between the parent organization and the stores was slowly growing. The expansion of the number of stores and of sales volume in major cities created a need for merchandising and operating specialists at the group level. Most of the larger independent "A" stores gradually added internal staff. The number of "B" store zones increased from the original four in 1935 to eight in 1939, and it proved impossible to confine the zone officers to serving simply as "the eyes and ears of the officers"—the function they were originally intended to perform. Over time, they began to assume managerial responsibilities as they augmented their initially spare staffs with sales promotion, advertising, display, and merchandising specialists.

Meanwhile, the task of maintaining effective surveillance of store and managerial performance was becoming increasingly difficult. The office of retail administration and the functional offices assiduously reviewed the profit and loss statements and the merchandise condition reports which they received each month from each store, but while these could reveal problems they could not always identify causes. Closer personal contact with the stores was necessary, but the span of control had now grown so broad as to make such contact tenuous at best. Moreover, in an organization of the size Sears had now reached there were many matters which had to be dealt with at levels higher than the local, and trying to handle these from a central point was becoming awkward. By 1939 it was inescapably clear that a nationwide network of over 500 stores required some form of intermediate geographic structure.

Faced with this reality, General Wood decided to reestablish the territorial offices. This time, however, they would have responsibility and authority over functional activities as well as for sales and profit performance. The plans he and his associates developed called for dividing the retail stores and mail-order plants into five semiautonomous territories, each heading up to an officer who would be a virtual president within his own territory. The buying activity would remain in the parent organization, as would control of finance and certain other overall corporate functions, but otherwise each territory would be run very much as an independent entity.

Profiting from his earlier experience, Wood planned to move toward the new structure in a series of steps rather than in a single action. In this way he could not only see how it would work in practice but also make it easier for the company as a whole to adapt to the new arrangements. The first step was taken with the establishment of the Pacific Coast territory in 1940, but subsequent steps were delayed by the outbreak of war in 1941. Immediately following the war, the eastern and southern territories were created, and the southwestern and midwestern territories were added two years later. By 1948, the "territorialization" process was complete and the company was operating as five semiautonomous geographic divisions capped by a merchandising and corporate staff.

But this was not the General's ultimate goal. He viewed the formation of administrative territories as preparing the way for a far grander scheme:

125

the creation of independent regional corporations. He broached this idea to his associates at least as early as 1940 and raised it again from time to time during the war years and after.[30] His mature thinking on this score, outlined at a meeting of directors, officers, and senior executives in 1947, bears quoting at some length:

> In spite of its colossal growth, Sears Roebuck and Co. can gain still further and its sales, profits and opportunity for its employees and stockholders be still further increased.
>
> But you may well ask, even if you agree with me wholly, what is the end of all this. Can a company grow too big, will it become too unwieldy, will it become a great bureaucracy, will it get beyond the control of its officers? The adage of the prize ring is still true, "the bigger they are the harder they fall."
>
> Yet it is also true that a business organization is like an animal or plant—when it ceases to grow, it begins to decay. Part of the success of Sears is due to the fact that for 15 years we have been expanding, and have attracted a multitude of able young men. . . .
>
> I have realized that the company is too vast and complicated today to be administered by any one man, however able that man may be—it is too vast to be administered from any one point without danger of delay or bureaucracy.
>
> My answer to this is that all these dangers do exist, and that to my mind there is only one possible answer—so my final answer is to divide the Company into four or five regional companies, with the buying organizations, factories, and factory investments in still another company, whose stock will be owned by the regional companies, each with its own officers and Board of Directors. We can appoint some of our younger and able men to Vice Presidents and Directors of these five or six companies. As a result I believe the growth and prosperity of the Company would continue. I believe the results would be similar to that of the Standard Oil Company of New Jersey which was dissolved by the Government in 1912. The constituent oil companies today, under the leadership of many different groups of officers and directors, have ten times the assets of the regional [original?] parent company and have more than ten times the profits. I believe our experience will parallel this. I feel we have enough able young men in the organization to carry on these constituent companies with ability and vigor, that we have in our present Directorate, older officers and key employees a wealth of experience and wisdom to guide their policies in the right direction.
>
> And if this step is taken, I look forward to another great era of growth and prosperity for the Company.

The following note, written in longhand on the General's copy of the speech, evidently served as his conclusion:

126

This step is not alone in Sears business interest but it is also in the public interest, in the interest of the people of the United States. It will mark a reversal of the 50 year trend toward consolidation, and I believe it may be followed in time by other companies.[31]

It was an ambitious concept, and it proved too ambitious for achievement. Although intensive studies were undertaken over a period of some eight or ten years, no practical means could be devised for overcoming the legal, tax, and financial obstacles that stood in the way, let alone the administrative and organizational problems of merging regional corporate autonomy with centralized merchandise planning and procurement. The Standard Oil precedent was attractive but of limited relevance. There were enough difficulties inherent in combining decentralized regional operations and centralized buying under one corporate roof; the complications of multicorporate autonomy were insurmountable. Wood had no choice but to rest content with a territorial structure that fell well short of his cherished goal.

The General soon had other reasons to be disappointed. It was his clear and emphatic intention that the new structure confirm and solidly establish the principles of decentralization to which he was so firmly committed. He saw the establishment of the territories as a re-creation of the halcyon days following 1935 when, in giving an unprecedented degree of autonomy to his store managers, he had unleashed a flood tide of energy and accomplishment. But in thinking that he was restoring organizational decentralization, he was badly mistaken.

Under the original plan, the territorial staffs were to be kept small and to consist only of the vice-president and a few staff assistants, primarily in the areas of personnel and employee relations, merchandising, operating, accounting, and public relations. Wood wanted these to be administrative structures close enough to the scene of the action to deal effectively with supralocal matters and to facilitate attention to stores in need of help. But he continued to believe in the virtues of maximum local autonomy and to abhor the evils of unnecessary overhead. Almost at once, however, territorial staffs began to grow. The new structure had been in place scarcely a year when General Wood addressed this topic in a communication to F. B. McConnell, who was then Sears president. That Wood was alarmed is evident:

The chairman and president of the company have decentralized their own activities and given very great latitude to vice presidents who are in effect the presidents of their respective territories, but if

127

the principle of decentralization ends with the president and chairman giving great authority to the vice presidents and if the vice presidents do not in turn pass that authority on to the retail store managers and the mail order plant managers, the system will fail. I do not want territorial vice presidents to centralize authority in their offices and in their staffs. Their staffs must remain a useful instrument but not the controlling element in the operating and merchandising of the stores and mail order plants in their respective territories.[32]

When McConnell sent copies of the General's memorandum to the territorial and functional officers, he added his own admonitory words:

I believe all of you know that I have been disturbed by the growth of our staffs . . . which has taken place since the end of the war. In a Retail Committee meeting held in August of 1947, I made quite an issue of this. . . . Then, because of merchandise allocations [required by still-prevailing scarcities], and, since we were in the midst of our post-war retail expansion, I felt the arguments for a continuation of the larger staffs were reasonably good.

This year, some small reductions in staff have been made, but my personal opinion is that they are still constituted with too many people. The mere fact that we have large staffs, I believe, tends to take the responsibilities from the field that belong to the field.[33]

At a meeting of all store and plant managers and parent executives held in May of 1950, Clarence B. Caldwell, now vice-president for personnel and as always a staunch supporter of Wood's doctrine of decentralization, warned, "Ironically enough, the very fact of territorial decentralization can result . . . in a high degree of centralization at the territorial level."[34] Two years later, Caldwell sounded a fresh warning: "From the point of view of parent, Sears is more decentralized today than it was fifteen years ago. But from the point of view of the individual store manager Sears today is a great deal more centralized than it was fifteen years ago. The territorial office has become a new focus of centralization—a centralization all the more undesirable because it is centralization on a provincial level."[35] Nevertheless, the tide of centralization moved inexorably ahead. Despite admonitions from the chairman and the president, and despite eloquent arguments on the virtues of decentralization from the director of personnel and other corporate officers, the size of territorial staffs and of group and zone staffs within the territories grew apace. During the few short years remaining of Wood's tenure of office, his very presence exercised some moderating influence, but on his retirement in 1954 the rate of territorial centralization gained new momentum. By the mid-sixties Sears was as highly centralized as it had once been decentralized.

This development was doubtless due in part to several factors over which no one could exercise much control. The introduction of computers, new advertising and sales promotional practices, changes in the legal environment (such as affirmative action and employee and product safety), and the like all had impact on the Sears organization and the changes taking place within it. By far the most powerful cause for the rapid centralization, however, was the sheer drive of able and ambitious territorial executives anxious to turn in a good account of themselves. And this was precisely what they had been trained in the Sears tradition to do. General Wood had put his finger on the problem years before in his previously quoted 1938 memorandum to the officers and retail policy committee: "The natural human tendency for the men on top and for the bright young members of their staff, if they discover a weakness, is to set up a system of checks and inspection that will obviate that weakness." [36] Following their "natural human tendency," the territorial vice-presidents were more wont to take direct action—which often meant adding staff—than to rely on the slower and less certain practice of trusting the good sense and potential for growth of those at lower levels of the organization. Before long, centralization was firmly rooted and there was little anyone could do about it.

General Wood had no choice but to watch matters take their course. Back in 1938, when he had been very much in direct command of Sears, he had halted an incipient trend toward centralization by a single pronouncement. But once he moved up to board chairman, even though he retained the position of chief executive officer, the strong, semiautonomous territorial organization he had himself created left him too far removed from the troops to control the day-to-day course of events. And following his retirement in 1954, his earlier words had little apparent relevance to the realities with which current management was seeking to deal. He remained a respected and revered figure within Sears until the end of his days, but the time when he could have taken the reins had passed.

Perhaps the most insidious influence throughout this entire sequence of events was the fact that Wood's successors simply did not share his abiding faith in the capacity of well-chosen and -placed men and women to manage their own affairs. The General's confidence on this score may have led him to undervalue the need for systematic organization—in truth, he distrusted it from the start—but for all of his charismatic qualities he failed to communicate his central conviction to enough of those he left behind. When he departed Sears, there was no one to carry on the tradition he had labored so hard and long to establish. Some tried, most notably Houser and Caldwell, but they, too, were approaching the end of their tenure at the company.

There is no question but that some form of territorial structure was necessary. By the late 1930s Sears, Roebuck had simply grown too large and complex to be administered in the loose and sprawling manner General Wood preferred. But the new territories *could* have been arranged in much the same way the General had once structured the company as a whole. Without men of similar turn of mind—and similar personal strength—this was not to be.

The phenomenal success of Sears under General Wood's leadership was accomplished in large part through the efforts of capable men who grew up within the system the General had built. In a very literal sense, Wood built the business by building people. And a key element in this process was the simple, highly decentralized organization structure he had designed for that purpose. But while the system built strong executives at middle and upper middle management levels, it failed to build men capable of rising to the top.

Robert Wood had a vision. It was a large vision. And during the years of his ascendancy it was an eminently workable vision. Out of it arose not only one of the most successful enterprises of its day but also a unique institution that occupied a special place in American life, made a major contribution to the well-being of the American people, and embodied much of the essence of the American dream. But without the General's strength of character and sheer ability, perhaps it was inevitable that the vision fade.

8

Manager Policies

O NE ASPECT OF THE 1930 Frazer Report that especially pleased General Wood was its emphasis on the personnel functions of the territorial officers. To Wood, "management work" and "personnel work" were one and the same. He viewed the process of managing as consisting essentially of the selection, placement, rewarding, and replacement of people. This, in fact, was how he defined his own role, as expressed in a 1931 memorandum to his territorial officers:

> In outlining my conception of responsibilities and duties of the Territorial Officers, I am really outlining my conception of my own job, because, in your respective territories, you stand in my place. There is very little that the principal executive of a widely scattered, far-flung organization like Sears, Roebuck can do personally. This applies to me and likewise to you.
>
> As President of the company, about the most I can hope to do is to select, properly reward, and properly weed out the officers and key men of the Company, besides continuing along the lines of certain fundamental policies. To sum up, my principal job is that of a personnel officer to a limited class of men, the establishment and maintenance of proper policy and a close watch over the results of policy to the Company.
>
> This again applies to you. In your respective territories your first and most important duty is the proper selection, proper reward and proper elimination of personnel in your territory.[1]

In practice, however, it proved impossible for the territorial officers to confine themselves to personnel duties alone. Under the terms of the Frazer Report, they were also responsible for the sales and profit performance of the stores within their jurisdiction, and this drew them inescapably into merchandising, operating, and other administrative matters. The realities of the circumstances led J. M. Barker, the ablest and most articulate of the territorial officers (and the only one to hold the position of vice-president), to propose that they be permitted to add personnel assistants to their staffs. The General was reluctant to concur with this suggestion, due in part to his aversion to overhead and in part by his conviction that the personnel function was so central to the managerial function that he did not want his territorial officers to delegate any portion of it.[2] When Barker persisted, he alone among the territorial officers was allowed to hire a personnel aide.

Wood never succeeded in imposing his personnel-centered concept of management on his territorial officers, and this was undoubtedly a factor in his deciding to abolish the territorial offices outright in 1932. The Chicago-based office of retail administration he established to replace them, headed by Barker, was charged not only with coordinating the retail aspects of the functional officers' work but also with carrying on the personnel duties formerly vested in the territorial officers.

F. B. McConnell, who was named assistant to Barker, immediately became involved in manager-personnel activities, and the post of retail personnel manager was created to assist him. Although this position was two levels below that of president, because of the great importance Wood attached to the function he took an active interest in selecting the person to fill it. Unfortunately, neither of the first two appointments proved satisfactory and each held office for only a short time. In what may have been the best personnel decision he ever made, his next and final choice was Clarence B. Caldwell.

Caldwell was then thirty-eight years old, and his entire career up to that point had been spent in retail store management: first with two other chain organizations, and most recently as the manager of the Jackson, Michigan, Sears store, where he had been for about a year. He had written a rather frank memorandum to General Wood, pointing out a number of weaknesses in the company's retail operations, and was understandably apprehensive when he was summoned to Chicago to see the General. Upon being offered the position of retail personnel director, he reacted with astonishment.[3]

"But I don't know anything about personnel," Caldwell protested. "I'm just a store manager."

"That's exactly what I want," the General replied. "Hire whatever technical talent you need, but I want a man as personnel director who knows what it takes to be a good store manager. And I want a man who, when he tells other store managers there's something they ought to do, they'll do it—not because he's personnel director but because they know he's a good store manager and knows what he's talking about."

Caldwell assumed the retail personnel post in 1934 and soon became McConnell's right-hand man. He was firmly established in his new role when, in early 1935, Wood abolished the office of retail administration, moved Barker to financial vice-president, and appointed McConnell assistant to the president for retail administration and personnel.

That Caldwell more than met Wood's expectations over the coming years is clear. The General paid close heed to Caldwell's advice and spoke often in glowing terms of the accomplishments of his department. At the June 1948 National Personnel Conference, for example, he observed:

> In the type of organization we have, when so much is decentralized, the personnel department is one of the keystones of the company. I remember some fifteen years ago when we decided to "turn the stores loose," more or less, I said that this scheme would work if we had a strong personnel department, and would not work if we did not, and it *has* worked since. The freedom of action that I would like to see given to the retail stores, mail order plants, buying departments, or any other will work only when you have good men and women. It is my opinion that people work better when they are free to express themselves and to carry out their own ideas and then be judged by the results. But to do things this way, it is essential that we have a strong personnel department.[4]

Because of Wood's unflagging insistence on the centrality of the personnel function, reinforced by Caldwell's constant support of this philosophy, there developed within Sears a strong tradition of personnel as an integral part of the managerial process. This was in sharp contrast to the way the personnel function was normally viewed—as a technical specialty. Caldwell hired technicians when he needed them, but when it came to filling key positions on his staff he relied primarily on proven retail executives who kept the personnel function in proper managerial perspective. He often said that it was easier to teach a good Sears man what he needed to know about personnel than it was to teach a good personnel man what he needed to know about Sears.

Under Caldwell's leadership, the personnel department evolved into one of the strongest departments in the company. Initially, it was concerned almost exclusively with executive personnel matters, and its energies were concentrated on the task of meeting the seemingly insatiable demands of the rapidly expanding retail system for qualified managerial talent. Personnel field men with good Sears retail backgrounds were brought into the department and assigned to the several geographic areas into which the company was divided. It was their task to work with the store managers and zone officers to build reservoirs of promotable people, to lay out job rotation schedules for them, to counsel with them and evaluate their progress, and to participate in decisions regarding their advancement.

For administrative purposes, these activities were organized into what was termed the "Reserve Group Program." While this was an executive development program in every sense of the word, and a singularly productive one at that, it made little use of formal training methods and relied chiefly on direct job experience. Reserve Group members were rotated through those store positions deemed most important for their careers. At each step, they functioned not as "observers" but as practitioners, since a basic premise of the program was that experience had to be real and could not be contrived. It was not enough to put a man where he could watch what the occupant of a particular job did and then move him on to repeat the process elsewhere; the Reserve Group member was expected both to learn the job at hand and to assume full responsibility for its proper performance. It was considered axiomatic that only by doing the work himself, and only by having to hold his own in competition with others not favored as he was with special Reserve Group status, could the trainee actually get the feel and flavor of the work he would later be called upon to supervise.

Sears decentralized organizational structure was itself a major factor in executive development. The loosely knit retail system was not an easy one in which to live. Large measures of self-reliance, self-confidence, and personal capacity were required to function effectively within it; those who did not possess such qualities in adequate degree tended to be weeded out—in fact, had to be weeded out if the system was to work. People were encouraged, even pushed, to reach to the limit of their capabilities, and sometimes to develop capabilities they never knew they had.

The Reserve Group program included some organized effort and systematic procedures, but these were not its essence. Instead, it was built around dynamic forces which fostered the processes of growth and maturation. It left ample room for growth to occur *within* the individual, recognizing that while growth could be encouraged or inhibited by external conditions, it was the individual who had to do the growing. The program was a logical offshoot of the structure Wood had created for the management of the rapidly burgeoning retail system and its supporting buying organization and was one of that structure's greatest advantages.

With his personal retail background and practical, down-to-earth orientation, Caldwell was the ideal man to implement this program on a large scale. He and Wood thought alike on important points. Both understood that the future executive needs practice in making decisions, that he needs to become accustomed to carrying responsibility, that he needs to make mistakes and live with them, that he needs the courage that comes from facing new problems and solving them. Both believed that people of promise are more likely to be exposed to these kinds of conditions in an organization characterized by extensive managerial decentralization. And neither needed a psychologist to tell him that if people have to wait until middle age before having a chance to carry bona fide responsibility, they are not apt to develop into strong, self-reliant leaders and executives.

Wood did not hesitate to stand behind managers who evidenced the traits he was looking for—including a high degree of independence. The story is told that during the early years of the retail system a retired Army officer whom Wood had hired was assigned the task of visiting stores and checking on their operations. In one Ohio store, he started telling the manager that he wasn't doing things right.[5]

"Listen," the manager replied, "I'm making a profit in this store. I'm running it, and I don't want anybody coming in here telling me how to run it."

"You've got somebody telling you how to run it," his visitor insisted.

"You get out of my store or I'll throw you out physically," the manager said.

Upon returning to Chicago, the retired Army man went to see Wood.

"You've got to fire the manager of the [such and such] store," he began.

"Why?" the General wanted to know.

"Well, for insubordination. I went in trying to show him how to do certain things, and he told me that if I didn't get out of the store he'd throw me out."

"What store is that again?" Wood asked, reaching for the black book containing the P & L Statements. He flipped through them until he found the one for the store in question and scanned it while the other waited.

"Tell me again what that fellow said," Wood instructed.

"He said, 'Get out of my store or I'll throw you out.'"

135

"Well," the General replied, "he made ten percent before taxes. You got out, didn't you?"

Wood also made sure that Sears as an organization treated its managers fairly. In a 1939 speech before all store managers, he reiterated company policy on this matter: "We have established safe guards [sic] against injustice to you through the Personnel Department, through a special committee appointed for the purpose. No manager can be discharged without first being given every opportunity to make good, without a careful review by the Personnel Department, by a special committee appointed for the purpose by Mr. McConnell personally, by the President personally. No manager, if his work is satisfactory, can be transferred without his own consent." [6]

An essential feature of the Sears concept of executive development was that vacancies in the organization were to be viewed not merely as positions to be filled but as opportunities to provide people of promise with valuable experience—"creative experience," in the words of Mary Parker Follett, one of the pioneers in the development of theories of organizational behavior. I was once called upon to explain the placement process and the rationale behind it to a meeting of the American Management Association, at which time I said, in part:

> We regularly transfer men from one type of activity to another, solely as a means of rounding out their experience. For instance, we frequently have operating superintendents and sales superintendents trade jobs with one another. We transfer men from personnel to operating, to merchandising, etc.; we transfer them between retail stores and mail order plants, and between various field assignments and the parent organization. These moves are made not only to stimulate the growth and development of the individual, but because the fresh point of view brought to a job by a man trained in another type of activity or another branch of the company often enables him to make a positive contribution to the improvement of the job itself. [7]

Placement decisions were based not only on the requirements of the job but also on the needs of people. Positions were often filled by persons whose backgrounds did not make them obvious candidates but who could benefit from the particular types of experience offered. As a result, Sears employees gained access to avenues for growth that might otherwise have been closed to them, and the jobs themselves were frequently enriched by the introduction of fresh modes of thought and action.

The growth analogy was very much a part of Sears thinking in all matters related to executive development. As T. V. Houser noted in his book about the company, *Big Business and Human Values*: "Fundamentally, we respect the many-sided potentialities of human beings. In more concrete terms, the placement of people is not regarded as a matter of fitting square pegs into square holes; a much better analogy is planting good seed in a well-prepared seed bed, and then giving it the conditions that will enable it to attain the fullest growth with which it is endowed." [8] On some occasions, transfers were dramatic. The head of the candy department, the smallest of all buying departments, was promoted to general manager of the company's second largest mail-order plant, despite the fact that he had no previous mail-order experience. The general manager of another mail-order plant was promoted to vice-president and controller of the company without benefit of formal accounting training. Peter Drucker, who studied Sears closely during this period, once told T. V. Houser, "At no time during this process of making decisions about people do you play god and at no time do you say, this man is this and nothing else. Your careers in Sears are remarkably open-ended. If you look at any hundred people in your executive ranks, their career patterns defy definition." [9]

People who made personnel decisions at Sears developed a capacity to see in others a broader range of potential than was suggested by the experience or education they happened to have. They were more interested in what a man might become than in what he had been. They learned to recognize how experience gained in one field might be applicable to other not obviously related fields, just as Wood had recognized the value of Caldwell's store management experience to the job of retail personnel director. Wood himself, of course, was the example *par excellence* of what could happen if a man were given a chance: wholly without retail experience, he built the largest and most successful retail system the world had ever seen.

Clarence Caldwell was an astute judge of people. The conclusions he drew about them were largely intuitive and probably based on subconsciously perceived clues which he had learned to recognize as significant indicators of behavior and capacity. While he seldom made mistakes about people, he often found it difficult to explain how he arrived at his judgments, and his efforts to do so were sometimes amusing. He grew increasingly concerned, however, about the inherent risks of relying overmuch on subjective assessments. Although the early years of his personnel responsibilities were swallowed up by the overriding task of meeting the rapidly expanding retail system's demand for competent executives, by 1937 he was urging his staff to give more attention to defining the attributes desirable in prospective employees.[10] Continuing efforts were made over the following years to improve the interviewing skills not only of personnel staff but also of store managers and others in the field who were responsible for making employment decisions.[11]

By 1939 serious consideration was being given to the use of testing "as a supplement to interviewing and rating methods of determining aptitude and ability of applicants and employees."[12] On Caldwell's recommendation, General Wood in mid-1941 approved a research grant of $50,000 (a large sum for this purpose at that time) to the University of Chicago to develop batteries of tests for use in selecting trainees for the Reserve Group program. Under the direction of a distinguished psychometrician, L. L. Thurstone, the researchers compiled profiles of the psychological characteristics of Sears executives with proven performance records and then constructed tests designed to identify those candidates who had similar characteristics and, hence, were presumably most likely to succeed in the Sears environment. Toward the close of World War II, when Sears was on the threshold of its great postwar expansion, the personnel department was able to inform its director: "Our work with Dr. Thurstone of the Psychology Department of the University of Chicago during the past three years has enabled us to develop a program of aptitude testing which is far in advance of that of any other concern in the United States. We are now at a stage when we are able to test for executive and specialized capacities with a remarkable degree of accuracy, and testing has become an integral part of our whole selection and training process."[13] The tests proved of material value in the large-scale recruiting effort of the postwar years. Nevertheless, they were used with discretion, as indicated in this excerpt from a lengthy report generated in 1944:

> It is not intended that exclusive reliance be placed on test results in employing trainees. The report on test results and the doctor's report will merely be two items among the variety of factors which the interviewer will weigh and consider in evaluating the individual's probable value to the company. There can be no substitute for good judgement as the basis of any personnel decision. However, in conjunction with the personal interview, test results can be a valuable additional aid to sound personnel judgement. . . .
>
> Frequently, latent sources of future difficulty cannot be ascertained even by a skillful interviewer. . . . Psychological tests, because they are objective and penetrating, frequently can suggest to

the interviewer possible areas of weakness or strength in the applicant which might not otherwise be discovered or discovered too late. With such possibilities brought to his attention, the interviewer can make special efforts to verify or refute the evidence of the tests, with consequent improvement in the soundness of his final employment decision.[14]

Used as an aid to judgment and not as a substitute for it, psychological testing became a standard part of the company's executive personnel procedure and made an important contribution to the selection and advancement of the kinds of people needed to function effectively within the company's decentralized system of management.

From the late 1930s on, it was Sears policy that decisions on positions ranging from assistant store manager to just below the officer level required the concurrence of three persons: the supervisor to whom the position reported, that person's superior, and the personnel field man. The field man's voice carried special weight. He, in effect, "controlled the inventory" since it was his records which were reviewed by the group and he was usually the only one of the three who had personal knowledge of all the candidates under consideration. Thus, he was often in a position to say, "These two people are equally well qualifed for the job, but this one will work out better in this particular situation than that one." As a result, personnel field men imperceptibly over time acquired considerable power. So, of course, did Caldwell. But because he and his key staff took pains not to abuse their privileged position, they came to enjoy a unique degree of respect and confidence within the organization.

With the development of a strong central personnel function, increasing emphasis was placed on promotion from within. Caldwell frequently admonished the store managers to include in their hiring for rank-and-file positions at least a scattering of people who had the potential to move on to higher levels within the company. At a meeting of all store managers in 1939, for example, he urged: "We must recognize that from our sales force, our receiving rooms, our customer service desks, and other rank and file positions will come our future managers and other Company executives. However, this is only possible if, in our initial selection of people, we have chosen those of high caliber who possess the necessary qualifications to develop under proper supervision and training."[15] In fact, the store managers were expected to be the chief recruiters of potential executive personnel, not only for their own needs but for the system as a whole. In its plan of operations for the year 1940, the personnel department (Department 707) explicitly stated: "It would be impossible, as well as undesirable, for Department 707 to recruit more than a small proportion of all potential executive material. Primary reliance must continue to be placed on retail store executives, with Department 707 confining itself primarily to recruiting sufficient man-power to offset any deficiency in the number originating in the field." [16] The plan stressed that store managers were to "continue to be impressed with their obligation to the company for the selection and development of efficient, well-balanced, and well-trained organizations, containing the proper quotas of promotable men." [17]

As was true for all other aspects of managing the Sears retail system, decentralized authority and local responsibility were key features of the executive recruitment program. Managers took seriously the personnel department's charge to hire and train people of promise. They were encouraged in this by General Wood himself; as early as 1933, for example, supervisors and members of the buying force listened closely as he said: "I want to impress upon you the paramount importance of developing and instructing the younger members of our buying force. The only way to develop our younger men is to give them some responsibility, let them actually buy a portion of a line—one item if you please—but let them try their wings. I consider the training and development of these young men the most important job of the department manager." [18] Managers knew that their record on this score would be taken into account when they themselves came up for promotion. A demonstrated capacity to recognize and develop potential ability was considered an integral part of managerial competence, and those who failed to show it in sufficient degree were not likely to progress far up the promotional ladder. Managers learned to take pride in the number of good men they had "contributed" to the executive ranks of the company.

Although local recruitment efforts proved productive, the central personnel staff found it necessary to do supplemental recruiting to meet the pressing needs of the rapidly expanding organization. They looked chiefly to colleges and universities, but here, too, care was taken to involve the managers of nearby stores in the process. To hold down costs, local managers were often deputized to act as recruiting agents. First, however, they were cautioned to make sure that those who were hired were "given to understand clearly that they are to be employed on productive assignments

140

and that they will in no way be favored over men inducted through the regular channels." [19]

It was not until well after World War II that personnel acquired through organized college recruitment came to predominate in the Sears retail executive ranks. As late as 1947, only one store manager in five had a college degree, and just under half had never attended college at all. [20] Caldwell and his colleagues took a measure of pride in the fact that a college education was not a prerequisite for a successful Sears career. It is interesting that during this period there was no significant difference in the time it took college and non-college men to reach store management positions. [21]

Once individuals were recruited, no matter how, it became the responsibility of the personnel field men, in consultation with store managers, to identify those who appeared promotable, place them in the Reserve Group, and move them to higher levels as rapidly as they were ready. By the close of the 1930s, the company was no longer as dependent as it once had been on recruiting experienced retail executives from the outside, since almost all store managers came from the internal ranks. The promotion pace was steady, but it was not as frenetic as it had been during the early years of retail. Between 1925 and 1930, the typical new store manager had been with the company an average of only two years; between 1934 and 1939, most newly promoted store managers could claim an average of seven years of service. [22]

Wood was thoroughly committed to a policy of promotion from within, and not only because he viewed it as the best way to meet the company's needs for executive talent. He also considered it essential to the long-range survival of the Sears organization, as indicated by a talk he delivered to company executives in 1939: "It is my firm conviction that large corporations, like ours, tend to grow old and decay, that to keep them vigorous, up-to-date, in condition to meet the rapid changes of modern industrial life and to meet the severe competition of every line, there must be a constant flow of promotion, a constant rise to the top of young, ambitious, progressive men—men who have their futures before them—not behind them." [23] A policy of this sort involved long lead times, which in turn called for planning far in advance. Reasonably reliable estimates of future manpower requirements had to be made, taking into account both the company's plans for expansion and vacancies created by turnover and the promotional process itself. By the late 1930s the parent merchandising and administrative organizations were turning more and more to people with good Sears

141

retail experience, and these demands, too, had to be factored in.

As of the beginning of 1940, the personnel department estimated that the Sears retail system would be called upon to fill approximately 2,370 executive positions during the coming five-year period. At that time there were 1,258 identifiably promotable people within the Reserve Group.[24] The deficit was not nearly as great as the raw numbers suggested, since many Reserve Group members would be promoted more than once during those five years. But they in turn would leave behind them jobs that needed filling, so it was clear that a major recruiting and training effort would have to be mounted as the new decade dawned.

When assessing future requirements and the reserves against them, Caldwell and his staff had no way of predicting Pearl Harbor. With the onset of the war, both estimated needs and estimated resources proved wildly off, in part because the retail expansion program came to a grinding halt and in part because much of the Reserve Group melted away into military service. The retail executive organization, consisting primarily of younger men, was particularly hard hit by the draft and voluntary enlistments. Before the war was out, a fourth of the company's managerial employees were on military leaves of absence,[25] and the Reserve Group had ceased to exist as an operational entity. Vacancies were filled with the best talent available, a task that was greatly facilitated by the personnel staff's extensive knowledge of the people in the organization. All things considered, Sears weathered the war years well, largely due to the fact that the personnel machinery was securely in place and knew how to make optimum use of the human resources it still had. Once again, Wood was vindicated in his conviction that, given the chance and a suitable environment, people would prove equal to the challenges presented to them.

To the General, the war years were not merely a time for improvisation; they were also a time to prepare for the peace that would eventually return. Accordingly, he created a Post-War Planning Committee with subsidiary committees assigned to specific areas of activity. The mail-order committee produced a plan calling for the first new mail-order plant since the 1920s. The retail committee, envisioning a vast increase in demand for consumer goods to make up for war-inflicted shortages, submitted plans calling for the renovation, enlargement, or relocation of most of the company's existing stores and for the opening of many new stores. Plans for the parent buying departments called for substantial increases in procurement volumes as well as for the introduction of new and improved lines of merchandise.

142

H. Wendell Endicott, circa 1940, president of Endicott-Johnson Shoe Company, director of Sears, and close friend and mentor of General Wood.

James M. Barker, circa 1950, key figure in Sears early retail history, later chief company financial officer, and subsequently chairman of Allstate Insurance Company.

Thomas J. Carney, circa 1939, longtime mail-order executive and operating vice-president who succeeded General Wood as president of Sears in 1939.

Arthur S. Barrows, circa 1943, veteran merchandising executive who succeeded to the presidency of Sears on Carney's death in 1942.

Fowler B. McConnell, circa 1946, long-time mail-order executive, later vice-president for retail administration and personnel, who succeeded Barrows as president in 1946 and T. V. Houser as chairman and chief executive officer in 1958.

Lessing Rosenwald, circa, 1939, senior vice-president who succeeded his father as board chairman on the latter's death in 1932 and retired in 1939.

Theodore V. Houser, February 1952, key figure in developing Sears merchandising strategies who succeeded General Wood as chairman and chief executive in 1954.

General Wood, right, circa 1950, with Charles E. Humm, vice-president and controller.

E. P. ("Penn") Brooks, circa 1948, factory vice-president who took early retirement in 1951 to become founding dean of the Sloan School of Management at the Massachusetts Institute of Technology.

Edward Gudeman, March 1957, Houser's right-hand man who succeeded him as merchandising vice-president in 1952.

Clarence B. Caldwell, circa 1947, director and subsequently vice-president of personnel; architect of Sears personnel policies.

Edward J. Condon, circa 1939, director and later vice-president of public relations; architect of Sears public affairs programs.

In preparing its own postwar plans, the personnel department took into account the staffing implications of all these ambitious programs, along with the need to provide for the orderly reabsorption of the company's returning servicemen. In anticipation of the impending executive shortage, which it analyzed in some detail, the personnel committee warned:

> The need for new recruitment is only in part a result of the company's expansion program. *Even if it were not planned to open a single new store, or to convert a single store, and even if no increase in sales volume whatsoever were anticipated, there would still be a serious shortage of qualified check list* [i.e., managerial] *personnel.* The necessity for reorganizing executive staffs, and, above all, the curtailment of executive recruitment and training during the war period have created a substantial manpower deficit. The post-war expansion program will merely complicate and intensify an already serious problem.
>
> The deficit can be met only in part by returning military absentees. In estimating post-war requirements, ample allowance has been made for this factor. In all cases, estimated shortages allow for the return of 80% of those on military leave [actually, over 90 percent of managerial absentees returned]. *Our post-war executive personnel problem is thus not one of finding jobs for returning servicemen but rather of finding men for 1200 jobs which will be left over after four out of every five military absentees have been reinstated in their former jobs.*
>
> It is of the utmost importance that this impending executive shortage be clearly recognized. Check list vacancies cannot be filled on short notice. Years are required to train store managers and other key personnel. Only to a limited extent is it possible or desirable to fill such positions directly from the outside. If they are to be filled chiefly by promotion from within, recruitment and training must take place far in advance. Unless there is agreement now as to the probable post-war need, the day will arrive when we simply will not have the trained manpower available to fill important vacancies within the organization.[26]

The committee proceeded to lay out a detailed program of recruitment and training. With Wood's full support, it was ready for implementation by war's end and launched in timely fashion. As the new and improved operational facilities came on line, the personnel required for their effective and efficient management were ready to assume their posts (see Chapter 11 herein for a more detailed analysis of postwar expansion).

Both before and after the war, the General placed special emphasis on the importance of providing career opportunities for able people striving to make their way in the world. He had a particular interest in young people. This interest expressed itself in various ways, but none was so evident as the delight he took in watching young men grow up in the Sears organization. At a company-wide meeting of executives in 1939, for example, he said warmly, "The greatest pleasure I have had in recent years is watching the growth and success of you store managers, and of the younger men on the buying force." [27] And again, at a similar meeting some years later: "I knew many of you managers here present when you were just starting your business careers. Some of you have been with us through the entire period of our retail growth. Nothing in life has given me more satisfaction than to see your progress, to see your evolution from green kids, at small salaries, to skilled merchants, to prominent and respected citizens of your communities, with financial independence." [28]

The "green kids" may have started at "small salaries," but Wood paid his executives well—provided they produced results. He was a strong believer in financial incentives, and where possible sought to link compensation directly to profits. Store managers worked under bonus contracts that were individually negotiated each year; these were based on reasonable expectations as to sales and profit performance and took into consideration both local circumstances and general economic conditions. Although base salaries were low, bonus contracts provided for sharply increasing increments of compensation as successively higher levels of profits were achieved. As late as 1946, managers of the largest "A" stores were paid an annual base salary of only $6,000 per year but typically received year-end bonuses of from four to six times that amount, and much more when profits were exceptionally good. The relation of base to incentive earnings was not as disproportionate for buyers and their supervisors, since the profit contributions of individual parent buying departments could not be measured with the same precision as those of individual retail stores and mail-order plants. Nonetheless, sales and gross profit figures by merchandise line were taken into account when determining their bonuses, and a large part of the average buyer's or supervisor's annual income was also in the form of a single year-end payment. At higher levels within the company, the bonus pool out of which individual bonuses were paid was based on company profits for the year, and even officers of the company received the greater share of their annual income as bonus rather than salary.

Assuming, as always, good profit performance, the combined bonus and salary awarded all company executives from store manager on up was typically generous. This was deliberate because key executives were expected to live in a manner commensurate with the dignity of their positions. Store managers, in particular, were expected to assume leadership roles in their communities, and this required that they live in the "right" parts of town, belong to the "right" clubs, drive the "right" kinds of automobiles, and in other ways exhibit the behavioral characteristics appropriate to community leaders. Naturally, no one was so gauche as to put any of this into words, but everyone understood the rules, including those whose task it was to determine levels of store manager compensation.

Wood also held firmly to the virtues of capital accumulation. The assets of the Sears Profit Sharing Fund were invested chiefly in company stock, giving all employees an ownership interest in the business and, on retirement, a fund of capital which was more flexible and could be more productively employed than an ordinary annuity (see Chapter 9 herein). Stock options, in addition to bonuses, were an important part of executive compensation, and these were distributed liberally throughout the organization in sharply ascending proportion to levels of responsibility. The General was caustically critical of other major corporations—notably those within the automotive industry—for what he regarded as the excessively high salaries and bonuses paid to their top executives; he regarded these six- and seven-figure salaries not only as execrable public relations but also as inappropriate means for compensating top people. In his judgment, the economic rewards of the senior executives of public corporations should come in the form of appreciation of company assets, in the same manner as for the owners of privately held enterprises. It was Wood's ideal, in fact, that his executives look upon themselves and their work as though they were in business for themselves. Through his decentralized plan of organization, and through his bonus and stock option policies, he came remarkably close, psychologically speaking, to making this ideal a reality.

Under General Wood's leadership, Sears became an important vehicle of social mobility. As already noted, a college education was not a prerequisite for advancement to prominent and remunerative positions, as was often true elsewhere. Many able and ambitious young men of modest backgrounds achieved levels of career success and community standing which might otherwise have been denied them. Significantly, the Sears personnel department learned early to concentrate its college recruiting at state universities rather than prestigious private institutions where the socioeconomic mix of students was often quite different.[29] A study made in 1947 disclosed that a substantial majority of the company's store managers had come from rural areas and smaller cities and, in the manner typical of the upwardly mobile, had "left home" to seek their fortunes.[30] Many in fact found them at Sears, and much of the drive and élan which characterized the company during the Wood era was directly attributable to the high proportion of upwardly mobile people in its ranks.

One of these was Clarence Caldwell himself. With a small-town background and without the benefit of a college education, he carved out a notable place for himself at Sears. After establishing himself as a successful store manager, he was brought into the parent personnel department; initially responsible for retail personnel only, he became director of personnel for the entire company on F. B. McConnell's advancement to the presidency in 1946. With this broader mandate, he proceeded to apply to the mail-order and parent branches of the company the policies and programs which had proved so effective in retail. In 1952 he was elected vice-president for personnel and in 1955 became a director of the company. For health reasons, he was forced to retire in 1956 at the early age of sixty.

During his tenure as head of personnel, Caldwell more than fulfilled his charge of meeting the company's manpower requirements. But his greatest contribution was his ability to make operational General Wood's ideas about organizations and people. Of all Wood's lieutenants, Caldwell understood better than most the deeper reasoning behind and implications of the concept of decentralization. He saw clearly that the role of the store manager was basic to this concept. If a manager were to be held responsible for his store's performance, Caldwell insisted, he must have authority equal to that responsibility, and this meant that within broad limits of company policy he must be free to use his own best judgment even if he made mistakes from time to time. Caldwell often pointed out that mistakes were the price that had to be paid for building a strong, competent, self-reliant organization. Time and time again, he reminded parent and zone staffs that their task was to *assist* store managers and not to try to run their stores for them; no system of external controls, he maintained, could ever replace sound day-to-day judgment at the scene of the action.[31]

Portions of Caldwell's address to the 1950 On-to-Chicago meeting merit quoting at length since they so accurately reflect Wood's thinking and reveal much about Sears in its mature phase in the closing years of Wood's incumbency:

> Our constant aim must be to develop better merchants *in the stores*. No matter how wise we may be in parent, we cannot do as good a job of merchandising the stores at long distance as even a mediocre grade of management could do on the spot. And we are very

146

far from having a "mediocre grade of management" in the stores. . . .

Fundamental to the Sears way of doing things is a deep-rooted reliance on the experience and good judgement of the store and plant managers. But you can't have such reliance unless you've got the right kind of men in the first place. It is for this reason that such emphasis is placed by Sears on the proper selection, training, and assignment of key personnel, for if decentralized management is to work successfully, it must depend in very large measure on the quality of executive manpower at all strategic places.

A necessary corollary to the principle of relying on the experience and good judgement of the store and plant managers is that these men must be allowed a wide degree of latitude to accomplish their jobs. We cannot narrow that latitude or circumscribe too sharply their area of discretion, or impose too much supervision and control and expect them to develop the kind of judgment on which we can rely with confidence. We've got to decide what kind of organization we're going to have, and then we've got to operate in ways that are consistent with its basic principles. . . .

The essential evil of too much staff, of too close supervision, of too elaborate a system of controls is precisely that of hemming people in to the point where they come to rely too heavily on such supports and thus miss the opportunity of developing self-confidence and self-reliance.

If your people are to grow, they must have responsibility delegated to them. And I mean really delegated, not with a lot of strings tied to it. . . .

In any case, the top man must have a very great deal of confidence in his subordinates. This is absolutely crucial. If he does not have that kind of confidence, he cannot give them the range of latitude and discretion that is necessary, nor can he tolerate the mistakes that are occasionally but inevitably made under this kind of system. This is why the right kind of selection is so essential, and why the right kind of training and experience are so important. This is why, too, the company emphasizes such things as character and integrity, because without these confidence is impossible.

You've got to have confidence in your subordinates, because without that you can't run your store or plant in line with Sears principles. But you can't afford to misplace your confidence. You've got to use good judgement, because the company holds you responsible for your subordinates. The most important kinds of decisions you as an administrator have to make is [sic] in whom you will place your confidence and how far.[32]

Throughout his active career, Wood frequently stressed how critical it was to have the right man on the job. In Clarence Caldwell, he certainly had the right man. Caldwell took to heart Wood's philosophies and beliefs.

He fleshed out Wood's intuitive leanings and developed personnel policies and programs to give them practical effect. He shared Wood's conviction that management problems are really people problems, and that the way to build a strong organization is to staff it with strong people. Of the cadre of extraordinarily able men with whom Wood surrounded himself in his years at Sears, none served him better than Clarence Caldwell.

9

Employee Policies

A WIDELY DISPERSED SYSTEM of mail-order plants and retail stores, each functioning with considerable autonomy, requires that purposive measures be taken to avoid friction and divisiveness between employees and management, to maintain high levels of morale, and to provide motivation for superior individual and group performance. These considerations were of concern to General Wood from early in his association with Sears.

As he traveled about the country establishing the first Sears stores, he was struck forcibly by the unsatisfactory relations he observed between management and employees in the stores of other retailers. Years later, he recalled: "To begin with, the wages of the rank and file were terribly low, and there was no provision for taking care of the superannuated or old employees. In the upper ranks, there was no feeling of security, buyers shifted from store to store, their time with any one store was short. This was the rule. There were exceptions, of course." [1]

The General viewed good employee relations as good business, just as on more than one occasion he stressed that "good ethics is good business." He accepted as an article of faith that if the company treated its employees fairly, if it paid them well while they were working and made reasonable provision for their retirement, these policies would more than pay for themselves. That they did is clear from the record of Sears achievement. As Wood wrote in his *Reminiscences*: "There's no question but that the employees of Sears gave a far better return to their employer than is the case in the ordinary company. . . . [There's] a great difference in the results between the contented, happy employee and the discontented one; between the man who just works for his paycheck, and the man who really puts his heart in it." [2] His attitude had more behind it than the conviction that treating employees fairly was the best way to get the most out of them. He genuinely liked people and was sincerely interested in their welfare. He often felt required by the prevailing standards of the times to explain his motives in terms of "good business" or enlightened self-interest, but the fact remains that his warmly positive attitudes toward the men and women who comprised his organization were authentic. Natural and spontaneous, they reflected a deeply ingrained personal characteristic.

Wood took his concern for Sears people far beyond the executive level. During roughly the first fifteen years of the retail experience, he spent a great deal of time visiting the stores. He wanted to know firsthand what kinds of problems the stores were having and what changes needed to be made in company policies and practices to enable them to better serve their customers. He was not willing to leave this task to subordinates; he wanted to see for himself.

His store visits evolved into a set routine. First he would go to the store manager's office, where he would review the store's P & L Statement and the Merchandise Condition Report and discuss with the manager any problems these revealed. He would then ask for the employee record cards and focus particularly on those of the division managers (Sears term for the heads of selling departments in the stores) he wanted to see because of something he had learned from the store reports. He also gave special attention to the cards of longer-service employees and those who were identified by the manager as doing especially outstanding work.

With the store manager in tow, he would descend to the selling floor and move from department to department, questioning the division managers about things that might be going well or poorly and soliciting their suggestions. Along the way, he made a point of talking with longer-service people and those who merited commendation. In the course of these discussions, Wood made use of the rather considerable knowledge he had gained of each person's family background and employment history from his perusal of the employee record cards. An exceptionally rapid reader with a photographic memory, he used these traits to advantage for this and many other purposes.

Throughout this period, Wood visited virtually every store in the Sears system, many of them several times. During these visits, he learned much that came to be integrated into the highly successful Sears way of doing things and established a special kind of relationship with the people in the stores. Employees learned from personal experience and by word-of-mouth that their company's top executive was genuinely interested in finding ways to remove obstacles to their doing a better job, and that he was also interested in them as persons: in their ideas, their families, their futures. This was not something he learned from a book or did for effect, and his sincerity showed through.

For years after Wood stopped visiting the stores except on special occasions, it was not uncommon to hear one employee say to another, "And I told the General. . . ." In truth, he probably *had* told the General something at some point in the past, and the General had paid attention. (Similarly, "If the General only knew . . . " was a comment often voiced by employees discussing some local problem—again, years after they could possibly have had personal contact with him.) As a direct result of Wood's example, a closeness developed between Sears management and employees that was unusual in such a large and widely scattered organization. And out of this grew a feeling of confidence on the part of employees that top management cared about them as human beings.

This feeling was enhanced by another Wood practice. Each year, immediately following the annual meeting of the board of directors and the press conference at which the company's annual report was released, Wood and his officers repaired to the employee cafeteria. Gathered there were all parent and Chicago mail order employees able to crowd into what was the largest meeting room available. After presenting the sales and profit and results for the year just past and commenting on current business prospects, the General invited questions from employees. These were put into writing, collected, and brought forward to the podium. Wood then proceeded to answer personally many of the questions put to him; others which dealt with matters about which he was not fully informed, he referred to the appropriate officer. Wood called these yearly gatherings in the cafeteria his "Big Board" meetings, and he took great pride in them. They became company tradition and did much to strengthen the feelings of good will between management and workers.

General Wood's interest in the people who worked for Sears evidenced itself in many other ways. One of the most tangible of these was his commitment to the Profit Sharing Plan. Begun under Julius Rosenwald in 1916, when it was far ahead of its time and was looked upon by Rosenwald's business contemporaries as a dangerously radical departure from sound business practice, it was fiscally and administratively well established upon Wood's arrival. The General saw the utility of the plan to the development of good employee relations in his rapidly growing system

151

of retail stores. He expanded it, increased its benefits, and made it the cornerstone of his employee relations policies.[3]

The Profit Sharing and Pension Fund of Sears, Roebuck Employees (to give the plan its full name) was in many respects unique. All regular employees were entitled to join after a year of service, and virtually all of them did. Participating employees contributed 5 percent of their earnings, up to a stated maximum, into the fund. Initially, the company contributed 5 percent of its profits before taxes and dividends; when General Wood took command, this was increased to 10 percent. The company's contribution was divided among participants on a dual basis of individual contributions and length of service, with benefits heavily weighted in favor of longevity. Thus, for each dollar of their own contributions, employees with from five to ten years of service received twice the pro rata share of the company's contribution as employees with less than five years of service; those with ten or more years, three times; and those with fifteen or more years and over fifty years of age, four times.

For many years, funds deposited by both the company and the employees were invested almost exclusively in Sears stock, which of course earned dividends and, at least during Wood's tenure, increased mightily in market value. The practice of investing employee pension funds in a company's own securities is severely frowned upon today, but its wisdom in this case was demonstrated dramatically. Between the day Wood joined Sears in 1924 and the day he retired as chief executive officer in 1954, the market value of Sears stock, taking into account stock splits and stock dividends, increased by 1,140 percent. During the same period, the Dow Jones Industrial Average rose by a modest 202 percent.[4] This fivefold-plus superior rate of appreciation of Sears stock was a major factor in generating the exceptionally high level of benefits enjoyed by members of the plan.

Employees who spent the whole or a major part of their careers with Sears were likely to retire with comfortable accumulations of capital. There were some who drew out of profit sharing more than they had earned in salaries during their entire working lives. Significantly, the plan was designed to favor rank-and-file employees over executives. Participation was limited to stated amounts of income; until after World War II, this was $5,000 per year, but in 1952 it was raised to $10,000 and later to $15,000. In general, the upper limit of participation was geared to the higher levels of rank-and-file salaries, which meant that no matter how high an executive's pay might be, he could not benefit, dollar-for-dollar of individual contribution and year-for-year of service, more than the better paid rank-

and-file employee. When it came to profit sharing, the president of the company fared no better than a good salesman with a comparable number of years of company service.

The benefits generated by the Profit Sharing Plan unquestionably played an important role in Sears employee relations. But even more important than the benefits themselves was the fact that they served as highly visible evidence of top management's concern for employee welfare. By emphasizing the large degree of commonality between management interests and employee interests, the plan conveyed a message to employees that came through more clearly and far more credibly than it would have had it been expressed in words alone.

The policy of investing fund assets in Sears stock not only generated substantial capital gains but also resulted in the fund owning 26 percent of all outstanding stock by the time Wood retired in 1954. This fact had a subtle yet perceptible influence on employee thinking. There was a widespread feeling that in a very real sense people were working for themselves and that employees and management alike were pursuing the same goals. It was not unusual during those years to overhear one employee tell another, "Well, that's good for profit sharing," or an older employee admonish a newcomer for doing something "not good for profit sharing." In short, the Profit Sharing Plan acquired great symbolic significance for Sears employees.

The same was true for the executives and officers of the company. They, too, understood the underlying message of the plan: that top management considered employees important. This deeply influenced their attitudes toward and dealings with the employees within the scope of their responsibility. Once again, General Wood himself set the example. He frequently reminded his officers: "[You have] a greater responsibility than the officers of any other corporation in the United States, because the future of thousands of people lies in profit sharing, and if you don't run this company right and destroy their values, you've committed a crime." [5]

The Profit Sharing Plan and everything it symbolized in terms of concern for employee fairness, dignity, and welfare carried over into all other relationships between management and employees. This was expressed, among other ways, in a wide range of employee benefits: life and health insurance, sick pay, vacations, separation allowances, and the like. Sears, often at Wood's prodding and always with his support, led the way in establishing measures for employee security in areas such as these long before they became common practice in American industry.

153

General Wood insisted that all employee benefits, including profit sharing, be *in addition* to wages and salaries. These in turn were to be adequate in their own right. He often pointed out that, whereas the benefits would be useful in emergencies or for retirement, employees had to live in the here and now and should be paid accordingly. Managers checking competitive rates of pay in their areas, as they were required to do periodically, were instructed to consider actual pay only and to make no allowances in their analyses for differences between Sears benefits and those of the other companies surveyed. The General was very critical of the retail industry at the time for the low salaries then prevailing, and he urged his managers to be more liberal in their own pay practices. In 1930, when a six-day work week was practically universal in retailing, he proposed going to five days during the slow summer months with no reduction in pay.[6] This idea came to naught due to the Depression.

Although he was strongly opposed to the monopolistic features of the 1933 National Industrial Recovery Act, Wood directed the stores to maintain strict compliance with the wage and hour provisions of the retail code adopted in 1934. When the Recovery Act was declared unconstitutional in 1935, he ordered the stores to continue to comply on a voluntary basis. To that end he incorporated the relevant provisions of the code into an offical statement of company policy: the internally well-known "Bulletin 0–399." This was frequently amended in succeeding years to apply increasingly strict standards to the company's wage and hour practices.[7]

So far as rates of pay were concerned, Bulletin 0–399 prescribed only basic, storewide minima, leaving rates above those levels to the judgment of individual store managers. Based on an ambitious study begun in 1940 and completed in 1941, standard compensation policies specifying minimum levels of pay for all job classifications were issued and made obligatory for all stores. These often proved higher than prevailing local rates and were hotly opposed by some local managers, but Clarence Caldwell, with Wood's firm support, stood by his guns and the new plan was uniformly applied and enforced. Inquiries made at the time revealed that no other national or regional chain-store organization had implemented systemwide wage and hour policies of any kind.[8]

Adoption of the standard compensation plan could not have come at a more fortuitous time. Well established and running smoothly by the outbreak of the war at the close of 1941, it permitted a much more orderly administration of wages and salaries under wartime controls than would otherwise have been possible. And while other retailers lost large numbers

154

of their employees to higher-paying war industries as well as to military service, Sears salary levels were such that its personnel losses were not nearly as serious as they might have been.

During the war years, levels of pay were raised as rapidly as controls would permit, and when plans were drawn up for the presumably control-free postwar period significantly higher levels were contemplated. Expectations on this score were related explicitly to the need for quality personnel to deal with the more intensively competitive environment foreseen for the peacetime years ahead. As the detailed and carefully formulated "Post-War Personnel Program" pointed out:

> If Sears is to recruit a generally higher caliber of personnel in the post-war period, it is imperative that wage rates be established which will be attractive to higher caliber people. The advance in wage rates must *precede* any general improvement in the quality of recruits; the sequence cannot be reversed.[9]

And again:

> In the long run, a high wage policy *coupled by insistence on high quality people* will prove a definite economy. All our experience has demonstrated that well-paid and well-qualified people create lower wage costs per unit of sales. Our entire post-war personnel program must be founded on this premise.
>
> The retail industry is traditionally a low-paid industry. As a result, the better qualified younger people in the community tend to seek other lines of work as they enter the labor market, and retail salespeople are typically those who are less qualified or who take retailing as a second or third choice after failing in their efforts to enter a more attractive field.
>
> Because of general retail wage practice, an excellent opportunity exists for Sears to exercise leadership in the improvement in wage standards and thereby not only help improve conditions in the industry as a whole, but in so doing, secure the advantages which will accrue to the concern which takes the pioneering step.[10]

In the years immediately following the war, Sears more than fulfilled the leadership role it had outlined for itself. According to figures compiled by the personnel department and cited in a letter sent by then president F. B. McConnell to all officers of the company in early 1949, the average earnings of Sears rank-and-file employees increased by 128 percent between 1939 and 1948. During the same ten-year period, according to the Bureau of Labor Statistics, the cost of living advanced only 75 percent, resulting in a substantial improvement in the real wages of Sears employees. The 128 percent increase at Sears compared with a 96 percent increase in retail wages generally and a 97 percent increase in those paid by the manufacturing industry.[11]

Throughout the whole of General Wood's tenure as chief executive, Sears remained at the forefront of the retail business in its compensation practices. Not only was this achieved without cost to profitable performance; the higher pay scales themselves contributed to profitability by enabling the company to attract and hold quality employees. Just as the "Post-War Personnel Program" had predicted, a high wage policy, coupled with care in employee selection and placement, proved "a definite economy."

Prior to the war, encouraged by Wood to formulate rational and soundly based policies and practices for all aspects of personnel operations, Caldwell had established and placed me in charge of a research and planning function within the personnel department. One of the first major undertakings of this new unit was the development and implementation of the standard retail compensation plan discussed above. Other activities included studies of employee turnover and the demographic characteristics of company personnel, projections of future executive and employee requirements, the development of improved methods of selection and training, and analyses of the adequacy of employee benefit plans.

A particularly significant phase of the work of this unit involved the introduction of systematic means for discovering and evaluating employee attitudes and morale. This effort originated at the direct behest of T. J. Carney, Wood's successor as president. At the time, both Carney and Wood were growing increasingly uncomfortable with the fact that they were out of touch with the day-to-day goings on within the rapidly expanding retail system. Carney had come up through the mail-order organization and had only limited firsthand knowledge of the stores and their people. Wood, by now chairman of the board, no longer paid regular visits to the stores or enjoyed the close relationships with field personnel that had characterized the earlier retail years.

One day in the fall of 1939, Carney summoned Caldwell and me into his office. To this day I vividly recall what transpired during that meeting.

"When I was general manager of a mail-order plant," Carney began, "I could walk out on the floor two or three times a day, talk to the people, and really get the feel of how things were going. Even when I became operating vice president with ten mail-order plants to look after, I could still visit each plant several times a year, and while my contacts with the people were not what they had been, I felt I was still in touch.

156

"But here I am," he continued, "in this big office, president of this huge organization spread from one end of the country to the other. I can't walk out on the floor and talk to people like I used to, and I now simply have no way to keep myself as informed as I want to be about how people are thinking and feeling about their jobs and the company.

"We have a very good system of reports," he reminded us. "From the Merchandise Condition Reports, I can get a good idea of how things are going in the merchandising end of our business. The P&L Statements tell me all I need to know about how well managers are building sales volume and controlling expenses. But I don't have anything that gives me any idea about one of the most important things in our business: how satisfied our own people are with their work and the kind of treatment they get from their bosses and the company."

Carney explained that General Wood felt just as he did—isolated from what was happening in the field. Then, fixing his two attentive listeners with his one good eye, he went on:

"Now, you're a couple of smart fellows. What I want you to do for me is to develop a system that will give me something of the kind of information about what is going on in the minds of employees that the Merchandise Condition Reports and the P&L Statements give me about other aspects of our business. Both General Wood and I need to be kept informed about all important things going on in our far-flung operations. We're pretty well covered in all respects but one. We need a reliable and continuing flow of information about the state of affairs in the one remaining absolutely vital aspect of our business: how we are getting along with our people. I want you to look into this carefully and come up with a plan that will give General Wood and me what we need."

Caldwell promptly reordered the priorities of his research and planning unit and placed Carney's charge at the head of the list. It seemed clear from the outset that the best way to find out what employees were thinking was to ask them, and carefully constructed questionnaires appeared to be the most convenient vehicle for this purpose. The services of an outside firm, Hauser Associates, were retained to help design the questionnaires and to administer them, thus assuring employees of the confidentiality of their individual responses. Before the end of 1939, a number of experimental surveys had been made of representative stores, and the results were encouraging. While recognizing that the technique required considerable refinement, Wood and Carney felt that a good start had been made and that the surveys were giving them at least some of the information they wanted. The project continued on a gradually expanding basis until Pearl Harbor, when it was suspended for the duration of the war.

During the war years, Wood directed a number of his staff departments to utilize whatever time they might have left over from their otherwise pressing duties to prepare for the period of peace that would eventually come. Among other things, the personnel department addressed the subject of improving the employee survey program. A particularly fruitful development was the establishment of a close working relationship with the University of Chicago's Committee on Human Relations in Industry, a group of distinguished social scientists headed by W. Lloyd Warner, a leading figure in the newly emerging "human relations" field. Executive director of the committee was Dr. Burleigh B. Gardner, who came to play a significant role in Sears personnel research work.

Sears awarded a series of contracts to the committee for the study of various aspects of the company's organizational phenomena. Warner and Gardner found the extensive data on employee attitudes and morale contained in the prewar Hauser surveys to be of special interest, and they enthusiastically undertook an assignment to work with Sears on developing more useful and reliable methods for compiling and interpreting such data. The outcome was a highly sophisticated system for objectively assessing prevailing levels of morale and for evaluating trends in employee attitudes.[12] After the war, the new surveys became standard company practice and continue to this day as a key feature of the Sears employee relations program.

Both the Hauser surveys and those formulated by the Committee on Human Relations in Industry proved invaluable in many ways. The former provided a factual basis for planning the company's postwar activities, including improvements in employee benefit policies; these were ready for introduction as soon as the regulatory and economic environment permitted, and the employee response was positive. In the years that followed, the latter provided the means for keeping policies and practices up-to-date in light of changing conditions.

The surveys themselves contributed significantly to employee goodwill by serving as tangible evidence of management's ongoing interest in what people thought about their jobs and the company. Survey data were used not only for statistical purposes but also for training store managers and other executives. Individual store and other unit results were reviewed in depth with local executive staffs. Specific local problems were identified, and local executives participated in planning needed corrective actions. Each unit survey was handled much like a "case study," with the significant difference that the "case" was not something out of a textbook but their own, real-life organization for which major responsibility rested on their own shoulders. The surveys and the way they were handled provided a rich learning experience with beneficial results for all concerned.

Equally important, the very fact that surveys were conducted in all units on a recurring basis carried a clear message to those in the managerial hierarchy. There could be no doubt in anyone's mind that top management was concerned with the quality of working relationships within the organization and held accountable those who were in a position to influence that quality. All up and down the line, Sears people responded positively to top management's clear expectations in this significant area.

While from the first the surveys disclosed that many problems existed and that morale varied widely among different company units, they gave ample evidence that, on the whole, employees were remarkably well disposed toward the company. For example, when some 12,000 employees responded to questionnaires distributed in 1948, it was found that 72 percent thought Sears was either "better than average" or "one of the very best" places to work and only 3 percent thought Sears was "poorer than average." Ninety-five percent said they would rather work for Sears than almost any other company they knew.[13]

Another valuable result of the survey program was the deeper understanding it provided of the underlying dynamics of employee attitudes and morale. A 1950 report containing an analysis of survey data disclosed that there was no simple explanation for the generally favorable responses: "Rather, our studies indicate the existence of a highly complex set of interdependent factors which combine in subtle and obscure ways to produce a particular level of employee satisfaction or dissatisfaction." Among the factors identified as working in Sears favor were its philosophy of decentralized management, a "flat" organizational structure, opportunities for advancement, the quality of supervision, and employee policies and benefits (particularly profit sharing). The analysis stressed that these factors did not create themselves but instead were the results of conscious and deliberate management policy and reflected a fundamental management philosophy. The report concluded:

> Our studies suggest that the problem of employee morale is far more complex than is customarily appreciated. There are no simple cause-and-effect relationships, and often the influences of primary importance are subtle and obscure. Nevertheless, it is clear that the

quality of personnel relations prevailing in any organization is not a matter of chance. The following points in particular would seem to merit the special attention of management:

(1) One of the great advantages of the simple and relatively informal structure is that such a structure not only permits but enforces a maximum of informal, face-to-face relationships and keeps impersonal "institutionalized" relationships at a minimum. This type of structure likewise provides a high degree of freedom on the job, utilizes a larger measure of the individual's capacities, requires the exercise of personal judgment and initiative, and encourages the development of native abilities.

(2) Such a system requires an unusually high order of administrative ability if it is to operate successfully. In essence such a system is a democratic system, and democratic leadership requires far higher skill than the authoritarian variety.

(3) Basic to all other factors is the attitude of top management itself toward the people who comprise its organization. The nature of this attitude will largely determine the structure of the organization and the quality of relationships that prevail within the structure.

(4) High employee morale is a by-product of sound organization. It is not a result that can be achieved by and for itself; above all, it is not a result of "being nice to people" or plying them with favors. Nor is high morale something to be achieved at the expense of good operating results. The same policies, attitudes, and practices which are best calculated to produce good operating results over the long run are precisely the policies, attitudes, and practices which produce high levels of employee morale.

(5) Good morale and good results are not mutually exclusive. They are two aspects of the same thing: sound organization and capable leadership.[14]

"Sound organization and capable leadership" are precisely what General Wood provided for Sears, Roebuck over a period of thirty highly productive years. He was rewarded not only with phenomenal sales and profits but also with the knowledge that Sears employees—the men and women he cared so much about and took such an active interest in—were pleased with their relationships as well. How Sears people felt about their company is aptly summarized by this response to the 1948 employee survey: "Sears has so many advantages for its employes [sic], I couldn't write them all on this page. In my opinion anyone who kicks about how Sears treats its employes and its benefits, would kick if someone gave him his pay check while he stayed at home in bed."[15]

A discussion of the employee relations policies of a major American corporation during the years 1924–54 cannot ignore the subject of unions and collective bargaining. General Wood was not unique among the big businessmen of his time: he looked on unions and their doings with high disfavor. While approving the wage and hour provisions of the National Industrial Recovery Act, he opposed its famous Section 7-A which granted new organizing and bargaining rights to labor, and after the Recovery Act was thrown out by the Supreme Court he argued strongly against the passage of the Wagner Act. As for his own home base, he directed that vigorous efforts be made to resist any efforts to organize Sears employees.[16] Like many liberal-minded employers before him who took a sincere interest in the welfare of their employees, he honestly believed that Sears people did not need a union to protect their rights and interests and that the intrusion of "outsiders" would be detrimental in the long run to both the company and the employees themselves. That his purpose in seeking to maintain a nonunion status for Sears was not dictated by exploitative motives is well documented by his record of maintaining wage, hour, and benefit practices that were far in advance of prevailing retail standards.

Anticipating that attempts to organize Sears employees would follow passage of the Wagner Act, Wood employed Nathan W. Shefferman, a man who appeared knowledgeable in the ways of organized labor. This move made sense because there was then no one within the company who professed any knowledge at all of what seemed an arcane and esoteric field.

Nathan Shefferman was an interesting, complex character. Son of a rabbi, sometime efficiency expert, briefly a practicing phrenologist, self-taught psychologist, personnel consultant, peripatetic lecturer on inspirational themes, and anonymous "Friendly Voice" dispensing advice on personal problems on a New York radio program, he was attracted by the reformist ideals of Roosevelt's New Deal and succeeded in finding a place for himself on the staff of the newly established National Labor Relations Board. He came to the favorable attention of Lessing Rosenwald, who served as an employer representative on "peace panels" set up by the Board to help resolve labor conflicts.[17]

Shefferman had a strong moralistic streak which expressed itself in a marked concern for justice and human dignity, at least in the abstract if not always in concrete terms. He was generous to a fault and lavished gifts and favors among those whose friendship he felt he needed. He had a quick wit, an engaging personality, a magnetic platform presence, and a knack for getting along well with businessmen and labor leaders alike. He also had a host of intriguing ideas for promoting labor-management peace, and it was these—together with the moralistic fervor with which he voiced them—which Rosenwald and Wood found attractive. On joining Sears in 1935, he worked first as an assistant to Rosenwald, then to Wood, and then to Carney when the latter became president in 1939. He continued to operate independently of Caldwell until the latter's elevation to company-wide director of personnel in 1946.

In addition to assuming responsibility for dealing with the numerous organizing drives directed at Sears during the second half of the 1930s—a task which, from the company's viewpoint, he attacked with a high rate of success—Shefferman took on an assignment from Rosenwald and Wood to form an "independent union of Sears employees" (company unions had not yet gained the opprobium they soon would). But while Shefferman at first advocated the idea, he eventually had second thoughts: "After completing the plan and proving its workability in several places, I advised Sears against participation and even encouraging the formation of an independent union on the grounds that it would make the employees organization-conscious and make them ready to be taken over by bona fide unions. Sears listened to me." [18]

Sears point of greatest vulnerability to unionization was its trucking operations. Movement of merchandise into and out of the stores, mail-order plants, and warehouses "was the company's very life blood," and anything that threatened to disrupt that movement was obviously a mortal danger. Recognizing this strategic fact, Shefferman persuaded the company to get out of the trucking business and turn the work over to independent contract haulers. Because these haulers worked for other companies as well as Sears, it was difficult for even so aggressive a union as the Teamsters "to interfere with the myriad of other customers of the operator by shutting him down" in an attempt to strike at Sears. [19]

Shefferman recommended, and Sears followed, a similar course of action for other operations that seemed to be likely targets for unionization, such as certain categories of merchandise installers and maintenance workers. The problem, however, could not always be finessed by the simple expedient of divestiture, and during the highly active period of labor agitation in the years immediately following passage of the Wagner Act, Shefferman was called upon to fend off a number of organizing drives. Most of these were directed against local and regional warehouses and such behind-the-scenes activities as shipping, receiving, and mechanical service. Some drives were directed toward salespeople and office employees, but in general they focused on the presumably more easily organized blue-collar workers.

In countering these organizing efforts, Shefferman displayed considerable ingenuity and skill, particularly when it came to creating "vote 'no' committees" of employees opposed to joining the union. Because of the generally good relations that existed between the company and its employees, such committees were readily formed and usually turned out a strong "no" vote. Shefferman had a keen sense for spotting and exploiting weaknesses in the unions' efforts and a sure feel for timing which often threw the organizers off balance and forced them to operate from positions of diminished strength. While no statistics were kept at the time and the record is impossible to reconstruct at this late date, it is clear that the company was more often successful than not in its efforts to hold off the unions. As the man in charge, Shefferman got the credit.

He did not always win, but when he lost he took pains to limit the scope of the union victory. From the outset he managed to keep Sears from becoming a party to a collective bargaining contract. He accomplished this incredible feat by insisting that the results of each bargaining process be set forth in a "third party letter of understanding"—a letter containing the terms of the agreement that was addressed to both the company and the union but signed by a third party, usually a lawyer acceptable to both sides.

In reaching agreements, such issues as wages, hours, and working conditions were seldom problems since Sears practices were almost always already superior to those of other retailers and were often superior to the unions' existing contracts. Three other issues, however, proved difficult to settle, at least initially. Under Shefferman's directions, backed unswervingly by General Wood, Sears adamantly refused to agree to a union shop, maintenance of membership, or check-off of dues.* The company stood its ground on these points and the unions in time accepted them reluctantly as the price they had to pay for any sort of agreement with Sears.

But it was a high price. A union that reached an agreement with Sears

---

*Under union shop agreements, all employees in the bargaining unit must join the union, usually after a short grace period. Under maintenance of membership agreements, new employees are not required to join the union unless they wish to do so but those who are already members must maintain their memberships. Under check-off arrangements, union dues are automatically deducted from worker paychecks and deposited to the union's account.

on such a basis ended up having very little security within the company. Employees in the bargaining unit could join or not as they pleased, and those who did could drop out whenever they wished. Each month, the union business agent had to go hat-in-hand to collect dues from members who could pay or not pay as they saw fit, with no encouragement either way from the company. There was little incentive for workers to maintain their memberships or keep their dues current because the company took pains to ensure that other employees received no less favorable treatment than those in the bargaining unit. Thus, membership and interest in a union often dwindled, sometimes rather quickly, to the point where unionization was hardly more than a fiction. In more than one instance, a union simply walked away, and the company realized its absence only when the business agent failed to show up at contract renewal time. It was not uncommon for a union to decide that the Sears bargaining unit did not merit the trouble and expense of trying to keep it going.

The leaders of organized labor found that Sears was an adversary not to be taken lightly. Because of the company's advanced personnel practices and generally high levels of employee morale, Sears employees were difficult to organize except in isolated instances under special conditions. Any organizing efforts which might be mounted were sure to meet with skillful countermeasures that often stymied even experienced organizers. And in those relatively few instances when victories were achieved—usually at considerable cost in both time and money—the results, so far as the unions were concerned, were of questionable value. Union leaders surveying fields to conquer learned by experience that their efforts could be much more fruitfully directed toward other targets; by and large, trying to organize Sears was simply not worth the candle.

Sears success in this area did not go unnoticed. Overtures gradually began to be extended to Shefferman by other businessmen who were interested in learning more about him and his work. With the encouragement of General Wood, Shefferman in 1939 established a consulting firm, Labor Relations Associates (LRA), as a means of making his services available to a larger clientele than Sears alone.[20] From this point on, although he remained a Sears employee until reaching company retirement age in 1948, Shefferman devoted most of his time to his new firm. According to one source, it quickly became "the largest and most prominent [in its field] and served through the years up to three thousand clients."[21]

While Sears was one of LRA's clients, it made relatively little use of its services. Shefferman continued to advise Sears officers on labor relations policies and to keep them informed on developments in the union field, but from the early 1940s on the company came to rely more and more on its own Sears-trained people for dealing with new labor problems as they arose and for servicing agreements already in existence. In the five-year period 1948–52, for example, Shefferman and his LRA staff handled a total of only four contract negotiations while Sears staff handled an average of nearly 200 renewal negotiations per year.[22]

Over time, Sears had grown uneasy about Shefferman and his methods. Clarence Caldwell in particular came to believe that much of the apparent success for which Shefferman was given credit was due not to any special skill on his part but instead to the company's basically sound employee relations, which Shefferman had played no part in developing. It became increasingly clear in Caldwell's mind that while Shefferman might have been able to deflect certain organizing drives, the tactics he had employed in the process were gravely detrimental to the company's longer-term interests. His convictions on this score were strengthened by reports he received from local executives.

Shefferman's most effective tactic was the creation of "vote 'no' committees." This practice, and some of the inducements offered "loyal" employees to lead such efforts, may have been effective when it came to winning union recognition elections, but they often left the local company unit deeply divided and bitterly disillusioned. Also disturbing to Caldwell were Shefferman's cozy relationships with certain union leaders, notably Dave Beck and Jimmy Hoffa of the Teamsters and some of their key lieutenants. From the beginning of his association with Sears, Shefferman had been given a free hand to secure merchandise at wholesale for these and other friends who were supposedly in positions to do favors for Sears, but the nature of these "favors" was never precisely identified.

Despite his misgivings, Caldwell continued to call on Shefferman and LRA on occasion. In 1953 he retained their services in connection with an organizing drive mounted by the Retail Clerks Union in Boston that particularly worried him. The fact that Caldwell's health had begun to fail may have had something to do with his feeling the need for outside assistance; it is certain that it prevented him from exercising his usual degree of supervision over the course of events. As a result, the Boston situation got seriously out of hand. Over the protests of local executives, LRA operators employed highly questionable tactics which came to public notice and were fully aired subsequently in testimony before the Senate Select Committee to Investigate Improper Activities in Labor Management Relations, popularly known as the McClellan Committee.

The experience of being hauled before the Senate Committee and having questionable acts for which it was responsible paraded out for public view (the hearings were avidly covered by the press, radio, and television) was deeply embarrassing to Sears. The Senate Committee and its staff, led by its general counsel, Robert F. Kennedy, looked forward eagerly to the session at which the official Sears representative would be called upon to give an accounting. That Sears with its enviable reputation for uprightness and probity had been caught red-handed in dishonorable behavior was intriguing to say the least. It was "rather like the preacher getting caught in the henhouse," as one observer commented.

Sears came through the experience better than might have been expected. By the time of the hearing, both General Wood and Clarence Caldwell had retired, but Caldwell's successor, W. Wallace Tudor, appeared on Sears behalf. In a prepared statement remarkable for its candor, Tudor faced the issues squarely: "Now, Mr. Chairman, in our relations with the unions, we have made some errors. Certain actions were taken on our behalf which were mistakes, which never should have happened and which will never be permitted to happen again. We will explain that which is explainable, defend that which is defensible, and freely admit that which is neither." [23] After tracing the history of Sears relationship with Shefferman and LRA, Tudor continued:

> I want to state, with the utmost candor and conviction, that many of the activities engaged in by Labor Relations Associates and certain company personnel acting with them were inexcusable, unnecessary, and disgraceful. A repetition of these mistakes will not be tolerated by this company.
>
> The fact that our employees were at that time and are now receiving wages far in excess of employees in competing Boston concerns, whether organized or not, in no way justifies what took place.
>
> At the same time, I think it is fair to remind this Committee that Boston and other scattered LRA excesses were isolated episodes, contrary in principle and practice to the employee relations program of Sears, of which we are justly proud. [24]

Tudor went on to assure the Committee that Sears no longer employed the services of either Shefferman or LRA and that steps had been taken to guarantee that the kind of things that had happened would not happen again. "A repetition of these mistakes will not be tolerated by this company," he asserted bluntly. His unequivocal mea culpa was a far cry from the dramatic confrontation which the Committee and the news media had anticipated with such relish, and it defused the entire situation. In the book he later wrote about the McClellan Committee, Robert F. Kennedy summed up the matter: "[Mr. Tudor's] attitude and forthright admission blunted the sharp criticism the company might otherwise have received from the Committee. As a practical matter, when someone says that mistakes have been made, asks for no sympathy and pledges in good faith that the errors will not be repeated, it is difficult to be critical." [25]

A minor sequel to this chapter in Sears history was in some ways both amusing and revealing. Concerned that the hearings might have had a harmful effect on Sears public image, I immediately arranged for a sampling of public opinion. The pollster reported that few people were even aware that anything in particular had happened. Among those who admitted to some knowledge that improper practices had been exposed, however, there was a marked tendency to ascribe them to Montgomery Ward! To quote a typical response: "Yes, I heard something about some funny goings-on at a mail-order company, but Sears isn't the kind of company that would do that sort of thing. It must have been Montgomery Ward." [26]

The Shefferman story has been recounted in some detail because over the years some scholars and critics have assumed that the Shefferman activities on the record are representative of Sears policies and practices. In turn, some observers of the labor-management scene have concluded that Shefferman and his tactics were largely responsible for the fact that Sears, Roebuck remained remarkably free of unionization during the heyday of the growth of trade unionism in America. But this gives Shefferman both too much credit and too much blame.

For one thing, most unionization of Sears employees took place during the period when Shefferman was assistant to the president in charge of labor relations and exercised unquestioned command over Sears activities in the labor field. A comprehensive review made in 1950 disclosed that of 192 union agreements then in force, 121, or about two-thirds, had originally been entered into "prior to 1941," the bulk of them in a five-year span when Shefferman's authority was unchallenged. In the succeeding ten years, during which Shefferman was available for information and occasional advice but most labor matters were handled chiefly by company people working under Caldwell's direction, far fewer new organizing

167

drives were successful.[27] From Sears perspective, events took a distinct turn for the better once Shefferman began devoting the majority of his attention to his other clients.

It is equally clear in retrospect that Caldwell was correct in assuming that much of Shefferman's success was due to Sears basically sound employee relations policies and the generally high level of employee morale rather than to any special expertise on Shefferman's part. If Sears employees were hard to organize, it was mainly because the organizers found so little ill will and resentment toward the company on which to build; if Shefferman had a high "win rate," it was chiefly because the cards were stacked in his favor.

The ultimate responsibility for originally hiring Shefferman and for giving him such a wide scope of authority rests, of course, on General Wood. But the combination of aggressive unionism and new federal legislation had posed problems with which Wood and his senior officers were totally unfamiliar and about which they were very uncomfortable. Shefferman seemed to offer what they needed, and his early apparent coups seemed to confirm that they had made a wise choice. Although none of this is intended to serve as an excuse for what proved to be Wood's poor judgment in this matter, it does help to place it in a somewhat more objective light than some observers have elected to do.

Wood did not want unions. He was sincere in his steadfast belief that Sears employees did not need unions and were better off without them. But he underestimated the strength of his own basic policies. Not only could Sears employees get along without unions; Sears itself would have gotten along fine without redundant means for combating unions, especially when those means conflicted with the spirit of the basic policies which were serving it so well. The truth of the matter is that the situation improved greatly once Shefferman turned his focus elsewhere. It was Sears misfortune to be "caught" on one of the few occasions on which his services were later utilized. Embarrassing as it was at the time, the event had the unquestioned benefit of causing Sears to terminate once and for all the Shefferman relationship and to rely from that day forward on its own resources.

Without intending to suggest that the extent of unionism within a company is an index of the quality of its employee relations, it is relevant to note here that in 1950, toward the end of Wood's tenure in office, Sears had only 192 collective agreements in force. These were concentrated in only eighty-four of the company's then 1,090 (nonfactory) operating units, and in most cases applied to a relatively small portion of the employees in

168

each such establishment. About 14,500 employees were in bargaining units covered by these agreements, but only an estimated 9,300, or 5.3 percent, of the company's hourly employees were actually union members, and an even smaller number were current in their union dues.

A much more reliable index of the quality of Sears employee relations during this period is provided by the results of the company's employee attitude surveys. That these were strongly positive is a sound basis on which to judge Wood's abilities on this score.

From early in his Sears career, General Wood recognized the importance of good relationships between management and employees. His instinct for what was good business was strongly reinforced by his own outgoing personality and genuine interest in and concern for the employees who comprised his organization. Under his leadership and undergirded by the policies he pursued, he succeeded in building a strong, close-knit, highly motivated human organization which played a major role in Sears remarkable record of economic achievement.

10

Public Policies

G ENERAL WOOD RECOGNIZED early on that broad public acceptance and support were essential to a company which aspired to become an integral part of American life. He knew that certain constituencies
"external" to the enterprise would be vital to its success and was keenly
sensitive to elements and trends in the company's environment which were
likely to inhibit or support his business purpose. But rather than try to
shape public opinion to fits Sears needs—a practice common among other
big businesses of his time and since—he approached the issue in a radically different way.

Realizing that attitudes are based on experience, and that public attitudes toward Sears would be determined far more by the kinds of experiences people had with the company than by any claims the company might
make about itself, Wood sought to *adapt company behavior to meet public
expectations* and thereby gain the support needed to accomplish his business purpose. Over time, he designed a series of public policies * aimed
not at "selling" a corporate image but instead at enabling the company he
headed to fit comfortably and function effectively within the value struc-

---

*The term "public policies" is used here to encompass the strategies a company em-
ploys in its relations with constituencies external to its principal business activities but important to the successful pursuit of its business purposes. The term in this connotation was unknown in Wood's time; he himself used the phrase "public relations" to describe these
strategies. Today "public affairs" is coming into favor in business circles as a way of describing this general area of business practice. I believe "public policies" preferable to either of
the other two terms because it focuses more clearly on the manner in which Wood sought to
relate the company he headed to the broader American society and particularly to its external
constituencies.

ture of American society. Broadly speaking, these focused on accomplishing three distinct but closely related goals: strengthening Sears markets, making friends in influential circles, and building a broad base of public goodwill and support. Frequently, particular policies contributed to all three primary purposes, and in practice the policies often intertwined in mutually supportive ways, but their significance is best apprehended by keeping in mind their individual thrusts.

The need for such policies became apparent at the outset of Sears venture into retail. The new stores were carefully located to be readily accessible to the largest number of people and were therefore highly visible; in addition, thanks to Wood's buying strategy and the integration of the mail-order/retail distribution system, the values offered by Sears stores were usually superior to those available elsewhere. Visibility combined with values posed a double threat to established merchants, and Wood and his associates knew that opposition from them represented a serious potential danger. This was especially true in the smaller and more tightly knit communities into which Sears began moving in 1928 in response to Montgomery Ward's strategy.

Local merchants, most notably those in the smaller towns, constituted a vocal and politically potent force with considerable influence in state legislative circles. Movements were already underway in the late 1920s to restrict the rapidly growing chain-store systems; these movements would gather great momentum during the 1930s, spurred on by the Depression and its aftermath. The Sears retail system was thus politically vulnerable, and it was evident to Wood that means would have to be found not only to minimize opposition from other business leaders but also to convert at least some of it to positive support.

The attitudes of one group—local bankers—were particularly important, but here the company unfortunately got off to a bad start. During its first few years in retailing, it concentrated its banking business in a narrow circle of banks: the Chase in New York, the First National in Chicago, and a major bank in each of the other mail-order cities. As new stores were opened, local banks were used for the deposit of daily sales receipts, but once balances exceeded a small minimum they were transferred to a central point. In Sears view, this was a logical and efficient practice, and it was similar to the procedure followed by all other chain stores. Logical and customary as it may have been, it was bitterly resented by local bankers and earned Sears and chain stores in general vast amounts of ill will on the part of this powerful group.[1]

According to J. M. Barker, the General sensed that something was wrong, but he apparently left it to Barker to study the matter and determine what needed to be done. Soon after becoming vice president for retail administration in 1932, Barker basically restructured the company's relationship with the banking community.[2] He began by carrying substantially higher balances in local banks; in describing this new policy, he later recalled: "We have consistently tried to be liberal with the local banks with regard to the minimum amount of funds which we leave on deposit with it [sic]. This may involve some additional expenses . . . to provide these excess bank balances at a time when the company may be borrowing money. We have felt, however, that such expense was justified."[3] With Wood's approval, Barker instituted other practices to further cement relations with local bankers. Rather than continuing to borrow exclusively from a few key banking centers, for example, Sears started offering local banks an opportunity to share in the loaning activity. As Barker pointed out: "The local banker is, in most cases, in proportionally as much need of earning assets as is the large city banker. . . . Our experience has been that most local banks consider it a privilege to be able to share in our company's loan."[4]

When he became chief financial officer in 1935, Barker began involving local store managers in negotiations with local banks in order to build up "the local manager in the mind of the banker as a man whose influence is important to the banker in the conduct of the company's financial affairs." He also encouraged local bankers to call on him personally whenever they happened to be in Chicago, and he attended as many bankers' conventions as possible to extend "the sphere of [his] personal relations with country bankers." Barker was convinced that "good deposit balances and direct borrowing relations with local banks make the local bank look at [Sears] as having the same type of relation to him as do his local merchants" and that "the policy of loyalty to local banks which have served the company well is also worthwhile."[5]

Barker and Wood were entirely sound in their judgment that local bankers were useful friends for a company such as Sears to have. From having been bitter adversaries of Sears, they became strong supporters. While dividing up its banking business among hundreds of banks scattered throughout the country involved a certain amount of cost and inconvenience, this proved a small price for Sears to pay to gain the backing of this key constituency.

Under Wood's leadership, Sears undertook to forge other useful alliances as well—not in any explicit or formal sense but in recognition of the fact that there were matters of mutual concern to the company and to key components of its economic, social, and political environment. The means adopted for this purpose took a variety of forms. Some were designed to integrate the stores and mail-order plants more closely into the business and civic life of the community, and thus change the perception of Sears from intruder to valued local citizen. Others were directed toward strengthening local and regional economies, which contributed to public goodwill while simultaneously improving Sears markets. All measures were pursued in ways likely to result in the creation of closer relationships with key leadership groups. And each was intended to accomplish not only its overt purpose but also an essentially political one: the building and maintenance of a public and governmental climate favorable to the company's abilities to perform its economic function.

In this context, the term "political" is in no way pejorative. It merely recognizes that a system of free economic institutions depends for its survival on public acceptance and support. It is interesting to speculate on what American business would be like today if more business leaders had had the General's "political" perspicacity and skills; perhaps it would not have nearly as many problems as it does.

Wood was one of the first businessmen to think in terms of corporate social responsibility. In Sears *Annual Report* for 1936, he wrote: "In these days of changing social, economic, and political values, it seems worthwhile . . . to render an account of your management's stewardship, not merely from the viewpoint of financial reports but also along the lines of those general broad social responsibilities which cannot be presented mathematically and yet are of prime importance."[6] He then proceeded to outline the ways in which Sears was seeking to discharge its responsibilities to what he considered the company's chief constituencies: customers, the public, employees, sources of merchandise supply, and stockholders.

In an address before an assembly of all parent and field executives in 1939, Wood stressed Sears obligations as a corporate citizen of the communities in which it operates:

> Sears have [*sic*] endeavored to pioneer in another direction. In the past most chain stores, in fact most large national corporations, have performed useful economic functions, but too often have neglected their social responsibilities. It has been my ambition to have Sears stand for something different, to have Sears become, through its plant and store

173

managers, a useful citizen in every community in which Sears has a plant or store, to be interested and assist in anything that tends to build up the community, locality, or state. Mr. Condon [the company's director of public relations] nationally, and you locally, have a great opportunity in demonstrating to the people of the United States that a corporation has a soul, that it can be a useful and generous citizen.[7]

Shortly thereafter he elaborated further in a speech before the American Retail Federation:

> The retailer, as well as other businessmen, must realize that he has social responsibility as well as an economic responsibility. It is not enough that he be a good merchant; he must be a good citizen, locally and nationally. . . .
>
> The American businessman, whether he be engaged in the production, distribution or transportation of goods, has been essentially a specialist and not disposed to be interested in matters beyond his own business or field of activity. That viewpoint has to be changed. If our democracy is to survive, every businessman has to take his social responsibilities, his duties as a citizen more seriously, has to devote more time and thought to these responsibilities and duties.[8]

In Wood's ranking of corporate responsibilities, the customer always came first and the employee second. Depending on his audience and the occasion, third place belonged either to the stockholder or the community. In what may have been the most mature and comprehensive statement of his business philosophy, he did not even mention the stockholder in his order of priorities; after listing the customer and the employee, he went on to say: "Next comes the community, the towns and cities in which are located our mail order plants, stores, and factories. We must be good citizens, first, last and all the time. Sears managers must do everything in their power to make their town or city a better place to live in, and to contribute freely and willingly in money and in time to the welfare of that community."[9]

Wood was determined that Sears would be second to none in the concern it showed for the well-being of the communities in which its stores were based. Some of his policies were aimed directly at dispelling the "absentee owner" onus characteristic of chain-store operations of the time. Sears men on the way up were likely to be transferred frequently, as part of their training, until they reached store management; thereafter, they typically remained in the same store for extended periods of time, often until retirement. Except for those who were promoted to higher corporate levels, Sears managers were generally expected to build their futures in the communities to which they were assigned. The rate of company growth during the General Wood years was such that most of them could anticipate very good futures indeed, and they and their families were apt to be quite content to settle in and put down their roots.

Aware of the leading role in community affairs played by the heads of major local department stores—during the early Sears retail period, most of these enterprises were still family-owned—Wood encouraged his managers to emulate them. Sears managers were sufficiently well paid to enable them to move in top local circles and into leadership positions. They lived in the "right" parts of town, belonged to the "right" clubs, and otherwise comported themselves in a manner befitting community leaders. Many became presidents of chambers of commerce and chairmen of the boards of YMCAs and boys clubs; they headed hospital drives, served on boards of education, and responded to other calls to civic duty. Because they had personal stakes in their communities as well as their company, and because they lived in their communities long enough to become deeply enmeshed in local affairs, Sears managers were able to achieve positions of business and civic leadership enjoyed by few other chain-store managers, whom Wood referred to disdainfully as "birds of passage." [10] He was "very proud of the fact that many of our managers have been singled out as outstanding citizens of the communities in which they live." [11]

Sears stores were expected to give liberally to local charities, and they were usually at the top of the list (at least on an employee per capita basis) when it came to contributing to broad-based causes such as United Fund drives. This was due in part to yet another policy which distinguished Sears from other chain stores. The Sears manager did not have to refer requests for funds to headquarters; he had the authority to decide how much his store would donate and to sign the pledge card without further ado. This simple and commonsense practice, combined with the typical generosity of the Sears contribution, yielded highly favorable reactions in local civic circles and went far toward confirming Sears reputation for community responsibility.

That Wood urged his managers to become part of their communities and formulated policies that made it possible for them to do so did much to neutralize the opposition of local merchants toward Sears. It was hard for them to remain antagonistic toward a fellow merchant who had become "one of their own"—a status few other chain-store managers achieved. At the same time, Sears managers and their families enjoyed more comfortable and satisfying lives than most other chain-store managers.

175

Still another factor contributed importantly to the relative ease with which Sears was accepted in the towns where it chose to locate. The Sears store usually became, in fairly short order, the largest store in town and, because of its size and broader range of merchandise offerings, tended to widen appreciably the trading area it served. This benefited other local merchants as well as Sears, considerably muting any latent hostility toward Sears in the immediate vicinity. It was the merchants in towns too small for Sears stores who took the brunt of Sears entry into retail.

To the General, good corporate citizenship meant far more than participating in community affairs and contributing to local charities. He believed that it was also incumbent upon Sears to strengthen the economic base of the areas it served. He outlined his rationale in his 1939 address to the American Retail Federation:

> The retailer, more than anyone else in the business world, sees how closely his well-being depends on the standard of living and prosperity of the people of the community which he serves. In an industrial town, wage cuts, lay-offs, strikes are quickly reflected in reduced retail sales and loss of profits. . . .
>
> Such being the case, it is not only good ethics but intelligent business for the retailer to be a leader in any attempt to build up the community of which he is a part. . . .
>
> And the building up of a community means a lot of things—an intelligent study of the needs, of the problems of the people, above all of the problems of its government. . . .
>
> What does it mean to study the needs and problems of the people of a community? Many communities today are faced with declining, not growing industries—with decline of employment, not increase of employment. What can be done to preserve these industries, to revive them, or if that cannot be done, to replace them with new industries? Because the retailer is not a manufacturer makes it none the less his problem, for it is his community and the employees of the industry are his customers. . . .
>
> The bulk of retail sales is founded on the purchasing power of the masses. How many retailers concern themselves with the living conditions of the workers in their communities? If housing is inadequate, rents are high, it not only hurts the worker and the community, but it directly affects the retailer.[12]

It is important to note that Wood was not indulging in abstractions but drawing on the concrete experience of his own company. He had seen what Sears could do, and he knew that it was capable of doing even more. He was convinced that businessmen were obligated to seek certain ends that were not just good for business but good in and of themselves. It was not enough for a business to take from its surroundings; it also had to give.

In his speech before the American Retail Federation, Wood placed special emphasis on the role of the retailer in the agricultural community. He reminded his audience:

> In an agricultural trading town, the retailer's sales and profits vary directly with the farm income of his trading area. . . .
>
> [The] changes in agriculture, soil depletion, the failure of export markets may cause a decline in farm income which in turn affects the sales of every retailer in that community. Such is the case today in many communities in the southeastern states, where the economy was built on cotton, and where cotton growing, on account of the loss of foreign markets and lower costs of production in Texas and the southwest, is passing out of the picture. The retailer is not a farmer, but it is to his vital interest to find a substitute for that vanishing farm income, either in the form of a changed agriculture or of new industries.[13]

It had now been many years since Sears had functioned exclusively as "buyer for the American farmer," but the American farmer still constituted a significant portion of its market and the farm economy was an essential component of the general economy on which Sears prosperity depended. Wood was determined that the needs of the farmer not be forgotten or ignored, and in this he was carrying on a long-standing Sears tradition.

Sears had taken a number of steps designed to strengthen the agricultural economy well before Wood joined the company. In the early years of this century, Julius Rosenwald had become increasingly concerned that so large a part of American agriculture was failing to utilize the improved methods developed by the schools of agriculture in the land grant college system. In an effort to bridge this gap, he offered in 1912 to contribute $1,000 to any county which would add to that sum sufficient money to employ a trained agricultural expert to advise farmers on more efficient practices. The program was an immediate success. In 1912 and 1913 a total of 110 counties received Sears grants,[14] and in 1914 the Smith-Lever Act made the county agent system an integral part of the country's national agricultural policy. Its impact on American farming has been incalculable. And Sears, of course, reaped benefits of its own—not only in improved sales but also in the favorable regard it gained in rural, small-town America.

In 1923, while Wood was still at Montgomery Ward, Sears established the Agricultural Foundation for the stated purpose of helping the farmer "farm better, sell better, and live better." The Foundation launched a series of projects to further these ends. Contests were held to find solutions to rural problems. A crop intelligence service was formed to translate the abstruse statistics generated by government agencies into terms more readily understandable and usable by farmers. A counseling service was begun to supply advice by mail to individual farmers and their wives on such everyday farm problems as how to treat sick livestock, deal with insect infestations, and safeguard family health—activities subsequently taken over by the Extension Division of the U.S. Department of Agriculture.[15]

In April of 1924 the Agricultural Foundation put into operation a new radio station designed to provide farmers with weather, crop, and marketing information along with education and entertainment. The new station, WLS (World's Largest Store), became popular with farmers almost overnight. In addition to its regular programming, it advertised special company activities and engaged in a variety of humanitarian projects, including fund raising for disaster relief following floods and tornadoes, appeals for toys for needy children at Christmas, and other public service functions.

Despite its success, WLS was not looked upon with favor by Rosenwald's two key officers, Max Adler and Otto Doering. They had trouble reconciling the putative increase in company sales with the highly tangible costs of running an expensive radio station, and they strongly opposed its continued ownership and operation by Sears. But Charles M. Kittle, who joined the company in 1924, became a quick convert to the station's merits and WLS survived, at least for the time.

Wood, who joined Sears the same day as Kittle, was apparently too engrossed over the next few years with launching his new urban-oriented retail system to take much interest in a radio station devoted exclusively to rural programming. After Kittle's premature death at the beginning of 1928, Wood agreed to the sale of WLS to the *Prairie Farmer*, a respected midwestern farm publication which found the station a profitable investment.[16]

Meanwhile, the Agricultural Foundation sponsored a number of projects designed to increase farm income by improving farm products and practices. These included a national seed-corn show in 1925, a single-stalk cotton show in 1928, and a national canning contest in 1929. The Raw Fur Marketing Service (begun in 1925), the Raw Wool Marketing Service (1929), and the Dressed Poultry Marketing Service (1930) were administered by the same people who managed the Foundation, but these were conducted as company rather than Foundation activities because of their direct relationship to sales promotion. Raw furs and wool and dressed poultry were supplements to basic farm income, but farmers had often been victimized by the unscrupulous practices of commission agents through whom these products had traditionally been sold. Better organized and more ethical marketing channels yielded higher sales proceeds, and these were frequently applied directly to purchases from Sears. Both Sears and the farmers were happy.

Although General Wood was impressed by the Agricultural Foundation and its work, he was unable to give it more than passing attention during his first few years at Sears. There was much in what the Foundation was doing and in the thinking behind it that struck a responsive chord in his mind, however. And the experience gained from its efforts laid the groundwork for what would soon develop into a distinctly creative and uniquely successful program that would serve Sears and its constituencies extremely well in the years to come. A moving force in this program was E. J. Condon, former chief announcer for WLS whom Wood chose in 1927 to head Sears new public relations department.

As assistant to the president as well as director of public relations, Condon assumed the duties of handling publicity for the new stores and orienting the stores to their communities. He also continued to play an active part in the public service work of the Agricultural Foundation. An articulate, able, imaginative young man with a notable capacity for inspiring confidence and making friends, Condon was excited about the possibilities of finding ways to strengthen Sears economic base by addressing urgent social needs. As it happened, he was the ideal person to give form and substance to Wood's evolving concept of corporate social responsibility in an imperfect society.

General Wood was particularly interested in the South, for personal as well as business reasons. His wife, Mary, was from Georgia, and together they owned a farm near her family home in Augusta. He knew from his grasp of demographic trends that the population of the South was expanding more rapidly than that of any other part of the country, and he established more stores in that region than were fully justified by the current size of southern cities; he saw the South growing and wanted Sears to grow along with it. He also saw that the South had two major problems: it was in dire need of manufacturing industries, and its farms were suffering from the blighting effects of one-crop agriculture. Characteristically, the General resolved to use Sears resources to help solve both obstacles to economic progress.

Because his buying strategy called for the establishment of close, long-term relationships with sources of supply—sometimes including a share in ownership—Sears was in a position to exercise considerable influence on them. As suppliers began needing additional capacity to serve Sears steadily mounting requirements, many were encouraged to locate new plants in the South. These in turn attracted others necessary to their support, and in time an environment was created that brought still more industries into the Sun Belt. The result was a radical restructuring of American industry.

While Sears cannot claim all the credit for industrializing the South, it is clear that it played a significant part in the rapid growth of manufacturing in this area that followed the Great Depression. Per capita income in the southern cities grew at a more rapid rate than in the nation as a whole. Of course Sears prospered, but so did nearly everyone else.

The curse of one-crop agriculture proved to be a more intractable problem. For years southern statesmen, educators, and agricultural leaders had crusaded for crop diversification and livestock improvement, but to little avail; customary practices in the rural South were too deeply imbedded to be sloughed off easily. It was probably Condon's representative in the South, J. C. Haynes, erstwhile customer correspondent in the Atlanta mail-order plant, who first saw that the best way to change rural habits would be to educate rural youth. Whether this idea originated with Haynes, Condon, or someone else—perhaps Wood himself—is impossible to determine at this late date. What is important is that Haynes received Condon's go-ahead and Wood's hearty endorsement; thus encouraged, he and Condon turned their imaginative talents to working out a practical program.

One-crop agriculture had stymied the development of both plant crops and animal herds. The most promising approach to both seemed to be from the animal side; if progress could be made with farm animals—and especially with cattle, hogs, and poultry—then progress on the plant side would be likely to follow. (Raising animals in the barnyard required the growing of more than cotton in the fields.) Condon and Haynes began their program modestly: with a series of contests for members of 4-H Clubs and Future Farmers of America chapters in selected southern counties. Contestants were club and chapter members who ranged in age from twelve to eighteen. Sears supplied the prizes, but the contests themselves were supervised and the winners chosen by judges named by the county agents and vocational agricultural teachers.

A three-tier system of contests gradually developed. At the first level, prizes were awarded to the boy or girl who wrote the best essay on "Advantages of the Cow-Hog-Hen Plan of Farming." Club or chapter winners were awarded 100 baby chicks each on the condition that they would agree to participate in a second round of judging at the county fair, where they would display the three best hens they had raised from the chicks they had won. Winners at this level received a purebred gilt (young female pig) as a prize. Again, there were conditions: each recipient had to agree to feed and care for the gilt, breed her at the proper time to a boar furnished by Sears, and contribute a choice gilt from the first litter to the prize pool for the following years. (Not surprisingly, the project soon became known as the "chain litter program.") The grown pigs were shown at the next fair, and winners this time around received a purebred dairy-type heifer. Most of the heifers awarded not only developed into fine dairy cows but also produced high-grade calves for a period of years.

Begun in 1935, the program soon spread throughout the entire southern states region and into other parts of the country as well. New competitions were mounted on a wide variety of subjects. Individual clubs and chapters and groups of units in defined areas—e.g., counties—were given considerable leeway, under the supervision of county agents and vocational agricultural teachers, in determining the kinds of contests they would hold and the criteria they would use in choosing winners; the only thing most contests had in common was their focus on local needs for increasing agricultural productivity and improving the quality of rural life. Judging was done by panels of local and regional experts. Sears public relations representatives continued to oversee the program in a general way but left its actual conduct up to the appropriate authorities. The company underwrote the cost—which was minimal once the initial investment had been made in getting a local or regional program started—and, of course, was represented at the award ceremonies, typically by a store manager or other company executive; at higher contest echelons, an officer of the company was usually present.

In 1941, when Sears made its last attempt to take a nationwide census of the rapidly multiplying progeny of the cow-hog-hen program, it was estimated that the total amount of livestock donated, plus their offspring, came to 692 cows, 2,645,000 hogs, and 13,650,000 chickens. The activity was accelerated to meet the wartime need for increased food production, and it was estimated that by 1950 these figures had at least doubled.[17] By then the program had become an established feature of the American agricultural scene. In 1948, the dean of the College of Agriculture of the University of Georgia had this to say about it: "A vast amount of good has been done, and Sears, Roebuck is responsible for the training of some outstanding leaders in the field of agriculture, and for the improvement of the agricultural program in the Southeast. In Georgia, the financing of livestock projects is bringing about a better balance in agriculture than we have ever had in the past and has already added untold millions to the total income of the state." [18]

The program was capped by the distribution of registered Hereford bulls to selected local 4-H clubs and FFA chapters, first in Georgia and eventually in seven southern states. The bulls were placed in the care of especially deserving members—a highly prized honor—and used both to maintain the bloodlines of heifers won by club and chapter members and to improve the overall quality of farm herds. By 1950, 350 top quality Hereford bull calves had been given to vocational agriculture high schools—fifty in each of seven southern states, resulting in many hundreds of thousands of dollars worth of new livestock annually for southern agriculture.[19] The "chain" concept was preserved by adding selected male progeny of the original bulls to the area's breeding resources, and so on for succeeding generations of cattle. The cumulative impact on the quality of southern dairy herds was substantial.

While the cow-hog-hen projects were the centerpiece of Sears agricultural program, they were not the only means employed to help the agricultural economy in the South and elsewhere. In 1937, for example, Sears donated a grand champion bull, Advance Domino III, to Utah State College with the understanding that qualified 4-H and FFA members would be able to use his services without charge to upgrade the bloodlines of their beef cattle. Through artificial insemination, thousands of young men and women were able to improve substantially the quality of their herds, thus adding millions of dollars to the value of Utah cattle. When Domino died, his passing was noted editorially in the Salt Lake City *Deseret News*. After estimating the millions of dollars his services had added to the value of Utah cattle, the eulogy concluded: "He accomplished great things for the cattle industry of Utah, and in his death his memory becomes one of the greatest symbols for livestock improvement the West has ever known." [20]

In 1924, the *State Journal* of Topeka, Kansas, devoted a lengthy editorial to Sears agricultural activities that included this comment: "Claude

King, 4-H Club agent for Shawnee county, reported earlier this year that a total of somewhere around 10,440 head of pure-bred pigs had already resulted from the Topeka project. Mr. King said, 'The Duroc hogs in this county, as a result of this project, are second in quality to none, even including those breeders who have been in the business for years. These pure-breds served a great purpose because before 1939 there were only two farms in the county raising good pure-bred hogs.'" [21] In 1950 the Texas A&M service specialist stated that over 90 percent of all pigs exhibited in fairs throughout the state were from Sears-donated stock. [22] And in 1952 the extension poultryman of Georgia State University reported: "I devote most of my time to the 4-H poultry chain sponsored by the Sears-Roebuck Foundation. Eight-thousand five hundred boys and girls have been trained in the state of Georgia in managing flocks of birds as they should be managed. The mongrel flock that was so well known in the state of Georgia is fast being replaced by pure-bred birds." [23]

The Sears livestock program produced significant human as well as economic values. Wendell Endicott, director of Sears and General Wood's great friend, reported with more than a touch of hyperbole on a tour he made of Sears southern agricultural projects in 1948:

> Could one help but be impressed when he stood watching a young lad of 13 or 14 years building a brooder house or a chicken coop out of such material as he could gather together that would conform to the scientific principals [sic] he had learned at school. How assuredly would he explain to me the intricacies of proper food and heat regulation. He was soon to be awarded 100 chickens. It was serious business to him—he was to be a farmer—that was to be his start.
>
> Could one help from being thrilled when a lad of 15 or 16 jumped into a pen and, with a friendly slap on her big fat sides, proudly showed us his pure blooded sow that he had won. "Sally" had been served by a blooded boar and was to produce in April. Yes, that young lad had raised his own corn for feed. He had built and fenced in his own pig yard. He had built his own house for Sally—he had put in proper guardrails so that Sally wouldn't hurt her babies when they arrived. He had different troughs of different types of feed that Sally required. Yes, he had learned all that at school. It might perhaps have been a bit crude and rough but it was scientifically correct. It was no hit and miss job. He had a record of his costs and he knew how to handle his piglets. He was going into the pig business— that was his start.
>
> Cliff was 16. He had been a 4-H member. Today he belongs to the F.F.A. Chapter. He had his pigs and his heiffers [sic]. His capital had grown to a value of almost $1500.00—quite wonderful for a boy

that age. Furthermore, he was entrusted with the care of the Chapter's Hereford bull (a Sears project). Cliff, as did others, showed us their "green" winter pastures which they had cultivated themselves. They knew its value to hens and cattle. They had studied all that with agricultural vocational instructors. I was constantly amazed at these youngsters' scientific knowledge of grasses and feeds and care of livestock. Cliff is to be a farmer—this was his start.[24]

These young people, and thousands of others like them, could look forward to a future that would be vastly different from the hardscrabble farming into which they had been born. Most of their accomplishments were due to their own determined efforts, but the Sears program gave them encouragement and tangible assistance at a crucial point.

Especially impressed by what he had seen in Georgia, Endicott concluded his report with this summation:

> Sears can place heavy bets on this territory and don't forget it. More and more pure-bred cattle will be bred and raised and scientifically cared for. More and more all-year-around green pasturage will be cultivated—more and more will alfalfa and other proper feeds be experimented with and produced—more and more will reforestation be pushed forward to produce lumber and pulp wood. Private irrigation ponds are being built everywhere. . . .
>
> The pecan and peach groves (marvelously cared for) are magnificent. The community canning stations play their part as well but, above all, is the character of Georgia's youth built up through 4-H Clubs and F.F.A. Chapters. Added to all this is the growing industries. This is Georgia's renaissance and Sears has been—still is—and I sincerely hope will be an important factor in this great work of reconstruction.

By the time Wood retired as chief executive in 1954, the South was a markedly different region than it had been at the start of his Sears career thirty years before. Industrialization was well advanced, and one-crop farming was largely a thing of the past. Population and per capita income levels were growing at higher than national rates, and by and large the quality of life was greatly improved. Admittedly the Sears influence was only one of several which combined to transform the southern economy, but its impact was greater because it was organized and purposive whereas many others were diffuse and circumstantial. The particular effectiveness of the Sears effort must be traced back to Wood's vision and grasp of fundamentals and the imagination and skill of Condon and his staff.

The Sears agricultural program was administered with remarkable flexibility and tailored to the varying needs and circumstances of different parts of the country. Forestry projects were sponsored in the Pacific Northwest, in Maine, and in Georgia. An attempt was made, with indifferent success, to develop viticulture (grape growing) in the Ozarks. There were turkey projects in Texas, a farmers' market in Atlanta, dairy improvement projects in New York and Pennsylvania, and sheep projects in Illinois and Nebraska. Aid was given for the growing, processing, and marketing of special local products such as holly in West Virginia, walnuts in Tennessee, strawberries in Kentucky, and honey in a number of other areas. Soil, water, and wildlife conservation projects were organized in various parts of the country. The introduction of high-grade breeding stock laid the foundation for the beef cattle industry that is today an important part of Florida's economy. In 1950 the Sears-Roebuck Foundation, which had been established in 1941 to carry on significant parts of Sears public service work, was conducting sixty-two different types of programs in a total of 1,254 separate efforts; projects of one kind or another were underway in all forty-eight states and in 90 percent of all U.S. counties.[25]

The Foundation addressed the needs of future homemakers as well as future farmers by designing and sponsoring national home improvement contests for 4-H Club girls. In 1951, 180,000 young women in forty-eight states entered the competition; individual projects ranged from upholstering furniture to draping windows, redecorating single rooms, and completely remodeling houses.[26] Also aimed primarily at young women was a Consumer Education Service based on the self-confident premise that the more intelligently people bought, the more they would buy from Sears. Exhibits and booklets using the theme "Hidden Values" were prepared to instruct consumers on sound buying practices. Topics included what to look for when comparing merchandise, how to appraise materials and construction, and general tips on getting the most for one's money. The materials were distributed through some 3,000 state home demonstration agents and 15,000 vocational home economics teachers.[27] In 1949 alone the service reached over two million people.[28]

An especially interesting activity conducted over a long period of time and supportive of other Sears projects was the production and distribution of motion pictures. *The Golden Egg* dealt with poultry-raising. *The Green Hand* addressed the ideals and work of the FFA while *When the Road Turns Right* did the same for the 4-H Club movement. *A Stitch in Time* promoted better safety practices on the farm, an occupation more than three times as hazardous as manufacturing; it received a National Safety

185

Council award in 1945 and was circulated within the medical profession by the American Medical Association, which termed it the best film on farm safety ever made.[29] Other motion pictures were produced on a wide range of subjects of importance to farm life. Distributed without charge and with no requirement other than a signed statement of attendance, Sears films were seen in 1949 by more than five million people.[30]

But it was the scholarship program which in some ways proved the most important of the Sears undertakings. As was the case with so much of Sears public service work, this program originated in the South. Many years later, J. C. Haynes, Sears longtime chief of public relations in that region, recounted how it all began.[31]

The year was 1936, and the anti-chain-store movement was mounting to a crescendo, particularly in the southern states. Sears had received some favorable public notice from a grant it had given to Auburn University in Alabama to help train county agents, and General Wood felt that this suggested an avenue worth exploring. He talked with Condon, who then telephoned Haynes in Atlanta with instructions to "take whatever money you want and see what you can do to get something started"—hardly a precise directive. Haynes drove to the University of Georgia in Athens and called on the dean of the College of Agriculture, whom he knew.

"I can spend a little bit of money on something worthwhile," Haynes said to him. "What can I do?"

"Thank God for your presence here today," the dean replied. "Look at this stack of letters. These are farm boys who want to go to college but haven't got any money, and we don't have scholarships for them. It would be a great thing for this state and this country if we could help these boys."

"How many you got?" Haynes wanted to know.

"About a hundred."

"I'm not talking about that much money. You must need at least five or six hundred dollars for each of them."

"Give me a hundred dollars and I can bring a boy to college."

With Haynes's go-ahead, the dean then and there picked twenty applications out of the stack. Haynes returned to his office and sent the dean $2,000.

This was the start of something big. Deans of other agricultural schools quickly learned what had happened in Georgia, and requests for similar grants began pouring in. When a hasty survey disclosed that the number of scholarships available across the country "for outstanding farm boys desiring to study agriculture was shockingly small," [32] General Wood invited the deans of four midwestern agricultural colleges to meet with him and Condon in the Sears officers' dining room in August of 1936. The outcome was a plan for Sears to provide scholarships for academically competent farm youths who would be unable to attend college without financial aid. The only requirements other than academic ability and dire financial need would be a genuine interest in agriculture and an intention to pursue farming or a farming-related career. Recipients would be chosen in whatever ways the deans saw fit, the schools would handle all administrative details, and Sears would foot the bill. The program was launched with ten schools in the autumn of 1936 and was soon expanded to include the agricultural colleges in all forty-eight states, the territories of Alaska and Hawaii, and the commonwealth of Puerto Rico. [33]

The scholarships were Spartan. Those granted during the first four years of the program averaged $125 each and were given for the freshman year only; thereafter, the scholars were on their own. Sears was skeptical of both the scale and duration of the stipends, but the deans felt strongly about these issues and Sears acquiesced. In time the sizes of the scholarships were increased, and limited amounts of aid were given to a few scholars for their sophomore year, but the level of assistance could never be described as other than minimal. While initially the scholarships were awarded only to boys, the program was later expanded to include home economics scholarships for girls—on a basis no less Spartan.

The success of the program was far greater than might reasonably have been expected. In terms of the number of scholarships granted (if not in dollars of expenditure), it was the largest scholarship program in the country and was strongly endorsed by farm and educational leaders nationwide. The academic achievements of the scholars were notable, and their staying power even more so. A survey taken just before World War II disclosed that the academic achievements of Sears scholars were well above average and that two-thirds of all Sears scholars completed four years of college as compared with only two-fifths of all other entering agricultural students. [34]

In December of 1949 Sears hosted a two-day conference in Chicago for all agricultural college deans to discuss postwar agricultural education and to review the Sears program in light of postwar needs. At a luncheon meeting attended by General Wood, then president McConnell, and other company officers, Dean Kildee of Iowa State spoke for himself and the other deans in paying tribute to the records of the Sears scholars. [35] At the

187

1950 On-to-Chicago meeting, Dean Kivlin of the University of Wisconsin's College of Agriculture reported that the four-year grade point average of Sears scholars was one-third better than that of the university population and that their four-year completion rate was two and a half times better.[36] In a survey conducted in 1961–62, questionnaires were sent to 11,000 recipients of freshman agricultural scholarships during the twenty-year period 1936–56; responses received from 7,520 indicated that four out of five had graduated and three out of four were in occupations related to agriculture.[37]

A highlight of the program for many years was an annual "working holiday" to which the dean and the outstanding scholar from each school were invited. They came to Chicago for a week's round of lunches, theater parties, and visits to the city's great meat-packing plants, the commodities and stock exchanges, and other places of special interest to farmers. A regular event was a banquet at which Sears officers and senior executives played host to their youthful guests and their mentors. Not surprisingly, the several groups attending the banquet came away liking each other very much.

By at least one account, the returns Sears gained from its scholarship program were "truly enormous": "The goodwill won from educators, from the recipients of the grants, and through word-of-mouth publicity in farm areas has been very nearly incalculable. And the company's original purpose—to improve agriculture by extending a 'leg up' to potential farm leaders of the future—seems to have been met and exceeded."[38] Of all Sears public service efforts, this was the one in which Sears people themselves took the greatest pride.

Once, on a visit to Georgia, General Wood asked J. C. Haynes to arrange for him to meet the dean of agriculture and the current group of Sears scholars at the university in Athens. After a pleasant dinner, Haynes called on some of the young men to tell something about themselves. As Haynes recounted the story years later:

"One little boy said, 'I had written over here and I didn't have a penny and I'd been told I couldn't get anything and I was plowing corn on the bottom one afternoon and my sister ran down with a letter and said it was from Dean Chapman and he said I could get a hundred dollars and I set down on the plow and cried.'

"I looked over at the General and he had tears in his eyes and he said, 'Goddamn, Haynes, let's do more of this.' "[39]

While the agricultural colleges and the ubiquitous 4-H and FFA systems were the chief vehicles for Sears public service work for many years, the company and later the Sears-Roebuck Foundation were quite ready to cooperate with other groups who shared an interest in improving the economic base and quality of life of American communities. In 1951, for example, the dean of the Emory University School of Theology approached J. C. Haynes with an idea for a "Church of the Year" program. Pointing out that the members of rural congregations were "the kinds of folks you need as friends," he proposed that Sears offer prizes for those churches which made the most progress in self-improvement during a contest year. The suggestion was quickly implemented. Administered under the auspices of the Emory School of Theology and conducted in cooperation with various denominational bodies, the project started on a small scale in the state of Georgia but soon spread throughout the South and Southwest. Winners in each state received cash awards, with the grand prize and "Church of the Year" title going to the overall winner.[40]

Here again, Sears provided the necessary funding, including the modest administration costs. The Emory dean appointed panels of judges drawn from the ranks of religious and civic leaders and other prominent persons in each state and region. Their stature was such as to attract considerable public attention—far beyond that of the local rural community—when they made on-site inspections of state winners as part of the judging process. And the governor of the state was almost always in attendance at the final award ceremony. As the dean predicted, the program made many friends for Sears. A similar program was conducted in Oregon in cooperation with the Oregon Council of Churches, with comparable results but on a smaller scale.[41]

Another significant Sears-Roebuck Foundation project was the Community Service program developed after the war with the National Grange, a long-established and highly respected farm organization with about 8,000 active chapters in thirty-seven states. The program focused on mobilizing Grange members and other local groups to improve their communities. Participating Granges selected projects of special interest to their own membership, and each state Grange ran its own contest and picked its own winners. First-place winners from all states received substantial cash awards before moving into a round of national competition. A panel of judges narrowed the field to ten finalists, and another panel of judges determined who would win the grand prize: a new Grange hall.[42]

The latter panel was composed of outstanding figures in American rural life: deans of agricultural colleges, the head of the U.S. Department of Agriculture Extension Service, eminent rural sociologists, and the like.

189

Using a Sears plane to visit and inspect the accomplishments of the ten finalists, the annual safari received extensive press coverage and its progress was followed closely by rural and small-town America. State and national winners basked in considerable laudatory attention, but the sum total of community improvements made each year by competing Granges yielded far more tangible rewards. During the first two years of the program, 2,625 Granges entered the contest with as many separate projects for upgrading their communities. Across the country, bridges were built, roads graded, telephone lines strung, parks created, churches restored, hospitals financed, and land reclaimed. Literally thousands of communities are better places today because of the efforts of Grangers who worked hard to win prizes for their own local units. At the 1949 annual meeting of the National Grange, Albert Goss, National Master, commented in part: "The value of these projects—in physical contribution to community improvement—amounts to many, many millions of dollars. But that's only part of the story. The spirit of cooperation and understanding that resulted from folks working unselfishly together for the common good is something you just can't put a dollar value on." [43]

Through the 1940s Sears public service projects were directed almost exclusively toward rural areas. In the early 1950s moves were made to address the needs of urban areas as well. During the final years of Wood's tenure as chief executive, programs very similar in thrust to the one conducted with the National Grange were begun with the National Federation of Garden Clubs and the General Federation of Women's Clubs. [44] The former was concerned chiefly with local community and neighborhood beautification projects; the latter, which was planned over the last two or three years of Wood's administration and launched the year after his retirement, was far more substantial in scope and achievement. R. V. Mullen, executive director of the Sears-Roebuck Foundation, stated his high hopes for the Women's Clubs program at its inauguration in January of 1955: "The really important thing about this cooperative effort is not the prizes, nor the great achievements of the prize winners. Rather, the true purpose of the contest is to make people stop and look around their community, and say: "What do we need to do to make this town a better place to live in? Once they do this, we firmly believe that using the Women's Club as a rallying point, people everywhere can accomplish miracles in the field of community achievement." [45]

There is no doubt that the combined impact of the various programs described here was great. Together with the public service work of store managers and other company executives, they left a lasting imprint on American life and earned Sears, Roebuck a unique place among American business enterprises. Like most of General Wood's public policies, each was aimed at strengthening Sears markets while increasing public goodwill and support; in the process, significant public needs were served as well.

A further motivation for many of the projects—including the cow-hog-hen and scholarship programs—was the very real threat of anti-chain-store legislation. Between 1925 and 1948, 1,244 separate bills imposing penalties on multiple retail operations were introduced into state legislatures, and while only sixty actually passed it appeared at one point during the 1930s that crippling enactments were virtually inevitable. To safeguard the enterprise he was building, Wood took both defensive and offensive measures. For example, he once commissioned a thorough study of the possibility of converting Sears into a system of consumer cooperatives. The study concluded that such a course would present grave and probably insuperable difficulties, and the idea was dropped.

Two other approaches appeared more practical and were actually tried: the creation of "associated stores" and "agency stores." The former were franchise arrangements whereby Sears, for a fee, licensed individuals in selected towns to set up stores under their own names bearing the subscription "Sears, Roebuck Associate" and to sell merchandise bought at wholesale from Sears. The latter were established retailers whom Sears contracted to sell its merchandise, with expenses and profits divided equitably. Neither approach interfered with Wood's basic retail strategy: associated stores were usually located in towns too small for regular Sears outlets, while agency stores were regional chains operating in areas remote from significant concentrations of Sears stores.[46]

The associated store plan generated mixed results, primarily because many of those picked as associates lacked adequate managerial expertise, but the agency plan was eminently successful. Sears gained valuable experience through both ventures, and had the anti-chain-store threat fully materialized the company would have been able to move swiftly into either or both or some combination of these two directions. During the war years, however, it proved hard enough to keep Sears regular stores supplied without the added burden of the associated and agency stores, and the anti-chain-store movement had by then largely become a thing of the past, so the company liquidated both experimental systems in the mid-1940s. Those affiliated stores of both types which were located in good markets and doing well were absorbed into the regular Sears system; the others were dropped after suitable financial settlements had been worked out with the partners.[47]

Apart from Wood's uneasiness over the anti-chain-store movement but intimately related to it was his concern that Sears size would leave it vulnerable to attack. This worry surfaced early in his Sears career. In January of 1928, while awaiting Julius Rosenwald's decision on who would be the new president following the sudden death of Charles Kittle, Wood speculated over the possibility that the post might go to a non-Sears man through a merger of Sears and Ward's. He wrote in a letter to Wendell Endicott: "I honestly think a merger of Wards and Sears would be a very dangerous thing for both companies. The volume of business would be so enormous that there would be a tremendous reaction against such a mail order monopoly and we would suffer in legislation, taxes, and a great many other ways. It would go far toward disrupting the present goodwill that we enjoy."[48]

A dozen years later, as Sears approached annual sales of $1 billion, Wood called the attention of his board to "some of the more obvious" disadvantages of the company's large size:

> 1. The monthly publication of our sales heralds our enormous growth to the mercantile world. Distributors in general are even now uneasy and alarmed over our size. . . . [With] continued growth we will be exposed to constant attacks in one form or another. We are just now enjoying a respite.
> 2. I believe there is a deep-rooted feeling in the American people against remote control and absentee ownership. We were first limited to the Midwest in our business. We then spread to all parts of the country, but not on a scale that caused alarm. Today we operate on a large scale in every state of the union, but our ownership is largely in Chicago, Philadelphia, New York and Boston. Leaving out any question of attack, it is questionable whether it is good public policy for a very large corporation such as ours to concentrate all its executive direction at one point. While ours is a national business, all our executives, the great majority of our high-salaried employees, our merchants, our legal staff, our insurance agents are all concentrated in the one city of Chicago.[49]

Wood could "see only one satisfactory solution to the problem": to divide Sears into a group of regional companies, each having its own officers and staff, with centralized functions such as buying grouped into a service corporation owned by the regional companies. He further proposed that half the common stock of each company be sold to the public, to the extent possible in its area of service.[50]

The General was not only concerned with public distrust of corporate size; he also feared that Sears might grow too large to be effectively managed. Intrigued by the experience of Standard Oil, he frequently reminded his associates that after the old Standard Oil Company had been broken up by court decree each of the dismembered parts had soon outgrown the original corporation. He felt that the same thing could happen to Sears and that regional companies with strong regional ownership would enjoy greater public acceptance and be more profitable.

A first step toward dividing Sears into a series of regional companies was taken at the beginning of 1941 with the establishment of the Pacific Coast territory. The new territory was given a considerable amount of autonomy under its own vice president; it was not, however, a separate corporation but merely a geographical operating division. All plans to pursue this idea further were interrupted by World War II. As the end of the war approached, Wood again raised the question with his board and initiated detailed studies of the financial, legal, and tax aspects of breaking Sears up into a geographically dispersed group of autonomous corporate entities.[51] By 1947 these studies were far enough along to serve as bases for concrete proposals for reorganization, which were formally submitted to and approved by the Department of Justice and the Internal Revenue Service.[52] With everything in place, Wood was able to make the following interesting observation to his personnel executives in mid-1948: "Now the time may come when it will be said that we are getting too big and that it is not a good thing for the people of the United States to have a company as big as this, because one company will 'exercise too much power.' If that time ever comes to me, or my successor, we are in a position to say, 'If you want to break us up into five separate companies, it is possible.' We are not going to oppose anything Congress or the people of the United States ever desire. I do not know if that will ever come."[53] As it happened, neither Congress nor public opinion made this demand; the public policies fostered by Wood had much to do with that favorable state of affairs.

Sears might have gone ahead with the plan anyway had it not foundered on a number of practical difficulties. One problem involved dividing the assets of the old corporation between the spun-off entities in such a way as to provide each with adequate working capital. Another had to do with finding workable means for combining centralized buying with regional corporate autonomy. Faced with these and other obstacles, Wood and his

193

board elected instead merely to divide the company into administrative territories. This course only partially accomplished the two goals Wood had in mind. Geographical decentralization made it easier to manage the company's continued growth in size, but it did not provide the kind of entrepreneurial impetus Standard Oil had gained and the General greatly envied. It did place senior company officers in dispersed locations closer to the company's publics, but they lacked the presence and authority enjoyed by chief executive officers of fully autonomous corporations. And regional divisions, of course, did nothing to modify the public perception of huge corporate size. But Wood had to be content.

There were other ways in which he shaped corporate practice with public ends in view. For example, the laws of New York State, under which Sears was incorporated, for many years required the company to hold its annual meetings in the state. When this requirement was dropped, Wood occasionally scheduled the meetings in other key cities around the country, enabling more local stockholders to attend and attracting great local public attention. He also felt that it was very much in the company's interest for its stock to be in the hands of as many people as possible, and he took pains to keep the market price of Sears shares relatively modest; he did not want Sears stock to reach the levels reached by some companies, notably IBM. Accordingly, whenever the market price of Sears stock advanced much beyond $100 a share and held at that level for a reasonable period, he ordered a stock split. Had this not been done, a share of Sears stock selling for $171 at the beginning of 1925 would have sold for approximately $2,000 by the time Wood retired in 1954.[54]

Although measures such as these had comparatively little impact on public attitudes about Sears, they are worth mentioning here for what they reveal about Wood's thinking. Ever sensitive to the need for public acceptance and support for his company, he frequently went out of his way to implement practices that would benefit Sears constituencies, sometimes in subtle and indirect ways.

One policy that was evident to anyone who had anything to do with Sears was its customer policy. Wood never tired of reiterating the theme:

> The customer is our real employer. The moment we lose his confidence, that moment marks the beginning of the disintegration of this company. The confidence of the American people in the values, the fairness and the honesty of Sears, Roebuck and Company is the most precious asset this company has . . . our motto of "Satisfaction Guaranteed or Your Money Back" is a real slogan, to be faithfully ob-

served and promptly executed. If to this policy is added real values, prompt, courteous and willing service, both mail order and retail, we will retain our present customers and add new ones all the time.[55]

Deeply committed to this ideal, the General was careful to adopt administrative measures aimed at enforcing it. Without question, his "customer policy" was his most significant and most effective "public policy."

It should be noted that while many of the activities Sears engaged in during Wood's tenure generated vast amounts of publicity, they were not done for the sake of publicity. On more than one occasion, the General told his public relations executives to "go out in the field and do some good, but if I catch any of you issuing a publicity release I'll fire you."[56] This is not to imply that he wanted Sears to hide its light under a bushel; rather, he wanted its actions to speak for themselves, and if anything was said about them he wanted people outside the company to do the talking—which they did, willingly and often. Few other companies have ever enjoyed the amount of favorable public notice that came to Sears.

Sears never employed lobbyists to influence legislators and others in positions of power. It followed a far more effective course of action: It made friends in high places. Before the Supreme Court's one-man-one-vote decision in 1962, rural America had a disproportionately strong voice in state legislatures—a fact of great importance in relation to the anti-chain-store movement which reached its peak in the years preceding World War II. A few brief stories aptly illustrate the great political value of Sears rurally oriented public service programs.

On numerous occasions during the 1930s, different southern legislators made statements to J. C. Haynes to the effect: "I don't have anything against Sears, Roebuck but I'm going to drive A&P out of the state."[57] Their difficulty lay in finding ways to work their will on A&P without harming Sears, and Sears had too many friends.

One time in the late 1930s, Haynes was invited to breakfast with Governor E. D. Rivers of Georgia. On his way to the mansion, he was apprehensive because he knew that a bill would be introduced that day in the legislature to impose a tax of $100,000 a year on Sears Georgia operations.

"Governor," Haynes said, "you know we've tried to do this state a lot of good. You've told me a million times how much good we've done."

"Yes," his host replied, "I really hate the bill myself, but it's going to be introduced, so you'd better give me all the arguments against it you can."

After listening to Haynes, Governor Rivers took the matter up with legislative leaders and succeeded in reducing the tax from $100,000 to $2,000. He was able to eliminate it altogether the following year.[58]

In 1939 E. J. Condon paid a visit to St. Paul, Minnesota, to see a senator who had just introduced a particularly vicious anti-chain-store measure in the state legislature. Following an exchange of pleasantries— the two already knew each other through the cow-hog-hen program— Condon brought up the purpose of his trip.

"But why are you worrying about that?" the senator asked, looking surprised. "Mine's an anti-chain-store bill and shouldn't hurt Sears."

Immediately realizing what he had said, the senator blushed deeply. He had never thought of Sears as a chain-store operation and did not include it among those whose practices he so strongly condemned.[59]

It is clear in retrospect that had it not been for General Wood and his public policies, the anti-chain-store movement would have been far more successful than it was. The cumulative reserve of goodwill endured long after the threat of punitive legislation had disappeared. In the late 1950s Leroy Collins, then governor of Florida, came to the end of awarding a series of plaques and scrolls to the winners of a statewide conservation project sponsored by Sears. After giving out the last one, he turned to the audience and said, "I find I don't have anything left to recognize the company that has made all this possible." He then removed his own cufflinks bearing the Great Seal of the State of Florida and ceremoniously presented them to the Sears representative.[60]

In summary, looking back at the public policies implemented under Wood's leadership, it is evident that nearly all were essentially political in the best and most literal sense of the term. They may not have had overt political intentions, but they were expressions of Wood's political instincts and certainly had political consequences. Their success must be counted a political achievement of the first magnitude (see Chapter 12 herein).

11

Entrepreneurial Policies

ROBERT E. WOOD WAS MANY things during his lifetime: military man, businessman, politician, humanitarian, visionary. But first and foremost, he was an entrepreneur: a man who was willing to embark on new and untried ventures requiring creativity, courage, and commitment and holding both the promise of success and the threat of failure.

Sears, Roebuck and Co. was itself the most dramatic manifestation of his entrepreneurship. Building on the solid foundations laid by Julius Rosenwald, Wood completely refashioned Sears to conform to a strikingly original concept of what business could be and do and how it could be run. Under his leadership, what had once been an old-line mail-order house was transformed into a mammoth merchandising organization. It began by serving the needs of rural America and went on to target as its market the country as a whole.

What Wood did with Sears once he had shaped it into the type of company he wanted is also indicative of his entrepreneurial spirit. He used it as a base from which to move into what appeared to be a totally different and unrelated type of business: automobile insurance. He took Sears into both Latin America and Canada and expanded its domestic operations far beyond anything that had previously been dreamed of as part of an overall program of aggressive development following the end of World War II. Any study of his career would be incomplete without a close look at these major undertakings, since each sheds further light on his personal character and business acumen.

According to one account, the idea for entering the automobile insurance field was originally broached to Wood by one of the members of the car pool with whom he commuted to work; according to another, he got it from a neighbor with whom he played bridge. In any event, it "rang a bell" in the General's mind,[1] and a little checking soon convinced him that it was the right thing for Sears.

It was then 1931, and a large part of what the consumer paid for car insurance went toward covering the cost of selling the policy rather than protecting the buyer. Wood believed that selling insurance over the counter and by mail could materially reduce this cost, offering significant economic values to the automobile-owning public while still leaving an attractive profit. He drew up a proposal for his board. Many years later, he recalled that their response had not exactly been enthusiastic:

> I called a meeting of my outside directors. . . . Business wasn't good at that time . . . and I proposed we form this insurance company. Well, there were four of them—Edgar Stern, Wendell Endicott, John Hancock, and Sidney Weinberg—fortunately, they were all good friends of mine. But when I made the proposition, they were very cool indeed, and they asked me two very pertinent questions. They said: "In the first place, why should we start anything new, when times are bad? In the second place, what the hell do you know about insurance?" Which was also true.
>
> "Well," I said, "I don't know much about insurance, but I do know this—that Sears has the largest tire and battery and auto accessory business in this country, and every car owner goes to Sears or knows Sears. In the second place, we've got this system of stores and instead of the agent pounding the pavement for a prospect, they'll come to our agent in the stores, and our cost of acquisition will be far less than with ordinary insurance companies."
>
> Well, they finally said—because they had absolutely no faith in the proposition, but they had some faith in me—what they said, in effect, was, "Well, go ahead, let your blood be on your head."[2]

Wood's instinct proved sound. Initially capitalized at $700,000, the Allstate Insurance Company, named after the Sears brand of automobile tires, lost money only in its first year of operation, and from the bottom of Depression year 1932 on has turned in increasingly handsome profits to its parent company.

To do business in the automobile insurance industry, Allstate had to be separately incorporated and duly licensed, but it was run at the outset much like any other merchandise department. It quickly became apparent, however, that insurance was a highly intangible product with unique selling and service characteristics and managerial requirements, and the new enterprise was given considerable autonomy. It is wholly owned by Sears, and its board—traditionally comprised both of Sears officers and strong directors brought in from other sources—is named by Sears management. Similarly, its senior officers are appointed with Sears concurrence. But the affairs of the company are left virtually in its own hands, and this has been the case almost since the beginning. When J. M. Barker served as chairman of the Allstate board from 1943 until 1957, he was always careful not to "mix into the administration" of the company unless he was "asked for judgment."[3] Allstate policies are sold through the Sears catalog, and there is an Allstate counter staffed by Allstate people in all but the smallest Sears stores, but the relationship of Allstate to Sears at the operating level is little different from that of a leased department such as the optical department or H&R Block.

Originally staffed by people drawn from various branches of the Sears organization (Lessing Rosenwald was the first chairman and G. E. Humphrey, a Sears officer, was the first president), the new company soon began to recruit its own talent. In 1934 it further strengthened its separate identity by moving out of the Sears administration building and taking over two floors in another building in the headquarters complex. By 1938 Allstate's space requirements had reached a point where they could no longer be accommodated in existing Sears structures, and the company leased an entire floor in the Civic Opera Building in downtown Chicago. Allstate built its own building soon after the end of the war, but this too was outgrown before long, and progressively larger facilities were constructed in the years that followed to house the burgeoning enterprise. Meanwhile, branch offices were opened in key cities throughout the country.

Growth in personnel paralleled Allstate's physical expansion. Starting with a dozen or so employees in 1931, it had a payroll of 560 in 1940, 3,700 in 1950, and 9,260 in 1954, the year of General Wood's retirement. While the company's personnel policies resembled those of Sears in spirit, they were fashioned to meet its own specific needs, which differed in important respects from those of its parent. There was virtually no interchange of personnel between the two companies, and even at management levels people in each considered themselves only distantly related to those in the other. The organization structures of the two companies also differed markedly: Allstate was as highly centralized in its management as Sears was decentralized. In keeping with Wood's philosophy that those who were held accountable for results should be given wide latitude in determining how they accomplished them, he left Allstate's management alone. Besides, he was content with the new company's performance—as he had good reason to be.

Starting with a single product type—automobile insurance—Allstate quickly expanded its offerings to include fire insurance and a wide variety of casualty coverages. (A brief foray into life insurance in the mid-1930s was terminated as unsatisfactory.) The basic principle of providing better values at lower cost proved as successful in selling insurance as in selling merchandise, and in a few short years Allstate had become one of the giants in its industry. Premiums written grew from a little over half a million dollars in the first full year of operation to nearly $5 million in 1940, $66.3 million in 1950, and $209.2 million in Wood's last year as head of Sears. After a small net loss the first year, profits in 1940, 1950, and 1954 were $0.5 million, $5.7 million, and $15.8 million, respectively. Beginning with an initial capitalization of $700,000, the company had net assets of $267.4 million at the time of Wood's retirement.[4] Despite the dire foreboding his board had expressed twenty-three years earlier, Wood's head was anything but bloody, and he made no secret of the fact that Allstate was among the accomplishments of which he was most proud.

The creation of Allstate Insurance Company serves as a prime example of Wood's entrepreneurial instinct. The original idea may not have been his, but he seized upon it and made it his. Under the management he put in place and then left largely on its own, Allstate introduced a number of innovative practices, including the use of simplified language to explain policy provisions, installment selling, and new methods for rating risks. These and other departures from industry custom helped to enable Allstate to offer quality insurance protection at lower than customary rates—some 10 to 15 percent lower, according to company claims.[5] But Allstate's most significant innovation was the concept upon which Wood had based the business: that of bringing the customer to the salesman through the catalog and the store. This not only saved salesmen's shoe leather and time but also materially reduced the costs of insurance acquisition, which theretofore had constituted a major portion of the cost of coverage.

If Allstate was the most lucrative (other than Sears itself) of the General's entrepreneurial endeavors, the expansion into Latin America was the most romantic. It, too, was undertaken in the face of skepticism on the part of his board. Charles A. Meyer, who was associated with the Latin American operation from its beginnings and who headed it from 1955 to 1960, tells this story of how it all began.[6]

It was Christmas Eve of 1946 when Meyer, who was then a young buyer, was called down to Wood's office. Wood got right to the point. "I'm opening stores in Latin America," he said. "How would you like to be my assistant?"

"Yes, I know we are," Meyer replied, "because I'm preparing a merchandise list—"

"No, you misunderstand me," the General interrupted. "*I'm* opening stores in Latin America. No one on the board except Wendell Endicott and Edgar Stern approves of what I'm doing."

Convinced of the soundness of his plans, he had decided to move ahead despite his board's misgiving—and once again events justified his actions.

General Wood's interest in providing merchandising service to Latin America had its inception during his years on the Panama Canal. Deeply offended by what he perceived as the unscrupulous practices of East Indian and Lebanese merchants, who had a virtual monopoly on Latin American retailing, he drew up plans for starting a privately owned retail venture there. The idea was firmly vetoed by General Goethals, who was concerned about the possible conflict of interest it represented and who in any event did not want his young assistant's attention distracted by such seemingly extraneous matters. Nevertheless, Wood left the Canal believing that "there had to come a time when some farsighted merchant would be able to give value to a growing population."[7]

In 1929, some twenty years later, Wood responded to a letter from Wendell Endicott by stating that while Sears had no plans for entering the Latin American market, "it is possible that at some future time, we might."[8] During the late twenties and early thirties, Wood and the entire Sears organization were simply too caught up in building the new retail system and dealing with the problems of the Depression to consider taking on the formidable task of venturing beyond the U.S. borders. But the lure of Latin America was never wholly submerged by domestic concerns, and, as one senior executive reported, it was based on more than commercial considerations:

> Having travelled back and forth to Latin America over a period of years with General Wood, [I remember] he said a number of times that he never expected the balance sheet of Sears U.S. to be substantially affected by earnings of those [Latin American] operations. His thought, as he expressed it to me, was that it would help relationships

between the United States and those countries. Down the road, he thought this was highly desirable, and hoped that other companies would do something similar to bring the countries closer together.[9]

Wood's fascination with demographic trends was not confined to those of the United States, and he paid close attention to statistics on Latin America. As he focused on the changes occurring there, he saw a vast geographical expanse whose rapidly growing populations were poorly served by a disorganized and inefficient system of retail distribution. He also saw the gradual emergence of a middle class with a strong desire for consumer goods.[10] By the time he turned over the Sears presidency to T. J. Carney in 1939, Wood had begun to form in his mind specific plans for taking the company into Latin America, and he made his first move shortly before the United States was drawn into World World II.

Cuba was chosen as the testing ground. Its principal city and major port were close at hand, its people were better educated than the Latin American norm, and it had a middle class clearly in the making. Its proximity to the United States and frequent contacts between American and Cuban citizens had created a strong latent demand for U.S.-type goods. To help satisfy that demand, Wood decided in 1940 to open a store in Havana, and the building of a structure designed to Sears specifications was begun in 1941. Construction of the new store was not yet complete when Pearl Harbor was bombed, and its opening and operation alike were greatly complicated by wartime shortages and the difficulty of transporting merchandise across the Florida Straits under wartime conditions. But even though its merchandise offerings were severely limited, the store was a notable popular and business success from the start.

No important policy issues were raised in the way the Cuban venture was conceived and executed. Wood was not ready to lay a full-blown Latin American strategy before his board: he merely wished to conduct an experiment involving no greater commitment than the opening of one more new store. The Havana store was not significantly different from any of the other stores Sears was opening in major cities. It did, however, provide a means for testing—and validating—Wood's ideas about the possibilities of launching a major Latin American venture. During the war years, plans were worked out for placing additional stores in Cuba and for expanding into other Latin American countries, and when peace returned Wood was ready to move with his characteristic vigor. By the end of 1946, he needed an able assistant to help him keep his fingers on the increasingly active

Latin American operations, and he found him in the person of Charles A. Meyer.

Early in 1947, in a meeting attended by Sears directors, officers, and senior executives, Wood explained what he was setting out to do:

> Merchandising conditions are about the same in these countries as in the United States in 1900. We are as far ahead in distribution as we are in production. Latin American merchants operate on a very slow turnover, a very high markup and no clean-ups of stock. There is a very great demand for American goods and American merchandising methods. The opportunity exists for Sears to go into these countries, undersell local merchants by 25%, make very handsome profits, and confer a great benefit on the masses in these countries. "A" stores can be established in the large capital cities, "B2" stores in some of the smaller cities, and eventually mail order plants can be established in Mexico, Brazil and the Argentine.[11]

Mexico had been selected well in advance as the starting point for the ambitious new program. It lay just below the border, and its principal cities were within easy reach of the United States. While the Mexican economy was still primitive by U.S. standards, it was the most advanced of any Latin American country, and political conditions were stable. In addition, the Mexican government was actively encouraging economic development; this, coupled with a rapidly growing population and rising standards of living, gave promise of a vigorous market ready for the introduction of Sears-type retailing. All in all, Mexico appeared to be an excellent business opportunity in its own right as well as an ideal laboratory in which Sears could practice operating in a Latin American environment, which differed in many important respects from the environment to which it was accustomed. Anything learned there, Wood felt, would be useful as the company moved into other countries on his agenda.

The first store, located in Mexico City, was opened with great fanfare in February of 1947 and was an immediate success. Customers crowded in, clamoring to buy in all departments but especially interested in stoves, electric refrigerators, radios and televisions, and other appliances and hard lines which were staples of Sears U.S. business but had been largely unavailable south of the border. The new store was, in fact, stocked chiefly with Sears standard U.S. lines, shipped from the same sources as supplied the U.S. stores. No doubt Wood intended in due course to begin establishing local sources for this store and the others he contemplated, just as earlier he had encouraged the development of sources in the southern United

States, but this would take time and the market would not wait. Besides, it was American merchandise in which the rising Latin middle class was most interested, and Wood saw no reason not to give the people what they wanted. Shipping proven Sears merchandise from proven Sears sources would provide Latin consumers with substantial values, and they would have the benefit of the vast productive efficiency of U.S. industry.

It seemed a good strategy, and the enthusiastic reception given the Mexico City store appeared both to vindicate it and to bode well for Wood's entire Latin American program. Mexico and the other Latin countries in which he was interested had built up large reserves of foreign exchange during the war years, when they had realized lucrative proceeds from the sale of raw materials to warring countries but had been able to buy little from abroad. With the coming of peace, however, years of pent-up demand for foreign goods soon exhausted these reserves. In Mexico, the end came quickly. Before the new store had been open a year, the Mexican authorities imposed tight foreign exchange controls and import restrictions which made it impossible to continue to rely primarily on U.S.-made goods. Other Latin countries adopted similar measures, and it was clear that Wood's service-of-supply strategy was no longer tenable.

By this time, however, he was too far committed to his Latin plans to back away, and in any case backing away was not in his nature. He decided on a bold shift in direction: if Mexico and the other Latin countries could not pay for goods made in the U.S., he would supply them with U.S.-style goods made by U.S. methods in their own countries.

Wood not only adapted to the drastic change in circumstances but also made a positive virtue of his new necessity-dictated policy. From that point on, he proudly maintained that he wanted his Latin stores to "live off the country" and not be dependent on imports from the United States. He knew that the Latin manufacturing plants Sears used as sources might not be as efficient as their U.S. counterparts or have their economies of scale, but they would be great improvements over the production facilities the countries already had—if they had any at all, which they often did not. As he had done years before in the American South, Wood carefully fashioned his buying practices to foster industrialization of the host countries and strengthen their base economies.

He was fortunate in having moved first into Mexico because the Mexican economy was further advanced than those of her sister countries and the prospect of establishing local sources was less formidable than it would have been elsewhere. He was also fortunate in having rich organizational resources on which to draw. Sears ranks boasted a corps of buyers with intimate knowledge of manufacturing as well as merchandise. They had been well trained in the concept of buying Wood had introduced into Sears nearly a quarter of a century before, which defined the buyer's job as not only the selection of merchandise but also the selection of efficient and reliable manufacturing sources. Many had set up new sources from scratch and had worked with them to bring them up to desired levels of performance. Wood turned now to this experienced and highly capable buying organization to help find and train Mexican sources for the store he had already opened and the others on his drawing board.

This task proved not too difficult for lines of merchandise such as textiles, clothing, and furniture; these were fields in which local businessmen and craftsmen already had experience, and what was chiefly necessary was to teach them U.S. methods of manufacturing and doing business. Even here, significant improvements were achieved in fairly short order. Shop layouts were revised and work flow simplified; ways were found to reduce costs and eliminate waste; better cost controls and bookkeeping procedures were introduced. Mexican suppliers were encouraged to visit Sears U.S. sources to study their production methods on the spot, and some U.S. sources visited their Mexican counterparts to assist them on their home ground. Financial aid was given frequently, typically by advancing up to half the value of orders placed or by helping to finance the purchase of new machinery. Sears policy of paying for merchandise promptly on delivery was practically unheard of in Latin America at the time, and this in itself was a financial boon to many small, cash-poor producers.

In effect, Sears buyers took Wood's basic buying concepts and adapted them to the special needs of Mexico and, later, other Latin American countries. These concepts rested on the premise that Sears interests were best served by making it profitable for good sources to do business with Sears. The policy worked brilliantly in the United States; it worked equally well, if on a smaller scale, in Mexico and other Hispanic environments.

The task of developing local sources of supply for mechanical and electrical appliances and for hard goods in general was far more problematic. Mexican nationals had had little experience with these more esoteric lines, and the nationals of other Latin countries had had no experience whatsoever. The manufacture of these types of merchandise required extensive capital investment, for which few resources were readily available, and called for sophisticated management skills which were virtually nonexistent among even the better educated and more affluent elements of many local populations.

A variety of means were adopted to deal with these obstacles. In Mexico and to a lesser extent in other Latin countries, there were a few established metals and equipment manufacturers, some locally and some foreign-owned, and these could be built upon. In a limited number of instances, local entrepreneurs were encouraged to set themselves up in business, with help from Sears in one form or another. Several Sears U.S. sources were prevailed upon to open Latin facilities. And despite the strict import controls, it was possible to bring in from the States key components for certain lines of merchandise and assemble them with locally made components; for example, U.S.-made sewing machine heads, television chassis, and radio parts could be mounted in Mexican-made cabinets on assembly lines set up in Sears warehouses. The ingenuity of Wood's buying organization proved equal to the task, even in the manufacture of the most difficult merchandise lines, and the goods so ardently in demand were eventually supplied.

Although industrialization had already begun in Mexico prior to Sears arrival, it was greatly accelerated by Sears buying practices. As more Sears stores were opened in Mexico, the company's requirements grew apace and soon reached substantial proportions. Other Mexican retailers followed Sears in offering the newer lines of merchandise, and their requirements in turn gave added strength to the movement toward industrialization. The net effect was to build up strong native industries with high standards of performance in a relatively short span of time. It can safely be claimed that the process would have taken place much more slowly had not Wood responded to the challenge of severe import restrictions in the way he did.[12]

But Sears impact on Mexico was not limited to the impetus it gave to industrialization. More obvious and immediately apparent were the major innovations it introduced into the country's retail practices. Window displays were lighted at night rather than closed behind steel shutters; merchandise was open to public handling and inspection on racks and counters rather than being shut away in glass cases; goods were given price tags and descriptive labels. For the first time, Mexican consumers were exposed to truth in advertising and price lining (i.e., grouping merchandise into well-defined price brackets according to levels of quality). Perhaps the most dramatic innovation was the introduction of display advertising. Before, classified ad-type announcements simply stated that certain kinds of mer-

chandise had arrived and were available for sale; now, full-page advertise-
ments featured specific items that were attractively illustrated and described, with their prices prominent. Other merchants quickly followed
Sears example, and previously drab Mexican newspapers began to carry
page after page of well-laid-out advertising. It was an economic bonanza
for the newspaper publishing industry. Papers which had hitherto depended
on political patronage and favors for their survival soon found themselves
economically independent, and the Mexican press achieved a degree of
freedom it had never before known.

Despite complications created by legal strictures and government
practices which differed in important respects from those of the United
States, Wood insisted on applying to his Mexican and other subsequent
Latin ventures the same basic personnel and employee relations policies
which had proved so useful to the U.S. company. Wages, hours, and working conditions were deliberately set well ahead of competition. Base pay
was 10 percent above established rates for comparable work in local markets, and salespeople in commission departments could earn far more than
base. Major appliance salesmen moved into income brackets significantly
above those achieved by their counterparts elsewhere, and it was reported
that women in Mexico City who sold kitchen cabinets for Sears were
"among the highest paid business women in Mexico." [13] Employees did not
have to press for wage increases; merit raises were given as they were
earned, and across-the-board increases were made from time to time to
compensate for rising living costs. Contrary to prevailing practice, overtime work drew premium pay. As a 1953 study conducted by the National
Planning Association noted: "High pay has proved to be no extravagance
on the part of Sears. The ratio of payroll to sales in Mexico is about
the same as in Sears stores in the United States. Turnover of personnel
is very low; it is a rarity for any employee to leave Sears to take another job." [14]

In addition, a wide range of employee benefits was provided, many of
which were virtually unknown in Latin America before that time. The
most striking of these was profit sharing, tailored as closely as country law
would allow to the plan that had long been at work in the parent company.
The stores earned excellent profits, and employees benefited accordingly.
But even more important from the standpoint of employee loyalty and morale was the fact that the investment of the assets of the Profit Sharing Fund
in company stock gave employees a tangible ownership interest in the local
company, something in which they took great pride. Employees of no other

207

company in the Latin countries could boast a similar privileged ownership status, and Sears employees were the envy of their less favored friends.[15]

Just as Wood had visited the Evansville store and other early domestic Sears stores, he now made frequent trips to the new Latin stores. True to form, he did not want to rely on the reports of others for knowledge of how things were going. He wanted to see for himself, to talk directly to those at the scene of the action, to learn firsthand about his customers and how they lived and what they needed. His purpose was not so much to check on the stores themselves as to discover what they required in the way of support from the parent company and to find means by which they might better serve their customers.

By this time Sears had acquired a small fleet of wartime surplus DC-3 airplanes, and Wood often commandeered one of them for a swing through Latin America. He was always accompanied by an entourage: Sears executives who could assist the new stores in one way or another, outside members of the board whose strong support he wished to ensure, leading U.S. businessmen whom he wanted to impress. His trips took on the trappings of visits of state, with dinners in honor of the Sears party being hosted by leading citizens and high government officials of the various countries. New store openings were especially gala occasions. In Latin America it has long been customary for new business ventures to be blessed by the Roman Catholic Church; archbishops and bishops were frequently honored to perform this rite for a new Sears store, in the beaming presence of General Wood. His instincts for learning how to manage a new business and for building the internal and external support essential to its success were as sharp as they had been a quarter of a century before. And once again, he thoroughly enjoyed himself.

In the beginning Sears encountered few legal difficulties in moving into Latin American countries, but as nationalistic feelings escalated most of them came to require 51 percent or more local ownership. The trouble was, there was no one there to buy, except the very rich. And, as Wood maintained, "I've not gone into Mexico to help rich Mexicans." Moreover, he was determined to keep control firmly in Sears hands. Had majority ownership been acquired by local wealthy classes, they might have tried to block some of the innovative practices he was introducing (the employee policies would have been particularly vulnerable), and this he resolved not to let happen.

Deft legal maneuvering was sometimes necessary to stay within the law and still retain control. In some of the countries most important to

Sears, matters were helped greatly by the fact that Sears had established profit-sharing plans for employees modeled on the highly successful U.S. plan. Instituting these plans was itself no easy matter because the concept was quite foreign to the legal systems of the host countries, but this obstacle was overcome in Cuba, Mexico, and Venezuela. In these key countries, a critical advantage was gained when attorneys representing Sears were able to establish that employee stock ownership through the profit-sharing plans could count toward the local ownership requirement. Naturally, this was the sort of local ownership of which Wood thoroughly approved. The profit-sharing plans in these countries came to hold as much as 20 percent of the stock of the local corporation, and this worked very much in Sears favor. In cases when additional measures were necessary, stocks were placed in escrow to satisfy ownership requirements. By one means or another, Wood was able to avoid the loss of control which could have gravely endangered his undertaking.

In nearly every respect other than that of ownership, Wood was anxious to establish close identity with the host countries. For example, a significant measure of country identity was gained by employing distinguished local architects to design stores in keeping with national architectural traditions, a practice which met with warm approbation in the intensely nationalistic Latin countries.

Of greater long-term importance was Wood's plan for executive staffing. While in the early stages fairly sizable cadres of Sears personnel were required to get the new stores started, it was his intention that the stores and local corporate organizations be staffed with their own nationals as soon as possible. His ultimate goal was to limit the number of U.S. nationals in each corporation to three: the president, the controller, and the head of buying. As a practical matter, it took some time to reach this goal, but in fairly short order many store managers, buyers, and merchandising executives were natives of the host countries. Wood insisted on applying the same promotion-from-within policies that had served the parent company so well; they served the Latin corporations equally well, and in the process enabled many Latin nationals to achieve levels of responsibility and remuneration that might otherwise have been out of their reach.

Following the launching of Wood's full-scale Latin American program in 1947, entry into selected countries proceeded apace, and by the time Wood retired in 1954 Sears was doing business in Cuba, Mexico, Venezuela, Colombia, Peru, and Brazil, as well as in several smaller Central American and Caribbean countries. No stores were opened in Argentina, despite attractive inducements offered by Juan Perón, because of distrust of its political climate. And no serious attention was ever given to Chile, largely because of logistical considerations. In 1954 sales for all Latin operations combined, expressed in U.S. dollars, totaled $66.0 million and profits a respectable but not striking $8.2 million.[16] The thirty-six Latin stores and nine sales offices provided gainful employment to more than 8,900 employees, over 98 percent of whom were nationals.[17]

Wood's Latin venture was not only good business for Sears but also proved to be of material benefit for the host countries. The greatest benefit was the stimulus it provided for economic development and the emergence of an increasingly strong middle class. The following evaluation of the impact of Sears operations in Mexico, excerpted from the National Planning Association's study, has general applicability to all the Latin countries in which Sears opened stores:

> The effect [of Sears buying policies] has been to build up wholly native industries with standards of performance that would have been achieved much more slowly by any other method than that of the well-placed order for goods to be delivered.
>
> As for the middle class which is forming due to thousands of impulses—of which Sears payments to small manufacturers and to its own employees form only one—the broad effect of the Sears operation is to hasten the establishment of the middle class by giving a large proportion of the people a much wider choice of goods than they formerly had. Sears has done this in many ways by now familiar to the reader [of the NPA report]: by introducing new products, by lowering prices, by supplying more reliable products, by encouraging in customers the process of deliberation and choice through advertising, quality labelling, counter display, and day-and-night window display. These practices have affected not only the Sears clientele, already the largest retail clientele in Mexico, but also a large part of the buying public through the effect of its example on other stores.
>
> It is not just money that makes a middle class, but rather goods, especially durables, and a wide choice among them. More value for your money is more effective in bringing about a social change than just more money. More money is only too often spent for additional food, drink, and personal luxuries. But more value for your money can mean the purchase of furniture and appliances and all the wares that go to make up a home. Certainly this is what it has meant at Sears.
>
> The observer thus may fairly conclude that the Mexicans have reason to be satisfied with the part Sears has played in the revolution of which they are so justly proud. It is clear that Sears is going their way and to that extent is helping them, helping not only by adapting

itself to them but by adapting to their uses a number of methods that have been tried and found good elsewhere.[18]

Other Latin American countries into which Sears moved had comparable reasons to be satisfied. Sears even received grudging tribute from postrevolutionary Cuba. It was the last foreign corporation to be nationalized by Castro's government, and in announcing the takeover (which included the seizure without compensation of the 18.8 percent ownership of the Cuban corporation[19] held in the Profit Sharing Fund for Sears Cuban employees), Raúl Castro, Fidel's brother, called Sears the "least bad of all the foreign imperialists." General Wood took wry pleasure in this left-handed compliment.

While much of Wood's entrepreneurial drive during this period was focused on expanding Sears south, he was also interested in taking it north: Canada, too, provided intriguing and challenging vistas. But here the nature of the opportunity was markedly different and had to be approached in a markedly different way. The Canadian economy was as fully developed as the American, and its system of retail distribution approached that of the United States in efficiency and sophistication—approached but did not equal. For although Canada had its share of chain stores as well as mail-order houses, no one there had put together the mail-order/retail store combination which Wood had pioneered so successfully in the United States.

The General wanted no local partners in Latin America, but he realized that a well-established Canadian partnership would be a definite asset should he decide to enter that market. He found the kind of partner he wanted in Simpsons, Limited, headquartered in Toronto. Simpsons, as it was popularly known, was older than Sears and operated five department stores and four mail-order plants with related catalog sales offices. Closely controlled and very well managed, it enjoyed a superb reputation with the Canadian public and in Canadian business and government circles.

Quite by chance, Wood met Edgar G. Burton, head of Simpsons, sometime in 1951 or 1952 when both men were guests at the home of a mutual friend.[20] Wood had been familiar with Simpsons in a general way, but his meeting with Burton gave him his first chance to size up its top management. Although Burton was a generation younger than Wood, the two men took an immediate liking to each other. Wood found in Burton a man who shared his ethical concerns about ways of doing business and dealing with people. Shortly after their meeting, Wood wrote to Burton saying that if Burton were interested he would like to explore the possibilities of some kind of joint venture.

Burton responded with alacrity. He and his associates were longtime admirers of Sears and had noted with both interest and concern Sears aggressive postwar expansion and its move into Latin America; they had grown somewhat apprehensive at the thought that Sears might one day enter Canada and pose an uncomfortable threat. Burton welcomed the prospect of a partnership that could be structured in such a way as not to jeopardize Simpsons' established mail-order and department store businesses. He foresaw additional advantages in an arrangement that would make available Sears considerable merchandising and operating know-how and provide the means for rapidly expanding into the broad reaches of Canada where Simpsons was not yet represented. Wood, for his part, welcomed the chance to acquire a partner who was already firmly entrenched in Canada and had impeccable Canadian credentials. Accordingly, the two men instructed their subordinates to begin exploring in detail how a joint venture might be put together.

There followed a series of meetings between the technical staffs of Sears and Simpsons at which information and ideas were freely exchanged and various possibilities discussed. This process had not gone far before Wood called a meeting of his people to find out from them how matters were progressing. The Sears men began to present in turn their preliminary conclusions, and one after another they recommended against going ahead. After the third or fourth such report, Wood thumped the table and said, "Stop this. Stop it now. We're going to do it. Let's find out how to do it because we're going to do it." This unequivocal directive changed the course of the discussion. The Sears men went back to their offices and busily applied themselves to working out the details.[21]

The result was a joint venture, Simpsons-Sears Limited, owned half by Sears and half by Simpsons. Simpsons put its mail-order and catalog order office business, valued at $20 million, into the new company, while Sears put in $20 million in cash.[22] Under the terms of the agreement, Simpsons-Sears was to operate the four mail-order plants and system of order offices contributed by Simpsons and establish a chain of Sears-type retail stores across Canada. However, it was precluded from opening stores in the five major Canadian cities where Simpsons already had department stores. There was no corporate relationship between the two parent companies, although both were equally represented on the Simpsons-Sears board.

The Simpsons-Sears undertaking was launched in General Wood's last full year as chief executive of Sears. Other than providing the entrepreneurial concept and forcing its adoption onto an initially reluctant Sears staff, Wood had little direct involvement in the undertaking, but it clearly bore his stamp. Among other things, the original joint venture contract made provision for the establishment of an employee profit-sharing plan similar to the one he had used to such good advantage for so many years at Sears. Also, the means for integrating the new company's mail-order and retail businesses were based largely on the methods he had worked out years earlier in the States; his basic ideas on this score proved equally applicable to the Canadian environment.

The mail-order business of Simpsons-Sears, which had been Simpsons' contribution to the new enterprise, continued to be led and staffed chiefly by Canadian personnel. The new retail system, however, was closely patterned on that of the U.S. parent, and its key positions were largely staffed by U.S. personnel. Top management consisted of a combination of senior men from both companies. The first president was Edgar Burton, but in 1956 he moved up to chairman and from that point on the chairman and chief executive has been a Canadian and the president an American, an arrangement that has worked very well in practice.

In the beginning it was hard to find topflight younger U.S. executives with families who were willing to leave promising stateside careers for chancier ones in the fledgling Simpsons-Sears retail system, and in a number of instances positions were filled by men approaching retirement age who were not as well qualified as might have been desired.[23] Other difficulties arose out of the understandable frictions created when two groups of executives from different national and organizational backgrounds had to learn to work together. Fortunately General Wood and Edgar Burton liked and respected each other immensely, and since the new venture was under their surveillance these and other problems were soon surmounted.

One of Wood's most notable characteristics was his knack for composing differences between subordinates and welding diverse opinions into unified courses of action. This proved especially useful in the Canadian undertaking, and in reasonably short order the operation was running smoothly.

Although Wood was never involved in the actual management of the enterprise, he remained on its board of directors until he was well into his eighties. He attended board meetings faithfully, where he was often able to help the new company with sage advice drawn from his long experience. Even after he was no longer physically able to be present at board meetings, he followed Simpsons-Sears financial and operating figures closely and to the end of his life took great interest in the progress of the joint venture he had orchestrated.

Simpsons-Sears was not the most significant of General Wood's achievements, but it was the penultimate expression of his enterpreneurial spirit. He began by perceiving a need as an opportunity: Canadian markets were not being adequately served by the distribution facilities they had, and an integrated mail-order/retail business seemed the best way to serve them. Brushing aside initial objections on the part of his staff, he demanded that they look at the problems that were there not as reasons for refusing to proceed but as obstacles to be surmounted. He adapted his course to the realities of the Canadian scene, as he had earlier adapted his U.S. and Latin American courses to the realities they presented. And he insisted that the new venture incorporate and be conducted according to basic ethical values on which he had long ago learned to rely. Given all this, it came as no surprise to Wood or anyone else who had followed his career that Simpsons-Sears turned out to be an unqualified success.

An interesting consequence of the Canadian venture with which Wood was only marginally involved (he had by this time retired) was the establishment of Waltons-Sears in Australia.[24] J. R. Walton, now Sir John, owned and operated a department store in downtown Sydney with a few outlying branches that primarily sold furniture. Intrigued by Simpson-Sears, he conceived the notion of a similar undertaking in his own country and approached Sears with a proposal for a joint venture. Wood and Walton quickly took a liking to each other. Mrs. Walton, who was active in the business, accompanied her husband on his visits to Chicago and the Walton and Wood families became good friends.

Walton wanted Sears help in building what he visualized as an Australia-wide system of Sears-type retail stores to be supplemented later by a mail-order operation. Encouraged by Wood, Sears management was tempted by the possibility of replicating the Canadian experience in that far-off British Commonwealth. The upshot was the creation of Waltons-Sears in 1955. For a modest investment of $2.25 million, Sears acquired a 16 percent interest with an option to increase its holdings to 20 percent. The remaining ownership was in the hands of Australian investors, with the Waltons holding the largest share.

The undertaking foundered from the start. Toronto is closer to Chicago than New York is, but Sydney is literally on the other side of the world. The constant interaction between U.S. and Canadian personnel which played a major role in the success of Simpsons-Sears was simply impossible to duplicate. Moreover, the new venture lacked the personal involvement of General Wood; he was no longer active in Sears management, and in any event the distances were too great for a man of his age to handle. In the absence of Wood's mediating influence, sharp differences quickly developed between the two partners. They disagreed on policies for financing the business, on merchandise quality, and on rate of expansion, among other matters.

Impatient with the course of events, Charles H. Kellstadt, the new president of Sears, wrote Walton a stern letter laying down six conditions for Sears continued participation. Walton found some of these hard to accept and sought to negotiate, whereupon Kellstadt dispatched Arthur Wood (no relation to the General) to Sydney to work out the terms for Sears withdrawal. The Waltons were bitterly disappointed at this shattering denouement to their ambitious plans, but Kellstadt refused to budge from his position. Arthur Wood devised a settlement which was financially favorable to the Australian shareholders, and the separation was accomplished without ill will.

While the idea for Waltons-Sears originally came from Walton and not from Wood, the General gave it his strong endorsement, without which it is doubtful that anything would ever have materialized. The new company had only a brief and unhappy life, but it nevertheless represented an appealing concept; had Wood been ten years younger it might have worked. At any rate, the risk of failure is integral to entrepreneurship, and the fact that Waltons-Sears failed in no way detracts from the imagination and courage Wood evidenced in supporting Sears entry into the venture.

One of General Wood's greatest entrepreneurial triumphs, second only to his re-creation of Sears in roughly the years 1925–35, was his spectacular expansion of the business in the decade following World War II. In the last year of the war, Sears recorded total sales of $1.045 billion, all domestic. Ten years later, in 1955, Sears domestic sales had more than tripled to $3.307 billion, to which were added $75.0 million from Latin America and $19.2 million from Simpsons-Sears.[25] Part of the dollar increase was due to inflation, but even so the volume of goods moved virtually doubled. In physical terms, Sears growth in the ten years following the war was nearly as great as it had been in the sixty years preceding it.

No expansion of facilities had been possible, of course, during the war itself. Wood spent a good part of his time away from the company on war-related duties, and the management left in charge had all it could do to keep the existing stores open and running. But Wood was not content with a holding operation; he knew that the postwar world would in many ways be a wholly new one, and he wanted to be ready for it. He understood that the war would accelerate changes already at work. He watched the rate at which industry and population were moving to the West and South. He followed the buildup of savings in hands of consumers who earned good wages but had little to spend them on, and he sensed the huge magnitude of their pent-up demand. He observed the shifting demography of the cities and foresaw the explosive growth of the suburbs. He was aware of the significance of new consumer products that were waiting for the return of peace to enter the market. The prospect of a transformed postwar world excited his entrepreneurial instincts, just as they had been excited years before by the urbanization of America following World War I.

He used the war years to prepare Sears for the opportunities that lay ahead. One of the instruments he chose for this purpose was the Post-War Planning Committee. Created in 1943, this committee and its various subcommittees addressed such topics as the size and shape of postwar demand; the number, locations, and types of physical facilities that would be needed to serve that demand; possible sources for new product lines for increased volume of traditional goods; distributive logistics; employee and executive personnel requirements; and the like—in short, the entire range of contingencies which were apt to arise in the changed postwar world.

A primary task of the committee was to draw up detailed plans for a major business expansion and have them ready for implementation immediately on the relaxation of wartime controls. A particularly important aspect of this task was assigned to the store planning and display department headed by Sears veteran L. S. Janes. Relieved of their customary work of planning and overseeing the construction and fixturing of new stores, Janes and his staff, under Wood's specific instructions, turned their talents to designing the store of the future. Employing industrial engineering techniques, they studied customer flow in the stores and the movement of merchandise from receiving dock to intermediate storage to the selling floor. From this objective base, they focused on the design of display and counter fixtures to maximize the visual exposure of merchandise, to facilitate stock counting for control purposes, and to provide more readily accessible backup stocks; the planning of store layouts and department locations to improve customer service; and a variety of other means for converting stores into more efficient selling machines.

216

According to Sears *Annual Report* for 1955, two basic considerations guided this department's efforts:

1. To make it easier for customers to shop and complete their transactions. . . .
2. To secure the greatest possible return on the investment in store space.[26]

These aims were brilliantly achieved, and Sears postwar stores were applauded by customers and management alike. The new facilities were much better than the old, and they were also much more attractive because close attention had been paid to aesthetic factors in the planning process. All things considered, they were a far cry from the "warehouses open to the public" which Wood had envisioned years earlier. Sears would never again be the same, and neither would the retail industry.

When the war ended, Wood moved swiftly. He and the team he had forged knew which stores they wanted to relocate and enlarge, where they wanted to open new stores and what size and kind they would be, where they needed new or larger warehouses and other backup facilities, what new merchandise sources had to be developed, what additional executive resources were required, how much all this would cost, and where the money would come from. There was far more to do, of course, than could be accomplished in a short time, but Wood knew how to set priorities that would give Sears the competitive edge and maximize the return on the sizable investments he proposed to make. It was a bold program, but Wood and his men were playing for high stakes. They won because they were ready and their plans were sound.

In the decade following the war, Sears enlarged and improved 154 stores where they stood, enlarged and relocated 125 others, added eleven stores in cities where Sears was already represented, and opened 114 stores in cities new to Sears. It also built one new mail-order plant and opened catalog sales offices. These figures do not include the thirty-seven stores opened in Latin America during this period, or the twenty stores opened by Simpsons-Sears in Canada, or the four mail-order plants acquired in that joint venture, all of which were integral parts of the overall postwar expansion program.[27] Nor do they include the additional factory resources provided, or the numerous new warehouses and other supporting facilities built, or the extensive improvements made in the many stores, plants, and warehouses that were not enlarged or relocated but simply converted into more attractive and efficient components of the Sears system. It was a busy ten years.

During the period 1946–55, Sears capital expenditures totaled just under $405 million. The bulk of these were made in the first six years following the war. For the period 1946–51 inclusive, Sears capital expenditures came to over $305 million, an average of just under $51 million a year. They decreased during the following four years to under $100 million, or less than $25 million annually.[28] The sharp drop was due in part to the fact that by the end of 1951 Wood had accomplished most of his expansion program, but the chief causes of the slowdown stemmed from the rearmament effort growing out of the Korean conflict. American business in general was inhibited by government restrictions on building, material shortages, and, in particular, the federal excess profits tax. In its 1951 *Annual Report*, Sears expressed in no uncertain terms how it—and Wood—felt about this tax:

> The management recognizes the need for high taxes in this period of rearmament, but points out that such a tax burden penalizes efficiency and growth. In the case of Sears some of the increased earnings resulting from the expansion programs of prior years are only now being realized, and under the present tax law 82 percent must be paid to the government. The effect of this large tax assessment is to stop further expansion and to deny stockholders a fair return on their investment in additional facilities. To illustrate the impact of the excess profits tax on the Company: in 1950 and 1951 this tax approximated $43,900,000, an amount which could have built six of the larger "A" stores and nine medium size "B" stores, giving employment to approximately 6,000 additional persons.[29]

Despite these and other dampening influences, Sears expansion continued, if at a slower pace. Ten years after the war, it was a vastly different company than it had been before: it was roughly twice as large in terms of capacity, and its physical plant was far more attractive and efficient. Its sizable capital funds—which were provided in their entirety from earnings and the sale and leaseback of selected properties—had been invested to good advantage. Wood took great pride in the fact that Sears expansion was accomplished without necessitating any change in the company's capital structure, and year after year the *Annual Report* noted, with obvious self-satisfaction, "The Company has no long-term debt or preferred stock."

Substantial amounts of working capital were needed to carry the inventories required by the threefold rise in dollar sales volume, but these, too, were generated internally. A further drain on capital resources was the very large increase in accounts receivable, occasioned chiefly by the growth in sales volume but also in part by the growing proportion of goods sold on credit. Credit sales were financed primarily by the sale of accounts receivable to banks under a practice initiated in the 1930s. Wood had a deep-seated distrust of debt, and during his tenure in office he went to great lengths to avoid it.

General Wood approached the postwar era with relish as a time of opportunity and promise; it came late in his life (he was sixty-seven years old in 1946), but he seized it with all the vigor and enthusiasm of youth. In this he differed sharply from Sewell Avery, his counterpart at Montgomery Ward. Years later, Wood recounted a meeting he had had with Avery in November of 1945.[30]

"He called me up and asked if I would come down and have lunch with him at the Chicago Club. We sat down and he started without any further ado. He said, 'I want to get your opinion and I'll give you my opinion on what I think events will be . . .' I said, 'Sure, Sewell, I'll do it.'

"Well," Wood continued, "he said that he was a great student of charts. He said, 'I'm convinced from the study of past depressions that this country is going to re-experience history—within two years . . . I'm making all my preparations for it. I'm not going to expand any more, I'm going to cut in every way possible.'

"So I said, 'You've been very frank with me and I'll be very frank with you. I don't agree with you and I know you won't agree with me but I'll tell you how I think. I feel there's a tremendous foundation of purchasing power that's been held back by the war . . . I've made up my mind for the biggest expansion . . . and I've been buying sites for a year and a half.'

" 'Bob,' he told me, 'I think you're 100 percent wrong and I have no doubt you consider me 100 percent wrong.'

"But that was a fact. He pulled in and he didn't even paint the stores. He wouldn't keep up maintenance. Well, we got the jump. We went right ahead in '46 in big ways. For the next five years, he did nothing."

Sewell Avery had been president of U.S. Gypsum Company before joining Montgomery Ward in 1932. Caution generated by his knowledge that all major wars had been followed by severe business crises had enabled him to carry U.S. Gypsum through the panic of 1920–21 in a strong cash position. During the prosperous years of the 1920s, he had restrained the optimism of his Gypsum associates and that company had entered the Depression in much better shape than many other companies.[31] Reasoning from the fact that World War II was the greatest war in history, Avery confidently expected that it would be succeeded by the greatest depression in history. To his mind, the only way to be ready was to save every possible dollar.

But instead of a disastrous depression, World War II was followed by an economic boom. In the eight-year period between the end of the war and Wood's retirement, Sears sales increased by 84 percent while those of Ward's dropped by 9 percent. In profit performance, the comparison between the two companies was even more striking: while Sears was recording a 73 percent gain, Ward's profits fell by 22 percent.[32]

After Avery's forced departure in 1955, Ward's made an effort to regain some of the competitive ground it had lost. By then, however, the cost of acquiring land and constructing modern stores was far greater than it had been in the years immediately following the war. To date, more than a quarter of a century later, Montgomery Ward has not yet recovered from the consequences of Avery's misbegotten strategy. Both companies have experienced serious problems in recent years, but Sears is in a much stronger position to deal with them than Ward's. Wood was an entrepreneur, Avery was not; the consequences of this difference proved profound.

PART IV

THE MAN

12

The Politician

MANY OF GENERAL WOOD'S methods, styles, and patterns of thinking bore striking similarities to those of successful political leaders. His leadership style, for example, was highly personal. Wood spent a lot of time in the field, especially in the crucial early days of the retail business and during the start-up period in Latin America. On these trips, he did not quite duplicate the behavior of a political candidate working an airport crowd, but in visiting the stores he was never satisfied to limit his contacts to a few executives; instead, he always walked through the store and behind-the-scenes departments, stopping frequently along the way to chat with people about themselves and their jobs. People responded by feeling as though they had a special relationship with him. In a very literal sense, General Wood personified the company.

Another essential characteristic of the successful political leader is the ability to mobilize support for his policies. This requires an aptitude for articulating policies and policy goals, and a sure instinct for identifying the constituencies necessary for their achievement. Wood carefully and deliberately cultivated ties with those groups and interests Sears depended upon. This was evident in the way he moved to blunt the anti-chain-store movement: he converted Sears opponents into Sears supporters. The company survived the efforts to cripple chain merchandising largely because Wood won over critically important groups such as local bankers and merchants, agricultural leaders, educators, and state legislators. Without their backing, the new Sears retail system would have been in grave jeopardy.

General Wood sought to establish within Sears itself a polity not unlike that envisioned by Jeffersonian democracy. He created an organizational climate which fostered self-reliance and encouraged the exercise of initiative. In this, his philosophy and policies were not unlike those of American agrarianism, the driving force behind the settlement of the continent. Wood looked on his store managers and buyers in ways reminiscent of the ways Jefferson viewed his yeoman farmers: as hard-working, self-respecting citizens capable of taking care of their own affairs and subject to only minimal authoritative direction and control. He sought to give people a personal stake in Sears much as the farmer had enjoyed a personal stake in his freehold, and endeavored to create a system in which the furthering of personal aims and company aims was in some significant degree synonymous. The analogy, of course, is far from exact, but it presents interesting parallels in spirit if not in form.

Wood was distrustful of authoritative structures of command and believed in relying on the common sense and good judgment of those he placed in positions of responsibility. The Sears he shaped had a clear-cut organizational structure with well-defined lines of reporting. There was never any question as to who was boss or whether an executive was accountable for the performance of those under his or her supervision. Nevertheless, as economic organizations go, Sears was remarkably "open" in the same sense that free societies are often described as "open."

Wood understood, as few businessmen before or since have understood, that a large corporation is a *political* as well as an *economic* institution. The task of providing leadership to an economic institution is not dissimilar in many essential respects from that of providing leadership to a political institution. In both settings, the effective leader must reconcile conflicting interests, provide a framework within which divergent forces can work together for common goals, create a climate of confidence, and generate an atmosphere in which members of the polity are willing to subordinate parochial goals to overall purposes. An economic institution, no less than a political one, can survive and prosper only through the support of its citizens: the employees and executives who comprise its organization, the sources of supply on which it depends, and the customers it seeks to serve. Among General Wood's distinguishing characteristics were his ability to enlist the respect and loyalty of diverse groups of interests, his ability to compose and harmonize differences, and his ability to communicate a sense of mission and commitment to a vast, far-flung organization.

What Wood wanted and to a remarkable extent achieved was an organization of people who could stand on their own feet without depending unduly on administratively contrived support. His goal was to generate an environment that would instill self-confidence and foster self-reliance, not one that would operate through dictates coming down a chain of authority. In a sense that belongs as much to political as to business theory, he sought to establish a system of governance, not simply a system of management.

For example, he recognized that in the kind of relatively unstructured milieu he purposed to build, it was necessary to provide a clear sense of direction; only if goals were well understood, and only if there were values that could be held in common in pursuing these goals, could such an organization achieve the degree of coordinated effort required for successful performance. As has already been noted more than once, Wood took pains to keep the entire organization aware that the first responsibility of the company and everyone in it was to satisfy the customer. Naturally there were also obligations to employees and communities, and derivatively to stockholders, but the customer always came first and all policies and activities were to be organized around that central unifying principle.

So long as this point was kept in view—and Wood never allowed it to be forgotten—only a minimum of administrative machinery and authoritative direction were required to coordinate the activities of a very large, widely dispersed human organization. Knowing their common purpose, people could see how their work related to that of others, and coordination and cooperation were in large measure spontaneous. Sears internal structure and environment under Wood had many similarities to a system of free economic institutions. Here again, the analogy must not be pushed too far, but the fact remains that people in Sears had something of the sense that they were working for themselves.

In business as in politics, great leaders must be good educators. They must be able to communicate to their followers—to those whose support they need—the goals toward which they are striving and the means by which they must be achieved. The leader cannot do the job himself; he must have others who will loyally fall in behind him and help him carry out his purpose. He must be able to inspire his people and give them a sense of urgency and direction. These were tasks Wood performed superlatively well.

In particular, General Wood recognized the need for internal support for his policies, and he moved with consummate political skill to mobilize that support. Knowing that the retail and buying systems he built were dependent on the loyalty and hard work of the ambitious men and women in them, he set about consciously to win and hold that loyalty and effort. Through his policies, he sought, in effect, to create among his middle and

225

upper management group a "middle class" with a significant economic and ideational stake in the company's success. He paid them well and took care of them in other ways because he knew his success hinged upon them. He insisted that his managers, as well as Sears employees in general, be dealt with fairly, and he established administrative means to protect them against arbitrary and unjust actions by their superiors. He instituted a policy of promotion from within, not only as an effective form of training but also to ensure that the better jobs went to Sears people who had earned them and not to outsiders. Through his program of aggressive expansion, he provided assurance that there would be ample opportunities for able and ambitious men and women. He took great pride in the highly successful careers thousands of Sears people carved out for themselves, and he often told them so.

He knew how necessary good relationships between management and workers and high levels of employee morale were to the Sears organization, and he worked tirelessly to achieve these desirable ends. Here, too, he was facing a political problem, and he solved it by means which, given their setting, were essentially political.

In this context, special note should be taken of the political role played by the Profit Sharing Plan. The successful political leader makes skillful use of symbols, particularly those which express goals and values, and Wood used profit sharing in precisely this manner. It became the central unifying symbol around which the entire organization revolved. Through it employees were able to share in the profits and growth of their company, and the plan itself was tangible evidence that Sears was being managed with their interests in mind and not merely for the benefit of absentee stockholders. In fact, through profit sharing, employees were far and away the largest stockholders, and to them "profit" was never the dirty word it often is among employees. During the General Wood years and for a long time thereafter, Sears avoided the sharp conflict between management interests and employee interests common in most large companies, and much of the credit must go to profit sharing. Significant as the material benefits of the plan undoubtedly were, its chief value lay in the fact that it symbolized the unity and common purposes of the thousands of men and woman who comprised the far-flung Sears empire. Its political function was more important than its economic function.

Like a skillful political leader, Wood reassured his constituencies in time of trouble. In the depths of the Great Depression, he called his buying organization together—not, as he emphasized, to give them a pep talk, "painting a fake picture and telling you to be happy and cheerful," because that would be "like telling a prize fighter who is groggy that he really hasn't been hurt." Rather, he told them that he knew very well they had been hurt and could understand their mood of discouragement. And then he said: "I firmly believe that the spirit of man is superior to any combination of circumstances, bad as they may be, and that if you retain your courage, and your faith, you can overcome any obstacle." [1] He then proceeded to recount from his personal experiences how seemingly insuperable difficulties had been overcome: in the Philippines, on the Panama Canal, in World War I, and during the sharp postwar economic crisis. He not only spoke words of encouragement but spelled out the kinds of approaches his listeners should employ to surmount the problems they faced. He went on to stress that far more was at stake than their own welfare: "I wonder if you gentlemen realize the responsibility that is upon you. The entire buying organization numbers possibly two hundred people, yet upon the skill, capacity and resourcefulness of these 200 people and their ability to maintain sales at a profit, rest the fortunes of some 50,000 human beings in the employ of the company." [2] Thus he gave them hope, he gave them concrete suggestions for working their way out of their troubles, and he placed their task in a context larger than themselves. This was not only business leadership; it was political leadership in the best sense of the term.

Some years later, in the midst of the business downturn of 1938, he took similar steps to rally his retail store managers. After acknowledging that sales were hard to get and would probably "become harder as summer progresses," he went on: "I want every one of you to know that I have confidence in your ability to intelligently and effectively handle your store under these trying conditions. Do the best and smartest thinking you can. . . . These are days for good, thorough thinking, and careful execution of your plans. This cannot be done when one is worried." [3] Not quite "blood, sweat, and tears" or even "we have nothing to fear but fear itself," but close enough in a business context. Under circumstances in which other chief executives might have resorted to punishing pressures and threats, Wood reassured his managers that he had faith in them, that the difficult period through which they were passing would not last too long, and that, in the meantime, they were to keep up their own and their employees' spirits. Sensing the mood of his constituency, he moved to restore its confidence. Toward the end of the same difficult period, he exhibited another aspect of a political leader's skill: demanding that people set their sights high. In July of 1938, he admonished his retail organization that he expected the stores "to make up some of this drop in profits in the spring and second half of the year. . . . Assuming that conditions are better, I will accept no excuses from our managers for poor results this fall."[4]

An effective leader, whether business or political, must be able to cope with great emergencies by grasping their impact and mapping the course to be followed. Three months after Pearl Harbor, Wood addressed a memorandum to his officers that began "Our company is confronted with a new and unusual set of conditions due to the great world war now raging." He then proceeded to summarize the issues facing the company and outlined an organized means for dealing with them.[5]

The war years were hard for Sears, but the company came through them remarkably well—in large part because the men and women of Sears had the enormous advantage of a leader who possessed political as well as business skills. Wood's business acumen enabled him to see the worst business and managerial problems the company was facing; his political acumen enabled him to mobilize the human resources of his enterprise and master them.

Wood's political instincts were rooted in an understanding of political processes in general. He supported major elements of the New Deal when many of his business contemporaries did not; looking back years later, he simply stated, "The Securities and Exchange Act, the Utility Holding Act, the Social Security Act, were all things that had to be done."[6] In taking this position during the deeply troubled 1930s, he accurately read the temper of the times—and found the "stupidity" of those who failed to do so "incredible."[7] He also perceived the objective facts of the period. During the 1932 presidential election, he broke with the party to which he had always belonged because he saw Herbert Hoover's deflationary policies leading straight to disaster. Before Franklin Roosevelt's inauguration, he wrote the president-elect:

> There is only one great issue before the country today—whether at this time to continue the process of deflation or whether to inflate. . . .
>
> If we are going to continue the first course to its logical conclusion, we are yet far from the point, because, while commodity prices have been thoroughly deflated and labor partially so, there are many other elements in our business structure that have not yet been deflated. Railroad rates will have to come down from 25 to 50%, utility rates as well as telephone and telegraph rates will have to come down from 20 to 40% and newspaper advertising rates correspondingly; also services—that is fees of lawyers, doctors, dentists, etc. will have

to come down, and the wages for labor in the cities, while already reduced, will have to continue their downward course.

Conservatives—the bankers and those who have urged this course—do not yet realize what the full effect will be if we reduce railroad rates and other services correspondingly. It will result in wholesale bankruptcy and receiverships. Labor, while it has been patient, is not going to take further sweeping reductions. In other words, I doubt whether our financial, business and social structures will stand the strain.[8]

Clearly, Wood had a better sense than most business leaders of the time for the mood of the general run of men and women. And he had a far better grasp of the political impossibility of pursuing any further the course that President Hoover had laid down and most of his own business friends supported. The policy of price inflation through currency manipulation advocated by Wood was not unlike, in spirit and purpose, that which had been fruitlessly urged in three unsuccessful Democratic presidential candidacies by the great populist champion, William Jennings Bryan.

Wood's political philosophy contained a number of what appear to be disparities, but these were at the surface level only; at a more fundamental level they were thoroughly consistent. His conservatism and his liberalism alike had a common base. The two senators from Wisconsin, Robert M. LaFollette, Jr., and Joseph R. McCarthy, cordially hated what they saw in each other, but Wood supported them both, and his lack of discomfort evidenced the internal consistency of his political philosophy. He was the embodiment of big business, yet he had a deep and abiding distrust of "Eastern moneyed interests."

The key to his seemingly contradictory behavior lies in the fact that he was at heart a prairie populist in the upper midwestern American tradition. It was a condition he came by naturally: his father had been one of John Brown's raiders and an aggressive partisan in the bloody struggle to keep Kansas and Nebraska free before the issue was settled by the Civil War. Later, in Kansas City, the elder Wood and his son witnessed firsthand the unconscionable exactions imposed on midwestern farmers and merchants by the eastern-owned railroads. The 1890s and 1900s saw the Granger Movement reach the peak of its power and influence. The panic of 1893, which brought Wood's father to the verge of bankruptcy, was widely blamed on monetary policies dictated by eastern bankers. The year young Wood graduated from high school was the year William Jennings Bryan delivered his famous "Cross of Gold" speech.

Strictly defined, populism is "a political philosophy directed to the needs of the common people and advocating a more equitable distribution of wealth and power."[9] This definition comes very close to expressing Wood's own philosophy. It helps to explain his early empathy for Franklin Delano Roosevelt, whose patrician populism he found attractive. He was comfortable with the politics of such old-style progressives as Senators Burton Wheeler and Gerald Nye, with both of whom he was on friendly personal terms. He invited a son of Senator Wheeler to join Sears, where he lived out a working lifetime in a middle management position. After LaFollette was beaten by McCarthy in the 1950 Wisconsin senatorial race, Wood hired LaFollette as Sears Washington representative. And late in Wood's life, during the 1968 presidential campaign, he stated: "I disagree with most of [Hubert] Humphrey's ideas, but if fate put him in the White House, I could go to sleep knowing we had on the job an honest man who truly loves his country."[10] Wood's thoughts on specific policy issues may have changed over time, but his basic populist leanings stayed with him throughout his long life.

One astute observer described an important element of the midwestern strain of populism: "At its core lies an idealistic vision of America as the New Jerusalem, a fresh and gleaming experiment in civilization. This was the vision cherished by generations of immigrants who peopled the center of the continent. They left the Old Country (which might have been any place from Minsk to Dublin) in bitterness; and they believed profoundly that the American Dream could survive only if it avoided all contamination from the corruption, quarrels, and oppression which they had fled."[11] Though Wood himself was neither an immigrant nor the son of an immigrant, he grew up in a milieu profoundly influenced by the immigrant experience. He shared the conviction that grew out of that experience: that to realize its destiny America must make its own way. His sense of the American Midwest was especially strong: "Nowhere in the world is there anything to match our Mississippi Valley, with over 1,000,000 square miles of rich soil, with a temperate climate, ample rainfall, inhabited by an intelligent people. Nowhere in the world are there anything like our factories, with their modern tools and equipment, their intelligent labor, their managerial 'know how.' I have always returned [from my trips abroad] an enthusiastic 'bull' on our own country and its people."[12]

Otherwise by most definitions a conservative businessman, Wood supported those elements of the New Deal "directed to the needs of the common people and advocating a more equitable distribution of wealth and power" because of his long-held, deeply felt populist leanings. He accepted leadership of the America First movement because he was profoundly convinced of the folly of becoming entangled in the affairs of a corrupt and decadent Old World. Whatever their differences, LaFollette and McCarthy were products of the Wisconsin immigrant experience, with which Missouri-Kansan Wood felt thoroughly at home.

The General's populism may not have been as obvious in the way he ran Sears, but it expressed itself most significantly there. He saw Sears primary business mission as raising the living standards of the American people. In serving that purpose, he sought to provide good jobs and career opportunities to the thousands of men and women who came to comprise the Sears organization; to strengthen the economic underpinnings of hitherto disadvantaged regions of the country (and hemisphere); to improve the quality of life in American communities; and to assure young people that they could acquire the preparation they needed to make their way in the world.

His attitude toward people and his emphasis on administrative decentralization contained elements of both laissez-faire and populism. In both respects, he displayed a marked strain of agrarian romanticism. Confidence in the good sense and high potentials of people was one expression of his populism. He was against too-close supervision and control in his own organization as he was against undue governmental regulation and interference with competitive market processes. He had great confidence that people would work things out with minimal intervention and direction from higher authority. He was as fiercely opposed to overhead in business as he was to big government, which he considered a kind of overhead for society.

Thus, despite superficial indications to the contrary, Robert E. Wood was a whole person with an internally consistent philosophy and a coherent approach to the times in which he lived. In his own unique way, he incorporated many of the best features of the American experience—itself unique, mercurial, and symmetrical at its core. And he did so in very much the same way a great political leader—a statesman—might have done.

13

Personal Sketches

W HAT EMERGES FROM ANY study of Robert E. Wood is a picture of an interesting, complex man difficult to categorize in standard terms. This is apparent from the stories told about him both during and after his lifetime. Some may be apocryphal; all reveal something about the kind of person he was.

That Wood possessed extraordinary intelligence almost goes without saying. There is no known record of his ever taking an intelligence test, but if he had his IQ probably would have measured far above the general run of business executives, who typically score significantly higher than average. His superior mental capacity evidenced itself in many ways. For one, he was a very rapid reader. His wife, Mary, tells of his bringing briefcases filled with papers home with him almost every evening and going through them quickly after dinner.[1] People who worked with him were continually amazed at how fast he could read a report and grasp every important idea and fact it contained; some who observed him closely were convinced that he read vertically rather than horizontally. His ability to read store and company operating financial statements was nothing short of phenomenal. He could pick one up, glance through it, and immediately spot figures which were anomalous or otherwise important.

His memory for figures bordered on the incredible. On his trips to Latin America during the early years of that program, the General carried the figures of the Latin corporations in his head. Learning through experience that Wood had instant recall of those figures in which he was interested, Charles A. Meyer, who usually traveled with him, stopped bothering to carry along the bulky operating and financial statements.[2]

Arthur Rosenbaum, Wood's expert on price trends, tells a related story: One day the General left his office to board a cab for downtown Chicago. As he crossed the sidewalk, he met the manager of the Des Moines, Iowa, store, who was starting to hail a cab to the same destination. Wood invited the manager to ride with him, and on the way began discussing the latest Des Moines store P & L Statement, quoting exact figures to the decimal point from memory.[3] It is possible, of course, that Wood saw the man from his first-floor office window and took a quick look at his P&L Statement before encountering him "unexpectedly" outside, but even so the tale reveals significant traits of character.

Wood read widely, his scope greatly broadened by his reading speed. He not only kept current on reports relating directly to work—and on the latest census data, which remained a special interest—but read countless books as well. His favorite subjects were history and biography; as his wife recalls, he was never interested in "light" reading, by which she meant fiction.[4]

As far as his own writing was concerned, "his command of English was just amazing."[5] His syntax occasionally suffered from the haste with which he wrote, but his statements were always clear and forceful. His sentences were simple and direct, free of complicated constructions. His ideas were developed logically and without ambiguity. He was no great prose stylist, but he had a marked ability to express his thoughts precisely and well in terms that were meaningful to his audience. Neither his letters nor his speeches were ever very long; he seldom wrote letters or memoranda of more than one page, and even his most important addresses were usually under twenty minutes and never over thirty. J. M. Barker, a man of no mean intellectual ability himself and one with more than a touch of intellectual arrogance, termed Wood "a genius": "General Wood is one of those men who shortcut the processes of reasoning which lesser men have to go through and take the time to weigh. Genius shortcuts those lengthy processes and comes to a conclusion as to what the right thing is to do and if you had a genius of the sort General Wood has, you make mistakes but the greater part of your decisions are right. He is, of course, outstanding, has always been outstanding, in that regard."[6] And, in his "Reminiscences," Barker included this glowing description:

> In speaking of men of stature whom I have met, I ought to say something about General Robert E. Wood. He, like the other men of great stature whom I have known, has courage, determination, intellectual ability, vision and human understanding. He is one of the men who does not let himself be hampered by logic. As I read history and as I

have known great men, it seems to me that they shortcut the logical processes by which most of us think we arrive at our conclusions. As a matter of fact, we probably do not, but we like to go through the motions of thinking that we reason a thing out. Of course we have to take the premises for granted and that all too often vitiates the logical conclusions that we draw. The great men are not so hampered. They instinctively feel that such and such an action is what must be done at such and such a time. If you cross-examine them, they would be unable to tell you why. They just feel it, and most of the time it proves to be correct. I worked closely with General Wood on the development of the Sears retail during those years of the great depression. I do not know of anyone else that I have ever met who would have had the courage and determination that he did under those circumstances. It was fascinating to watch.[7]

Wood's impressive mental capacity was matched and supported by superb health and great physical stamina, both of which he retained until very late in life. He came through the rigors of the Philippines with energy to spare and was untouched by the yellow fever and other epidemics which killed thousands of workers on the Panama Canal. He had, said Barker, "the zest for life."[8] In the words of Mrs. Wood, "Rob was a man of tremendous vigor."[9]

The General took good care of himself physically. He was a fine horseman and rode frequently until he was well along in age. He was also an avid hunter and fisherman and often vacationed in mountains and other remote areas where he could indulge these healthful pursuits. For many years he belonged to the Coleman Lake Club in Wisconsin, where he often spent time himself and which he used for meetings with his key associates at affairs combining business and recreation. He enjoyed golf and was a longtime member of the Old Elm Club, an exclusive (and exclusively men's) country club in Lake Forest, Illinois. Once, in the summer of his eighty-ninth year, he was observed taking a golf lesson from the club professional.[10]

Wood worked long hours and hard, but he knew how to relax. He did not have to wait for his next hunting or fishing trip before he could turn his mind from the pressing concerns of the day. In spite of all the work he brought home, he managed a warm and close family life. He relished a good game of bridge and was an ardent gin rummy player. After World War II, when Sears acquired its own airplanes, he devoted a large part of his time in the air to aggressively played games of gin rummy. Inordinately pleased when he won, he was given to sulking when he lost; like everything else he did, he took the game seriously.[11] The General enjoyed a cocktail or highball before dinner, wine with dinner, and a liqueur afterward, but he always drank in moderation. He ate sparingly but with pleasure; excess weight was never a problem.

His active life extended far beyond the norm. He did not step down as chief executive officer of Sears until he was seventy-five years of age, and for a dozen years thereafter continued as an effective member of the board and was closely involved in all major corporate decisions. His intellectual and physical strength were disciplined by strong ethical and moral values; throughout his long career, Wood placed great emphasis on the importance of character and integrity. He frequently spoke of the triumvirate of traits he valued most—experience, ability, and character—and of these he ranked character at the top of the list. "I do not decry experience and ability," he once said, "but character is the greatest essential." [12] He repeatedly stressed the need for maintaining high ethical standards in the conduct of business. For example, while still at Montgomery Ward, he lectured his buyers:

> I want the best merchandise force in America. I want every member of the Merchandise Organization to know his business; to be a master of his line; to be an able and efficient merchant; to know thoroughly the principles of the mail order business. I want all this, but there is one thing I demand more than anything else of the members of this organization—and that is character.
>
> All the ability in the world is useless without character. I want merchants who are truthful; who are square; who are incapable of dishonorable or petty tricks; who have the respect of the seller; who are gentlemen in the broadest sense of the term. . . . I want no man in this organization who does not measure up, in his personal and business conduct, to the standards I have outlined.[13]

A dozen years later he voiced similar sentiments before a meeting of Sears buyers: "Sears is today not alone a large business, it is a great public institution. It behooves us to guard its reputation jealously. We must be absolutely fair in our relations with our customers, our manufacturers, our employees, to those under us. We must not be small and petty, we must be fair and generous." [14]

The men with whom he surrounded himself were equally notable for their ethical standards. J. M. Barker described one of them as being of "absolutely sterling character. There was fine ability, not genius but fine ability, and his people all worshipped him." [15] The editor of the short-lived

Sears World, a publication initiated after Wood's retirement, made a telling comment about Wood's merchandising lieutenant, T. V. Houser. In going about Sears, he said, he found "the most extraordinary personal respect for Houser that has nothing to do, apparently, with his ability as such but much more to do with his character." [16]

Charles E. Humm, who had originally worked with Wood at Ward's and who later succeeded E. J. Pollock as Sears controller, was remarkable not only for his keen grasp of figures but also for the way in which he carried out the special responsibilities of his office. He relentlessly surveyed all company operations to ensure the highest levels of financial probity, and, to preserve complete objectivity in dealing with his fellow officers, he carefully refrained from developing close friendships with them. He was the only Sears officer who kept a personal distance from his colleagues, and on at least one occasion in a conversation with E. P. Brooks, he expressed a sense of loss at having denied himself the pleasures of companionship which the others enjoyed. Yet he continued to enforce his self-imposed discipline throughout his long tenure in the sensitive controller position. Wood did not require this abstinence but he admired the stern integrity it reflected.

Wood belonged to a church but was not an active churchman. In both his business and personal life, however, he was clearly guided by religious principles. His high standards of ethical conduct, his insistence on fairness and equity, and his sense of honor were deeply rooted in religious values. Nor was he hesitant to profess his religious convictions; in a 1951 speech before the Rotary Club of Chicago, for example, he reflected:

> During long hours in the saddle while on military duty in Montana in 1903–04 I had to *think*. . . . While not particularly a religious man, I usually carried a Bible with me and in my idle hours in camp I would read and re-read parts of it—particularly the Book of Proverbs—and when you read that book, you realize there is precious little wisdom concerning our human relations that has been added since the days of Solomon. . . .
>
> I believe the world cannot be saved unless men have religious faith—it does not matter what faith—Protestant—Catholic—Jewish as long as men have a belief in God, are sincere in their beliefs, and try to practice the ethics of their religion in their daily life and in their associations with their fellow men. [17]

These are sentiments that those who knew and worked with General Wood heard many times, in private conversations and group discussions alike. Significantly, though, there is no record or recollection of his ever speculating on the nature of the Divinity or the relationship between God and man. He did not have a theology per se; he was not concerned with abstract concepts of good and evil. Instead, he was concerned with justice in the ways men and women dealt with each other. He was interested in religions for what they had to say about relationships between people and the obligations human beings have to one another. And because all the great religions of the world express very similar teachings on this score, he was ready to accept them all as of equal authenticity and value.

Wood not only voiced his convictions; he lived them. They formed the basis for his people-centered employee relations policies; his determination to build a corps of strong, self-reliant managers; and his insistence on fairness and justice in all dealings with suppliers, customers, employees, and the public. They underscored his attitudes toward people, attitudes which reflected a genuine interest in them as flesh-and-blood individuals. He took advantage of every opportunity that came his way, or that he could create, to talk with Sears employees face to face. He was known for taking his time to talk, not just to key people but to people in all ranks. In the words of Cyril J. Deutsch, one of his early store managers who in time came to head one of his important metropolitan groups: "The employees in retail always loved him. When he visited a store, he always talked with the porters, maids, maintenance men, as well as sales personnel and staff. He enquired about their children, wife, husband, parents, etc." [18]

Douglas Peacher, who later rose to high positions in the company, recalls that one time in 1940 when he was a young man in the Pacific Coast buying office he volunteered to drive General Wood to the home of his daughter. Along the way, Peacher was surprised to learn that Wood had taken the trouble to find out a great deal about him before starting on the drive. During World War II, when Peacher was in the Marine Corps, he received a letter from General Wood every time he was promoted, often with a few comments about the state of the business. [19]

Sears people having appointments with General Wood were commonly greeted with "Hi [first name]. How's your wife [name]? How's your daughter [name]? How's your son [name] doing at [name of school]?" They were always flattered and pleased. What most of them did not know was that his secretary, Jennie Mae Richardson, kept a carefully updated file on all key company employees. Before any of them came in for their appointments, Miss Richardson would review their folders with Wood so that

237

he could talk knowledgeably with them about their families and other personal matters that might be pertinent at the time. While he was careful to keep this file a secret from all but a very few, he can hardly be accused of engaging in a deceptive practice. He went to some pains to accumulate and have on hand for ready reference up-to-date information on Sears people, their families, and their affairs because he cared enough to want to know.

Wood was a dedicated family man. He believed in large families and had five children of his own. He frequently inquired of his younger executives as to how many children they had, and if they had none or only one or two he would urge them to get busy and have more. Frederick P. Boynton, Jr., a former Sears executive, recalls: "He used to promote big families among all his young friends and took great delight in his own. My father used to call him 'The Ancestor.' . . . [In one] of the last letters I had from him before he died he wrote proudly of his 27 or so descendants. I wrote him back I could never compete on numbers alone but I could beat him on Boyntons vs. Woods—we had four sons and no daughters [as against Wood's four daughters and one son]." [20] (Incidentally, Boynton misremembered the number of Wood's descendants. At the time of his death, the General had fifteen grandchildren and thirty-six great-grandchildren.)

Rising young Sears men in whom Wood took a particular interest were likely to receive an attractive salary increase with each new addition to their families. And he knew who they were: in his never-ending effort to control expenses, he insisted for many years on personally approving all salary increases for monthly paid employees. During the Depression, when it came time for annual salary reviews, he used a simple method for distributing the limited amounts available for raises. He divided the record cards of employees into three piles: married men with children, married men without children, and single men. First consideration went to those in the first pile, and tighter criteria were applied to those in the second. If there was anything left over—and often there was not—it was doled out sparingly to especially meritorious individuals whose cards were in the third pile. [21] The few women on the monthly payroll got short shrift during those difficult years.

Affectionate toward his own children, Wood often expressed his liking for young people in general. During a visit to the company town of the Chicago Tribune Company in Baie Comeau, Quebec, Canada, he was taken on a tour of the plant and the town by J. Howard Wood, the publisher of the *Tribune*. Afterward, he told his host, "Howard, I'm most impressed." J. Howard Wood was pleased, thinking that what had impressed him was the great paper mill or the excellent physical appearance of the facilities and town. And then the General added, "I've never seen such a good looking bunch of healthy kids."[22]

His fondness for children was also evident in his commitment to the Boys Clubs. He was a member of the board of Boys Clubs of America and served as president (and later honorary chairman) of the Chicago Boys Clubs. He made generous personal contributions to the Boys Club movement and Sears, at his suggestion, did likewise. When Wood retired from active duty in 1954, the Sears board could think of no more fitting tribute to his thirty years of leadership than to erect the General Robert E. Wood Boys Club on the West Side of Chicago in his honor. Wood was very pleased, and in the years that followed he visited the club many times, taking sheer delight in the presence of those active young people.

Robert E. Wood was a very human person, and as such he had his share of personal idiosyncracies. He was a man of many concerns, but his dress and personal appearance were not among them. During his four years at West Point he accumulated an impressive record of demerits, chiefly for infractions of the dress code and for failing to maintain his quarters in militarily proper order.[23] While he was still at Montgomery Ward, he sometimes stayed at the Highland Park home of his close friends, the Boyntons, while his wife Mary and the children were away visiting relatives. Wood was put up in the room the Boynton family had earlier used as a nursery. Frederick P. Boynton, Jr., who was then still a boy, remembers that "the maid would always clean up, but a short time later the room would be all messed up again, clothes over the backs of chairs, dirty socks under the bed."[24]

E. P. Brooks, who worked for the General both at Ward's and Sears, described the first time he met his future employer and friend. He had an appointment to interview General Wood at the Boynton home during one of the times Wood was staying there. It was a summer weekend and very hot. The young man was ushered into the living room and told to wait. Wood joined him shortly; as Brook recalls, "Breezing into the room came a man wearing golf knickers, one leg of which was hanging down, his fly partly open."[25] He was more presentable at work, but only marginally so. Brooks says it best: "He didn't give a damn the way he looked."[26] During his early years with Sears he was far too busy and impatient to take time to be fitted for tailor-made suits. He typically bought his clothes by having his secretary call the men's clothing department in the mail-order plant across the street from his office and asking them to pick out a suit of a certain type

239

or color off the rack and send it over to him before the end of the day. Although the department kept Wood's chest, waist, and trouser length measurements on file, the fit always left something to be desired.

Wood's carelessness in dress was a matter of concern to his friends on the upper-middle-class North Shore where he lived. When he became president of Sears in 1928, the senior Boynton and two other friends, feeling that a man in that position should cut a better personal figure, went to see a tailor who kept a shop across the street from the Chicago Club and outfitted many of Chicago's top business and professional leaders. They said to the tailor: "We're going to send General Wood down here to you and you make him three suits of clothes—*good* clothes!" [27] Wood went along reluctantly, and while the resulting suits were of fine quality and excellent fit, not even the best tailor—and not even Mrs. Wood—could keep them from becoming rumpled at the office and flecked with carelessly dropped cigarette ashes.

The first time Wood was invited by President Roosevelt to have dinner at the White House, he was too busy, or at least neglected, to buy or rent the evening clothes that were de rigueur on such occasions. He showed up in a rumpled business suit, tie slightly awry, and if he was aware that his attire was out of place he gave no visible sign. His dress was a frequent problem on more ordinary occasions as well. At home, Mrs. Wood was able to check him out before he left for the office. On his trips, those traveling with him had to make sure he was wearing matching socks and that his pants and coat were from the same suit. Wood simply had too many other things on his mind to be bothered by what he viewed as nonessentials.

His driving was something else that gave his friends cause for worry. The younger Boynton, who joined Sears on leaving college, remembers what it was like to drive back and forth to work with Wood. It was a distance of some forty miles each way over suburban and city streets. Boynton drove home in the evenings because Wood was tired at the end of the day, but Wood always took the wheel in the mornings. "He drove like a racer on a race track. Actually, he would race other cars carrying Sears people, seeing who could beat the others to the next checkpoint. He drove a Model T Ford—fast, but not very well. He was really a hazard on the highway." [28]

Wood was a heavy cigarette smoker in those days, and he had an annoying habit of putting his cigarettes out against the car window without bothering to open it. Often he was too busy talking to light a cigarette and instead chewed vigorously on the end, dropping tobacco shreds on his clothing and the car seat. When excited in the car or in the office, he frequently chewed on caramels still in the wrapper.[29]

In time, at his doctor's and his wife's urging, he gave up smoking but not cigarettes: he continued to chew them—rather messily. This habit, too, distressed his family and friends. Mrs. Wood finally hit upon a solution. With the aid of a Sears buyer, she found a manufacturer who could keep the General supplied with celluloid facsimiles of partially chewed cigarettes, complete with realistic-looking stains at the chewing ends. For many years thereafter, Wood reached often for one of his imitation cigarettes and chewed away in apparent unconcern as he conducted his business. The stained-end celluloid cigarette was not particularly attractive, but from a neatness standpoint the new habit was a considerable improvement over the old.

For a man educated at West Point who rose to the rank of brigadier general in the regular U.S. Army at the age of thirty-nine, Wood was a singularly unmilitary man. Despite the pride he took in the title "General," by which he was always known even after entering civilian life, he was never a military man in spirit. And despite a sentimental attachment and close friendships with top military figures such as Generals Douglas MacArthur and Hap Arnold, he never really liked the Army. He spent many years in uniform, but his actual military experience was limited to two years in the Philippines and three years on the Western frontier. Otherwise, virtually all his time in uniform was spent on assignments which did not differ in any essential way from civilian managerial work.

In civilian as well as military life, Wood displayed superb managerial and leadership skills—and a distinct personal style. He was an orderly and systematic administrator who organized his work carefully and exercised tight control over his time. Robert E. Brooker, once Wood's factory vice-president who was later to become chief executive of Montgomery Ward & Co., recalled how "Wood scheduled people in to see him at fifteen minute intervals, so you always knew how much time you had. You also knew that when your fifteen minutes were over you were through. You could cover a lot of ground in that time. The General was always well prepared for whatever was to be discussed, so you didn't have to go into a lot of detail. And he made his decisions quickly, even if very large sums of money were involved."[30] Wood did not allow extraneous matters to interfere with the plans he had made for the day. When visitors overstayed their time, he simply stood up. If the visitor did not leave at once, Wood turned his back and

241

walked to the window. It was rare for a visitor to still be there when he turned around again.

Wood combined the ability to see the broad picture—indeed, that was perhaps his strongest point—with the ability to grasp significant details. He was closely familiar with the practices of individual buying departments, and until the establishment of semiautonomous territories after the war he monitored the sales and profit performance of each individual store and mail-order plant. He kept vigilant watch over competitors' prices, particularly those of Montgomery Ward, and was quick to demand an explanation whenever Sears prices were out of line. He followed the affairs of the Profit Sharing Fund with care, as well as relationships with major sources of supply. Not much of importance happened anywhere at Sears without his knowing about it.

When Wood wanted information or an explanation, it was his practice to proceed directly to the point where he could secure the most complete and reliable account, without bothering to go through channels. He was an impatient man. When he wanted information, he wanted it quickly. When he made a decision, he wanted it acted upon at once. His characteristic expression on such occasions was, "Let's charge!" And he really meant *charge*—right now! Fast!

Over a period of time, Wood built up around himself an exceptionally strong cadre of lieutenants. It is interesting, however, that choosing the right person for the right job was not one of his greatest strengths.[31] He had a sure sense for recognizing ability after seeing it in action, but he was not always adept at predicting it in advance. In fact, he made serious mistakes in some of his most important appointments. His actual procedure, though he would not have admitted it and may not have been aware of it, was one of trial and error. His choice of Arthur S. Barrows to succeed T. J. Carney as president backfired badly and required decisive corrective action. He tried two directors of personnel before finding in Clarence Caldwell the man he wanted. Some of his choices for top positions in the Latin American corporations were little short of disastrous.

Wood implemented his retail system as rapidly as he could, but he was slow in promoting his retail executives to positions of power within the company. Long after the balance between retail and mail order had swung decisively in favor of retail, people in Sears higher echelons who had come up through mail order greatly outnumbered those who had come up through retail. All of the early territorial officers were mail-order men. Carney, who succeeded Wood as president in 1939, was a mail-order man,

242

as was F. B. McConnell who succeeded Barrows. Not until C. H. Kellstadt was appointed to the post in 1960, six years after Wood retired, did Sears have a retail man as its president.

In part, this imbalance in favor of mail order reflected the relative youth of the rising retail staff and the relative maturity of the established mail-order staff. A more important influence, however, was the fact that people such as the general managers of the mail-order plants were in positions where they could demonstrate their capabilities. Wood acknowledged and rewarded superior performance when he saw it, and without question the mail-order organization, which was well formed when he came on the scene, was well supplied with executives who had proven track records. Many years passed before retail men had reached the point where they could compete on equal terms.

Between the mail-order and parent buying organizations, which were both staffed with seasoned executives, and the retail organization, which in time developed a seasoned executive corps, Wood had at hand a good supply of excellent talent. He used this supply wisely and took pride in the organization he built from it. The story is told that one day at lunch Sewell Avery said to him, "We're in the same kind of business. Why are you so much more successful than I am?" to which Wood replied simply, "I've got the men." [32]

The General displayed a marked ability to draw the best out of the men with whom he surrounded himself. His basic philosophy was to choose people carefully and then treat them with dignity and respect. "I select a man for a job," he often said, "and give him great latitude to perform that job." [33] Unlike Sewell Avery, who was quick to fire his key people for the slightest cause, or no cause at all, Wood was slow to change his mind once he had given a man his trust. Sometime in the late 1940s, Avery and Wood engaged in the following revealing dialogue:

Avery: Bob, they tell me you don't fire a man even if he's made a mistake.

Wood: No, because a man can learn from his mistakes.

Avery: Well, he only has to make one mistake with me and he's through. [34]

Once, not long after World War II, I was called to General Wood's office where I found him in an irritated mood, chewing fiercely on his celluloid imitation cigarette. Before coming to the purpose of our visit, he told me why he was upset. He had just left a board meeting where approval had been given for Sears to go into the business of selling automobiles with what proved to be the short-lived Allstate car. "It's a mistake," Wood fumed. "It'll never work, and we'll lose a couple of million dollars, maybe a lot more. But [naming the officer who had pushed the program] is a fellow with a lot of promise. Still, he's got a lot to learn, and some of it he's going to have to learn the hard way. What he will learn from this will be worth whatever it's going to cost us." Irked at the prospect of the loss, he was nevertheless willing to make the investment.

The General believed in giving his men plenty of rope, but when it became clear that someone was not equal to the job he acted decisively. He was able to look at people objectively and to a large degree divorce himself from his own emotions. He strongly supported a few people whom insiders knew he disliked, and on more than one occasion he fired people of whom he was genuinely fond. In either case, he tried to base his decisions on facts. So far as it was humanly possible, he judged people on the results they produced and not on his personal feelings about them, which he considered extraneous.

His key subordinates frequently commented on the finesse and objectivity with which he handled reprimands. He did not hesitate to call a lieutenant on a shortcoming or mistake, but he usually did so in ways that left no wounds and strengthened not only the performance but also the loyalty of the person on the receiving end. Robert E. Brooker's testimony on this score is typical: "General Wood was always very fair in his criticisms. If he didn't like something he let you know it, but in a way that helped rather than hurt." [35] His criticisms were delivered without rancor or hostility and were devoid of any implication or condemnation. More often than not he would say, in effect, "You could have done better. You just haven't thought it out right." And he would often close the discussion with, "Anybody can get into trouble. It's the good men that get out."

Cyril J. Deutsch, who held key posts in the retail system for many years, considered Wood's manner of handling reprimands one of his most distinguishing traits: "[If] it was necessary to reprimand an employee he always, at the same time, had praise for some outstanding accomplishment the employee had achieved." [36] Dr. Burleigh B. Gardner, one-time executive secretary of the Committee on Human Relations in Industry of the University of Chicago, later president of Social Research, Inc., and in both capacities a close observer of Sears and Sears people, recounts an illustrative incident from his own experience. [37]

244

Gardner was interviewing Louis Pfeiffle, then the head of one of the buying departments, when Pfeiffle received a phone call. After hanging up, he rose.

"Excuse me, I'll be back in a few minutes," he said

"Well, I'll come back later," Gardner replied.

"Oh, no. This will only take ten minutes."

Gardner waited, and in about ten minutes Pfeiffle returned.

"What was that all about?" Gardner asked.

"It was the General."

"What about?" Gardner wanted to know.

"Well, he chewed me out because I made a stupid buy and lost a pile of money. I was wrong. The General told me so. I had it coming, and that's the end of it."

With that, Pfeiffle picked up his conversation with Gardner where they had left off, just as though nothing had happened.

Gardner later commented on the significance of what had occurred: "I've seen this sort of thing happen often to other executives called on the carpet by their boss. The guy would jitter for an hour after such an interview. With Pfeiffle there was no nervousness, no anxiety; as far as both he and the General were concerned, the matter was over." [38]

That Wood listened as well as talked was revealed on another occasion at which Gardner was present. It was sometime not long after World War II, and Sears was tightening up controls on inventory. The manager of a large store disobeyed some specific instructions he had received and was ordered summarily to Chicago to see General Wood, "obviously for a thorough chewing out": "So he went in to see the General, and an hour and a half later he came out. The General had his arm around him and was saying, 'We need more men like you in the company.' He had convinced the General that what he did was right for his store, even if it violated general policy." [39] Just as it was in Wood's nature to criticize objectively, he was also objective in his praise. Whichever it happened to be, it was deserved and the recipient knew it. In Wood's handling, both criticism and praise strengthened morale.

Wood worked hard to build and maintain a spirit of teamwork among his key executives, especially his officers. During the 1930s he often said, "There's nothing can really hurt us except bad anti-chain-store taxes or divisiveness and rivalry among our officers." After the war, when the threat of anti-chain-store taxation had largely passed, he still maintained that there were only two things that could cause severe damage to the company. One was action on the part of the federal government to break Sears up because of its size; the other was dissension among the officers. Actually, under his regime and for a long time thereafter, Sears was notable for the degree of harmony and internal goodwill that prevailed at the top of the organization.

But it was not only a harmonious organization; within the broad parameters Wood laid down as to strategic direction, it was a productive and creative organization as well. He was primarily concerned with long-range goals, and he largely left it up to his subordinates to devise means to achieve them. J. M. Barker recalls how Wood approached the whole idea of building a nationwide system of retail stores: "He didn't see in detail how he was going to implement [the retail idea]. Instinctively, he recognized that the idea was fundamentally sound and that if he pushed it hard enough, he could gather around him men—he didn't know who they were or how they'd do it—who could implement that stroke of genius." [40]

Over a period of time, Wood did manage to identify and put in place the men who could implement his basic strategic concept. Among these were Barker himself (retail administration and later corporate finance), T. J. Carney (operating), T. V. Houser and Edward Gudeman (merchandising), E. P. Brooks and Robert E. Brooker (factories), C. E. Humm (accounting and control), Clarence Caldwell (personnel), and E. J. Condon (public relations). It was an able group, not merely because they could execute Wood's plans but because they could originate the ideas to flesh them out. Many of the innovative practices Sears pioneered had their beginnings with these men and members of their staffs. Wood recognized good ideas when he saw them and gave them the support they needed for realization, and he was always careful to bestow credit and praise when and where they were due. As a result, the good ideas kept coming, and together these men and their subordinates played a large part in making Sears what it became under Wood's leadership.

Robert E. Wood is remembered today as the man who brought Sears into retail and made it a force to be reckoned with in the world. He was a man with a great vision who had the intelligence, skill, and strength of character to bring it to life. Because so few of the men and women who worked with him and knew him personally are still living, there are not many left to tell stories about what it was like to be in his presence, to share a joke with him, to feel the excitement of a new idea taking shape in

246

General Wood at the time of his retirement, April 1954 (Grant Compton for *Business Week*).

General Robert E. Wood, age 88, 1967 (Fred Schnell, Black Star).

his mind. Yet, in a very real sense, anyone who has anything to do with Sears, Roebuck and Co.—whether as a customer, a supplier, an employee, a stockholder, or a student of American business—feels the lasting influence of the warm, versatile, many-sided human being who was known as "the General."

14

The Legacies

G ENERAL WOOD HAD an exceptionally clear view of what he wanted, and with the aid of the able group of men with whom he gradually surrounded himself, he worked out means to achieve it.

First, he defined Sears business purpose as providing a service of supply for the rapidly urbanizing mass market which emerged in the years following World War I.

Second, he devised a dual strategy to effect that purpose: a buying strategy which integrated mass production with mass distribution to provide the merchandise values needed, and a selling strategy—an integrated mail-order/retail system—to make those values more readily accessible to the consuming public.

And third, to support these strategies, he fashioned uniquely effective bodies of policy in the areas of organization, manager personnel, employee relations, and public responsibility—all within a framework of creative entrepreneurship. Policies in each area incorporated individual features which were in themselves important contributions to managerial practice. Their effectiveness was greatly enhanced by the fact that they fit together into a coherent overall pattern and were mutually reinforcing.

The bodies of policy have a holistic quality a posteriori which they did not have a priori. There is no evidence that they were thought through in advance and crafted into a neat structure. Rather, they were hammered out, one by one, by Wood himself and his loyal lieutenants—men such as Barker, Houser, Caldwell, and Condon, among others. Each man drew on his own experience and insights and enjoyed a large measure of independence. Yet each was able to relate his efforts to those of the others because they all had common goals and a clearly formulated strategic context within which to work.

In quantitative terms, their accomplishments were impressive. From a little over $200 million in 1924, the year Wood joined the company, sales rose to just under $3 billion in 1954, the year he retired—a fourteenfold increase. Net profits grew tenfold from $14 to $141 million, and net worth ninefold from $126 million to $1.141 billion. Employment likewise recorded a ninefold increase from 23,000 to 200,000.[1] By the time Wood stepped down, Sears had become the largest general merchandise distributor in the world and one of the nation's largest employers.

But quantitative measures tell only part of the story, and not the most important part. Sears, Roebuck under General Wood contributed significantly to the emergence of a new American middle class and to upgrading the quality of life of American blue- and white-collar workers. Wood's buying policies played a major role in the decentralization of American industry and the resulting shift in economic and political power from the East to the South and West. His public policies were instrumental in converting southern agriculture from a one-crop to a multi-crop system and for substantially improving livestock bloodlines and animal husbandry. His store location policies helped to change the face of urban geography, encouraged the growth of suburbs, and paved the way for the vast proliferation of shopping centers which radically altered the structure of the retail industry. His move into Latin America set in train a course of events there which speeded progress in industrialization, improved living standards, and accelerated the development of a new middle class. He was cool to any suggestions for expansion into Europe, which he regarded as finished, a continent without a future. But in the western hemisphere, where to his mind the future lay, he left a deep imprint on his times and on the shape of things to come.

Wood's most visible legacy was the kind of organization he built. It was an organization characterized by concern for human values. Structurally, it was highly decentralized, in keeping with Wood's deep-seated faith in people and his willingness to entrust others with levels of responsibility well beyond prevailing managerial practice, which to his mind had little to recommend it. In a 1948 memorandum to his officers, he stated:

> We complain about government in business, we stress the advantages of the free enterprise system, we complain about the totalitarian state,

249

but in our industrial organizations, in our striving for efficiency we have created more or less of a totalitarian organization in industry, particularly in large industry. The problem of retaining our efficiency and discipline in these large organizations and yet allowing our people to express themselves, to exercise initiative and to have some voice in the affairs of the organization is the greatest problem for large industrial organizations to solve.[2]

Wood had an unshakable conviction that the organization should serve the needs and aspirations of its members as well as those of the business itself. "Many corporations," he once said proudly, "have made a few top men enormously rich. We are making 150,000 very comfortable."[3] And he was not talking in terms of money alone. He was adamant about how each individual Sears employee was to be treated:

> We must always consider our 150,000 employees as 150,000 individual human beings, with personalities of their own. Just as far as it is humanly possible, our officers, our merchants, our managers, all Sears men in key positions should do everything in their power to allow each and every one of those people under them to have a measure of self-expression, even those in the humblest jobs. I believe there is no limit to what can be accomplished by a force of employees who are given an opportunity for self-expression, who have faith in their leaders, who believe not only in their ability, but in their fairness and justice, and who in return give of their best, freely and willingly. If all of Sears is animated by this spirit, nothing can stop us.[4]

These were high aspirations indeed, but under Wood's leadership they were realized to a remarkable degree. By his own example, he demonstrated that American democratic capitalism is not necessarily a Utopian dream.

This, in fact, was Wood's finest legacy. The kind of organization he built had greater visibility, but his chief and most enduring bequest to his company and American business as a whole was his demonstration that human and economic values are not necessarily conflictive. In his thirty years at Sears, he proved that with proper care and nurture they can be made mutually supportive. He created a corporate polity based on concern for human and democratic values which may well be unique in American economic history. During the period Sears was under Wood's command, there were few corporations, in America or elsewhere, as successful as Sears by any measure of economic performance; at the same time, there were very few indeed—perhaps none in the large-scale category—which went as far as Sears did to protect and preserve the substance of human values.

This orientation pervaded all of Wood's corporate and personal relationships: with employees, with managers, with suppliers, with customers, with communities, with the public. In each case, his concerns were expressed in terms relevant to the functions and needs of the particular situation. These concerns evidenced themselves spontaneously and appropriately because they were deeply embedded in his personal character and did not have to be contrived for the occasion.

In each area of relationship, the response was warm and positive. Sears under Wood enjoyed a remarkable degree of confidence and respect in its dealings with customers, suppliers, employees, stockholders, and the public; there was probably no more solidly popular corporation in America than Sears, Roebuck and Co., and this was largely a direct result of the system of values with which Wood thoroughly embued all levels of the company. These values so permeated the warp and woof of the organization that they have survived to some extent the many changes, internal and external, which have occurred in the years that followed his active leadership.

But the lives of organizations are ephemeral. Much that was distinctive about Sears under Wood did not survive intact and unchanged in the years that followed. What has survived is the fact that there once was a living demonstration that human and democratic values can be recognized and fostered not only without cost to but as a means for strengthening economic performance. That which has happened cannot be made not to have happened. That Sears was once the kind of organization it was is a fact that cannot be expunged and has a permanent place in this country's institutional and cultural history. If such an organization existed before, there is hope not only that it can be created again but also that it can be replicated many times over. The major purpose of this book is to help make this happen.

One lesson of the Wood/Sears experience is the crucial importance of the kind of person at the top. Without Wood or someone like him in command of the company, much that he stood for gradually fell by the wayside. Against his great record of achievement must be set at least one great shortcoming: his failure to provide for his own succession.

Admittedly his was a hard act to follow, but it proved considerably harder than it might have been. He was succeeded in office by a series of chairmen, none of whom until recently remained in power long enough to leave his personal stamp on the company, and none of whom—again until recently—approached Wood's broad vision and commanding stature. With the General as the standard against whom everyone else was measured, a successor of comparable stature was a long time in coming.

Theodore V. Houser was the first to assume the post after Wood stepped down. Of all Wood's lieutenants, he was probably the best qualified to succeed him, but he deliberately cut his own tenure short. Houser bitterly resented the fact that Wood had delayed his own retirement until he was seventy-five years old, which meant that Houser was sixty-one when the chief executive office was finally vacated. He felt, with justification, that he had been denied the chance he deserved, and to ensure that the younger men coming along behind him would not suffer a similar fate he had his directors revise the company's retirement rule as it applied to the chairman. Wood, on moving up to that position at age sixty in 1939, had at the same time secured a board resolution exempting the chairman, alone of all company employees, from any retirement age requirement, thereby opening the way for him to continue in office another fifteen years. On at last becoming chairman himself, Houser changed the rule to make it mandatory that the chairman retire at age sixty-five. He effectively limited himself to only four years in the office Wood had held for twenty-seven.

Houser's brief reign set a pattern that was to prevail for the next twenty-four years, and perhaps longer. In the sixty-eight years between the company's founding in 1886 and the year Wood retired in 1954, Sears had three chief executives (not counting Kittle, whose tenure was abbreviated by his untimely death). In the twenty-four years following 1954, the top office was occupied by six different people, none of whom held the position for more than six years and two for as little as two; their average incumbency was just under four years, compared with the twenty-two-year average of Richard Sears, Julius Rosenwald, and General Wood. The chief executive office was a revolving door.

This was partly due to the manner in which each successive chief executive was picked. It was taken for granted that he would be a Sears man, someone who had come up within the Sears organization. This meant that the field of selection was restricted to those who happened to be officer-directors of the company at the time each succession decision was made. Wood continued as an active member of the board for twelve years after his retirement and had an important voice in each decision; during this period, no one to whom he had strong objection was named to the top position.

Beyond this, however, those who exercised the greatest influence on the outcome were the incumbent officer-directors. The outside directors, of course, had a say in the matter, but during the period in question they were strongly outnumbered by insiders. The net result was a situation in which the officer-directors chose the next chief executive from among themselves, and there is some indication that in situations where the choice had been narrowed to a few people the candidate with the shortest time to go before retirement had a certain advantage. Whether or not this was true, the fact remains that most of those who followed Wood as chief executives had little time left.

General Wood was not happy with the result, but for whatever reason he failed to change the pattern. On more than one occasion in private conversation—and sometimes not so private—he voiced his unhappiness with the way things were. One of his senior executives (not a corporate officer) reported an incident that occurred some years after Wood's retirement.[5] Wood was at a Boys Club fund-raising event where many Sears people were present when he began to talk in a voice loud enough for people at neighboring tables to overhear:

Wood: "I made a hell of a mistake when I retired."

Companion [sotto voce]: "What was that, General?"

Wood: "Putting all those old men in to follow me. None of them stayed more than three years [Wood's arithmetic was off but not enough to invalidate his point.] They didn't have time to put it in this end of the pipe and see it come out the other. I made a hell of a mistake over this."

"You could hear a pin drop," the man recounting the story continued. "I kept trying to get him to change the subject or at least lower his voice, but he ran the course on it. He thought that was a bad mistake, one man following the other, three years at a time."

Part of the problem may have lain in the fact that Wood's ability to predict performance left something to be desired. He could recognize both superior performance and poor when he saw it, but he had trouble seeing in advance how a particular person would do when moved to a new set of duties or a higher level of responsibility. There is also some indication that after moving up to the chairmanship Wood deliberately chose as his successors men who would not challenge his preeminence but instead would implement his ideas unquestioningly. Barrows proved to be an exception, but he was a mistake in more ways than one and did not last long.

253

J. M. Barker described the promotion of T. J. Carney to president in 1939 as "an example of the General's unwillingness to have anyone who would in any way detract from the uniqueness of his, R. E. Wood's, position. I remember too well Tom [Carney] saying to me one day, 'To all intents and purposes the fellow who's president of this company is R. E. Wood.' . . . [Carney] had no illusions at all about his being president in anything but name. He was being told what to do." [6] About the situation in general, Barker observed: "R. E. Wood, the genius, couldn't have anyone else with a touch of genius . . . as the top man in Sears. . . . Wood knew what he wanted to do and, unconsciously, to have somebody in as president who had other ideas irked him." [7] And again: "The General did not feel hospitable to a flair in someone else. You know, somebody else who would have a light in his eye and say, this is the way it should be done. This was a prerogative . . . that a man at the top who himself had a terrific flair . . . reserved for himself." [8]

Barker's testimony on this score is best taken with a grain of salt. He had no doubt whatever that his own genius was fully equal to Wood's, and it is very likely that he attributed his failure to be advanced to the presidency to Wood's unwillingness to have a man as strong as he so close to the top.

But while Barker's statements may be somewhat self-serving, they are not without independent corroboration. More than one of the retired senior Sears executives I interviewed in the process of collecting data for this book commented on Wood's apparent reluctance to bring really strong men to the top. "He wanted an easy-going president under him so he could still run the company" was a typical observation. E. P. Brooks, Wood's factory vice-president (who, incidentally, seldom saw eye to eye with Barker) tells how Wood blocked T. V. Houser's nomination to the Business Advisory Council of the U.S. Department of Commerce for several years because he did not want anyone from Sears other than himself in that prestigious body. The General was a skillful politician, and a common characteristic of successful politicians is a marked reluctance to allow potential rivals to arise around them. Perhaps Wood's political instincts extended this far as well.

It is a curious fact that Sears own highly productive system of executive development proved inadequate in preparing candidates for the uppermost levels of responsibility within the company. And it becomes even more curious when one considers that this system came into being during the years of General Wood's ascendancy, under the direction of Clarence

254

Caldwell and with Wood's strong support. It enabled Sears to meet the great bulk of its own personnel requirements from its own resources within a few years of Caldwell's taking over. During the period under consideration, it was especially effective in producing qualified candidates for virtually all positions up to the vice presidential level, and reasonably successful in producing vice presidents. Yet when it came to finding a president, it failed. In all fairness, this was probably too much to expect of it. It is very unlikely that any administrative system could in itself have produced another General Wood or an individual whose capabilities were anywhere nearly comparable.

A brief review of Wood's own career is instructive. For only short periods during his entire working life did he play a secondary or subordinate role to anyone else; he was almost always the boss in his particular sphere of activity. General Goethals was chief engineer and in overall charge of building the Panama Canal, but he turned over to young Wood virtually complete autonomy for everything except the actual construction itself. Wood's stay at Du Pont was short because he quickly saw that there was no way he could reach the top of that family-run company. As quartermaster general in World War I, he ran the entire service of supply for the American Expeditionary Force. He encountered difficulties at Montgomery Ward because he did not have the free hand that was so important to him, and he and Merseles, Ward's president, soon came to a parting of the ways. During his first three years at Sears he was technically subordinate to Kittle as president, but Kittle gave Wood his head and provided support rather than direction as Wood developed his retail program. And, of course, at Kittle's death Wood became in name as well as fact chief executive officer and unquestioned master of all of Sears.

Wood was not overly concerned with titles; he could work well in positions where he was outranked formally, provided he had the power and authority to act largely on his own in his area of responsibility. But in those instances when he found himself in a de facto as well as a nominal secondary role, without the independent authority he so highly prized, he was restive and uncomfortable and did not stay there long.

Sears, Roebuck and Co. could not have produced General Wood; it is impossible to conceive of anyone like him working his way up through such a complex, multilevel organization. If he had been recruited from college and placed in the Sears training program, he would not have lasted six months, if indeed he had been willing to take the trainee job in the first place. He simply did not have the patience to move ahead by orderly increments of responsibility, and even at an early age his abilities were far superior to those required of all positions except those at the top.

Wood was not the product of any administrative system designed to produce a great leader. He had a very high order of latent talents to begin with, and he had the great fortune to find himself in circumstances—first in Panama, then in World War I, and finally at Sears—where those talents could emerge and flower without irksome restraint; in circumstances, in fact, which stretched him to exercise every ounce of ability he had. His failure to provide a successor comparable to himself stemmed from his failure to create within Sears circumstances such as those which had allowed his own latent capabilities to come to light and flourish. Ironically, the circumstances he did create had quite the contrary effect.

Wood's great strength as a businessman lay in his ability to think strategically. But that ability backfired when it came to grooming a successor. Beneath the comfortable and secure umbrella of Wood's brilliant strategy, Sears officers and executives were able to devote themselves to the details of establishing orderly and assured sources of supply, a stable and well-motivated work force, well-located and well-designed retail stores and mail-order plants, and an efficient logistical system for the rapid and low-cost movement of goods from sources of supply to stores and customers' homes. The senior people of Sears were able to concentrate on and refine tactical elements such as these to high levels of perfection without having to concern themselves with basic business strategy; they were able to plan and tinker and improve within a secure strategic environment.

The very security of that environment discouraged strategic innovation. While Sears key people were encouraged to be and in fact were skilled innovators in their respective fields—merchandise, operations, personnel, and the like—they were not encouraged to and thus did not develop skills in strategic *business* innovation. New and improved product lines, more efficient ways of operating, yes; new businesses, no.

Wood neglected to provide for an orderly, systematic review and redefinition of Sears business purpose and mission in the light of changing conditions, and he did not push his lieutenants to consider the possibility that there might be other businesses in which the company could fruitfully engage. The only major innovations of this kind were Sears entry into the retail business in 1925 and into the insurance business in 1931, and these were both on Wood's initiative. The organization he built was superbly competent at executing a given strategic concept but lacked the capacity to accomplish strategic changes comparable in size and scope to the retail and insurance moves. In truth, an organization can accommodate strategic changes of this magnitude only once or twice in a generation; greater frequency would likely be disruptive. But the success of these two major strategic changes, compared with the sad condition Sears would have been in without them, illustrates dramatically the urgent need for periodic shifts in business strategy to adapt to altered conditions or capitalize on new opportunities. The organization built by Wood was incapable of even contemplating significant strategic innovations, and for a long time there was no one to succeed Wood who was capable of conceiving any new move which would do for Sears in the third quarter of the century what the retail and insurance moves had done before. A strategic thinker himself, Wood failed to develop strategic thinkers to follow him.

There were other circumstances and practices which contributed importantly to Sears success under Wood's leadership while creating serious difficulties for later generations of management. One of these was the policy of promotion from within. This was a principal means by which Wood mobilized and maintained the ardent, unstinting efforts of the younger people whose loyalty, enthusiasm, and energy were integral to the company's outstanding economic performance. Unfortunately, the policy was applied too literally and too uniformly, with the result that at Wood's retirement in 1954 there were very few people in executive or officer positions who had ever worked anywhere but Sears. By this time the pattern was so firmly established and had become such a fixed part of the Sears way of life that it was continued with little variation for the next twenty-five years. In an era when the company needed people in key positions who could ask hard questions and be receptive to unconventional answers, all levels of management, up to and including the very top, were characterized by an essential sameness in experience and outlook which seriously hampered creative adaptations and changes in the company's environment.

The potential for adaptive change was further impeded by General Wood himself. Although he formally retired at age seventy-five in 1954, he remained on the board of directors for another twelve years and continued to be consulted on all matters of major importance. The company did him the courtesy of giving him an office with a secretary at corporate headquarters for most of this period, and although he used this only occasionally he did so often enough to preserve an active sense of his presence in the minds of the officers who came after him—most of whom, in fact, considered themselves and were considered by him as "his boys."

Wood's ready accessibility—either at his corporate headquarters

257

office, at a small private office he set up in downtown Chicago, or at his home in nearby Lake Forest—and his willingness to give advice when asked tended to discourage significant departures from established business strategies. At a time when Sears should have been exploring innovations as consequential as Wood's entry into the retail and insurance businesses, the very great success of the strategies already in place discouraged significant deviation from or supplementation of them. Wood's continued personal presence at or near the arena of decision making was a further inhibiting influence.

General Wood placed a high value on harmony within the Sears officer group. Sears would be all right, he frequently adjured them, as long as its officers worked together as a team and no divisiveness or factionalism developed among them. The habits of thought and behavior thus established persisted long after him, and to this day Sears officers get along together with remarkably little internal friction. Under Wood's strong leadership, this harmonious condition served a useful purpose, but since then the urge for consensus has discouraged dissent and made it difficult for the company to depart from its well-established ways. These ways included a certain amount of improvement and innovation within a fairly well-defined framework; for quite some time, however, any significant deviation was likely to be buried.

Dissent—even violent disagreement—at the policy-making level serves a useful purpose because it forces examination of premises and consideration of alternatives. Without this element in the decision-making process, serious mistakes can be made and important opportunities overlooked. In an age when it could have been highly useful for some people in top management to have fought hard for certain courses of action opposed by the majority, the deeply ingrained tradition that a good Sears officer "goes along" proved a serious inhibition. This tradition in turn reinforced other influences which have tended to be resistant to significant strategic departures.

Robert E. Wood left behind him rich and vital legacies. He made important contributions to improving the quality of life for millions of people. He was an innovator of the first order, and he wrote a brilliant chapter in the history of American enterprise. He built an organization remarkable for its economic effectiveness and for the stimulating and rewarding way of life it provided its members. He demonstrated dramatically not only that it is possible to conduct business without doing violence to human values but that concern for human values contributes importantly to business success.

In the whole history of American business enterprise, very few have left nearly as much as he. It is unfortunate that he failed to create the conditions that would enable the great organization he built to replicate the high order of creativity he himself brought to it. But that, perhaps, is too much to ask, for each generation must produce its own creative leaders.

EPILOGUE

A T THE TIME OF General Wood's formal retirement in 1954, Sears, Roebuck and Co. had acquired tremendous momentum, and it moved ahead rapidly in the next several years to impressively higher levels of sales and profit performance. From just under $3 billion in Wood's last year in office, sales grew to $10 billion in 1971 and to nearly $18 billion in 1978.[1] Although more than half of this nominal sales increase was due to price inflation,[2] these were eminently respectable figures.

But they told only part of the story. Toward the end of the 1960s, it began to be apparent to astute insiders and knowledgeable observers alike that all was not well with Sears. Rates of growth were slipping while the costs of doing business were edging upward. Profit margins were narrowing, and the competition was threatening. Sears remained the world's largest retailer—nearly twice the size of the second largest—but it was losing market share. In the recession of 1974–75 it was harder hit than the retail industry generally and recovered more slowly.

Financial performance was lackadaisical. In 1955 the return on average equity had been 16.1 percent; by 1975 it had fallen to 9.8 percent.[3] Investor confidence was badly shaken, and the market price of Sears stock dropped sharply. Internally, there were serious problems of management and organization. The once coherent merchandising strategy had become confused to the point that trade journalists were describing Sears as having "an identity crisis."[4] Merchants in the field and at headquarters often worked at cross purposes. Managerial morale began to erode, and there was considerable confusion in executive and supervisory ranks. The organization itself was top-heavy, and people inside and outside speculated that Sears had grown too big to manage. With nearly 900 stores, some 1,700

261

catalog and sales offices, thirteen huge regional distribution centers, 124 warehouses, and over 450,000 employees, giantism was a real and present concern.

Aware of its troubles, Sears management acted. Efforts were made to develop and enforce a more cohesive merchandising strategy; to cut back on overhead and streamline organization; to improve headquarters-field communications; to gain better control over inventory and expenses; to correct problems which had developed in executive incentive systems; and otherwise to strengthen managerial functions. These measures brought about significant improvements in merchandising performance by the second half of the 1970s. Nevertheless, it was clear that something more was needed.

The situation Sears found itself in at this time was reminiscent of two other periods in its history: the mid-1890s, and the mid-1920s. During each of these earlier times, the company had seemed to reach an impasse, and in each instance it had taken a new leader with a new entrepreneurial vision to restore sound and vigorous growth.

The first of these was Julius Rosenwald. Prior to his arrival, Richard Sears was unable to understand why his own freewheeling, ad hoc merchandising practices were no longer as successful as they had been. He failed to see that a more systematic marketing strategy was needed to support his brilliant sales promotional capabilities. Rosenwald, coming in from the outside, recognized that the rise in the nation's agricultural output, coupled with the poorly met needs of rural and small-town America, was generating unprecedented merchandising opportunities. His redefinition of Sears business purpose as "buyer for the American farmer" launched the company on an era of tremendous progress and prosperity.

Useful as Rosenwald's idea was, however, it depended on a special set of conditions to stay viable—and those conditions changed. With the coming of the automobile and good roads in the 1920s, there was no longer a separately identifiable rural and small-town market for which Sears could function profitably as "buyer." Again it took an outsider, this time Robert E. Wood, to perceive where the greatest merchandising opportunities lay: in the rapidly growing urban areas populated by an increasingly prosperous working class and a newly emerging middle class. Wood knew that this market could not be effectively served by mail order alone and could only be tapped through a nationwide system of retail stores, using the mail-order plants as jobbers and the catalog as a supplement to retail selling.

262

This was the concept that heralded the beginning of a second enormously prosperous period for Sears.

In time, of course, these conditions changed too. And, as had happened twice before, Sears failed to change with them. Top management in the late 1960s and early 1970s failed to see the relevance to their business of the far-reaching structural adjustments the American society and economy had undergone since the heyday of General Wood. For Sears, the most significant of these were the maturing of the merchandising industry and the shift from a goods economy to a service economy—two closely related phenomena that profoundly altered the fabric of American life.

Under General Wood, Sears developed to serve a goods-producing and goods-consuming society whose character was shaped by manufacturing, its central economic function. In the 1920s and for many years thereafter, American families were busy acquiring automobiles and auto accessories, household appliances and equipment, wearing apparel, sporting goods, radios and televisions, and a host of other items which had largely been unknown to or unattainable by earlier generations. Much of this was original equipment: electric refrigerators, automatic washing machines, wall-to-wall carpeting. By the 1960s and 1970s, however, the market for goods such as these had become primarily a replacement market, and competitors had learned to serve it as well as Sears.

There was nothing patentable in General Wood's buying methods or innovative system of distribution; others could and did copy them. The competitive advantage Sears had enjoyed for so long gradually eroded. Meanwhile, the merchandising industry itself grew overcrowded; American consumers, once underserved, suddenly found themselves with more stores than they could profitably support. Where Sears and (to some extent) Ward's had once had the new urban market virtually to themselves, they now had to fight hard to hold their own against a host of importunate rivals.

The concurrent shift from a goods to a service economy meant that the typical Sears customer was spending proportionately less on the tangibles that were Sears stock in trade. From the 1920s through the 1950s, the bulk of the spendable income of the middle- and working-class American family had gone for goods to support its rising material standard of living; from the 1960s on, a larger and larger share went for education, health care, travel, and other intangibles. The central economic function of the country was no longer manufacturing but the processing and managing of information. Faced with the difficulties of maintaining growth and profitability, Sears senior people dug in their heels and sought to do better the things they were already doing, and they did these exceedingly well. They failed, as their predecessors had failed twice before, to see that with the fundamental changes that had taken place in American society what was needed was not so much better business methods as new business directions.

In particular, the post-Wood top management did not grasp the understandably distasteful prospect that the business they knew so thoroughly lacked the capacity to take the company into a great new period of growth comparable to those it had experienced under Julius Rosenwald and General Wood. Having spent their working lives in merchandising, they had trouble seeing the need to go beyond it. The key phrase here is *go beyond*. Julius Rosenwald did not discard Richard Sears's promotional genius; he combined it skillfully with his new merchandising concept. General Wood did not abandon mail order; he used it as the starting point for his phenomenally successful mail-order/retail system. What later Sears management took a long time learning was to accept the limitations of its established business and find means to utilize the strengths of that business to enter into other areas that would offer significant potential for renewed growth.

Each of the company's two former periods of remarkable prosperity had its roots in the way it responded to urgent needs created by major new developments in the structure of American society. The rapid increase in agricultural output in the last decade of the nineteenth century and the first two decades of the twentieth and the far-reaching consequences of World Wars I and II brought about great changes. These in turn gave rise to pressing needs within broad sectors of the American public which were poorly served by existing economic institutions. In both cases, Sears moved into the breach with dramatic results.

The present stage in the evolution of the American economy is characterized by the inability of existing institutions to serve the country's growing needs for more efficient, more accessible, and more adequate financial and real estate services. Sears recent advances into these fields are evidence that the company is again moving into a major hiatus which has developed in the American economic system. The results should again be dramatic.

Tracing the origins of these new developments within the company goes beyond the scope and purpose of this book about General Wood and the Sears, Roebuck of his era. It appears, however, that the first steps toward systematic exploration of possible new directions were initiated during the tenure of Arthur M. Wood (no relation to the General) as chief executive officer in the mid-1970s. But it was not until his successor, Edward R. Telling, took office in 1978 that the broad outlines of a distinctly new entrepreneurial concept began to take form discernible to the public eye.

Telling saw the opportunity for Sears to become "the great American corporation," which he conceived as encompassing merchandising, insurance, finance, and real estate. The merchandising and insurance businesses were already securely in place, and good beginnings had been made toward building financial and real estate services through the operations of Allstate Insurance and the Homart Development Corporation, the wholly owned subsidiary which had been created in the 1950s to handle shopping center projects in which Sears was interested. Apparently it was Telling's original intention to build his "great American corporation" from these existing Sears components. Then, in 1981, the opportunity arose to greatly accelerate the process by means of two strategic acquisitions: Dean Witter Reynolds, a leading full-line investment house, and Coldwell Banker, the nation's largest real estate firm—two moves which came almost simultaneously and shook the finance and real estate communities to their foundations.

There are those on Wall Street who look askance at Sears new policy, just as a half century before the financial gurus of their grandfather's generation scoffed at General Wood's audacious entry into retailing. But despite skepticism in some quarters that "while people will buy fertilizer and washing machines from Sears, they won't buy stocks and bonds," the company's future in the finance and real estate fields looks highly promising.

Sears starts with impressive credentials. The more than 25 million Sears credit cards now actively in use represent about 55 percent of *all* American households and about 85 percent of households with annual incomes of $30,000 or more, the sector of the population comprising the most active homeowning and investing groups. A high proportion of all Americans have had or will have at some time in their lives need for real estate brokerage and mortgage loans, and it is reported that of the 9.5 million households doing business with New York Stock Exchange firms, 7 million are current Sears customers.

The company's greatest asset as it moves into these new areas is the confidence in which it is held by the American people. Sears enjoys a level of trust that has been accorded few if any other corporations, and this will

265

serve it well in fields where confidence and trust are essential. The established real estate and financial communities have reason to be worried; the new Sears is a greater competitive threat than any they have ever faced.

Even this early in the game, there is a saying on Wall Street that "there is nothing to fear but Sears itself." Facetious though these words may sound, they contain more than a grain of truth. Traditional financial institutions are in turmoil, anxiously trying to find their place in the scheme of things now taking shape. Real estate until recently has been virtually a cottage industry, huge in volume but hopelessly fragmented in management and operations; it, too, is changing. The way is open for Sears to establish itself firmly in both fields, and it is doing so with notable vigor. It is perhaps just as well that Sears marked time for as long as it did before setting off in these revolutionary strategic directions; any major moves of this kind before the 1980s would have been premature.

One other element of the new Sears, Roebuck has so far drawn little public attention, but appears to have dramatic potential. This is Sears World Trade Inc., created to develop a field in which this country has never been particularly strong but for which Sears is remarkably well adapted. Given the company's close ties with thousands of U.S. manufacturers and its established commercial contacts throughout the world, Sears is in a position to provide a globe-girdling trading service that American industry badly needs but has never had before. This is a key element of the new Sears strategy that will bear watching in the years ahead.

It is fascinating to observe how neatly these new developments at Sears replicate what has happened twice before. Many appear to think that Telling's ideas represent a radical break with Sears tradition, but in point of fact they are in close accord with that tradition. Both Julius Rosenwald and General Wood refashioned the company to serve major needs of their respective eras that were being poorly served by existing economic institutions; both created new institutions. Building on the start made by Arthur Wood, Edward Telling is refashioning Sears to serve the needs for more convenient, more readily accessible, more efficient, and less costly financial, real estate, and world trading services.

It is too early to pass judgment on the new Sears strategy. On the surface it looks good. But it will take time to prove, and meanwhile it carries a very high level of risk. Interestingly, both the time required and the risk involved are also part of the Sears tradition. It took Julius Rosenwald five years to establish his strategy of serving as buyer for the American farmer. And it was not until 1935, ten years after opening his first retail store, that

General Wood felt comfortable that the company was moving in the direction he wanted it to go. In today's volatile world, the management of Sears may not have the luxury of a ten- or even a five-year period of trial and test; the task cannot be accomplished overnight, but it must be accomplished with dispatch.

The managerial and organizational aspects of what Telling must accomplish are awesome. Before embarking on its new direction, Sears was already a huge and complex enterprise. Grafting onto it a host of additional functions and services, many of them still in nascent stages of development, presents problems of a magnitude and difficulty never before faced by an American corporation. At the heart of the task is the integration of the greatly broadened range of activities into a unified whole. For example, Sears cannot afford to operate Dean Witter Reynolds and Coldwell Banker as autonomous units within a conglomerate. The Allstate experience provides a useful object lesson: Allstate's success was built on closely integrating the selling of insurance with the selling of automobile-related merchandise in the retail stores. Telling and his key associates must now find ways to integrate similarly the investment and real estate businesses not only with Sears established merchandise and insurance businesses but also with the many new activities in which it is engaged. The course ahead is rough and filled with dangers, both seen and unseen. Yet, as General Wood often said, "If your strategy is right, you can make a lot of mistakes learning how to make it work."

There is reason to believe that the new strategy is right, that while it is risky it contains within it ample room to learn how to make it work. It is likely that in retrospect some years hence Edward Telling's entry into these fields will be perceived as comparable in significance to Julius Rosenwald's reorientation of the mail-order business in the 1980s and General Wood's venture into retail in the 1920s.

Sears now seems well on its way to becoming as dominant in the consumer finance and real estate industries—and perhaps in world trading services—as in earlier stages in its history it was dominant in mail order and retailing; it may well prove to be one of the great growth companies of the closing decades of the twentieth century.

No business strategy is good forever. The very success of a particular strategy dooms it to obsolescence because its foundations are built on circumstances that are bound to change, and success itself is a heady wine that makes the need for new strategies difficult to see. Moreover, organizations become senescent; they wither and die unless renewed.

267

What we are witnessing in Sears today is a process of organizational renewal—for the third time in the company's long history. Julius Rosenwald renewed Richard Sears's flagging enterprise; General Wood renewed Rosenwald's drooping mail-order business; Edward Telling is renewing a company that was growing increasingly moribund. In each instance, the renewal process was set in motion by the infusion of new and creative entrepreneurial concepts. What is happening now at Sears appears to be only a prelude to yet another great period of growth and prosperity.

It took a long time for Sears to find a successor to General Wood. History may well record that it finally found him in Edward Telling.

Note on Sources

A substantial portion of the contents of this book is drawn from my personal knowledge, partially in the form of recollections and partially in the form of documentary materials accumulated over a period of many years.

I was employed by Sears, Roebuck and Co. during more than half the time General Wood was the company's chief executive officer. My position in the parent personnel and public relations departments brought me into frequent contact with him and enabled me to observe his actions and their consequences firsthand. From early in my employment, I developed a keen interest in Wood and his methods, and about 1940 I began collecting materials bearing on his managerial policies and practices—having in mind even then that I would one day write a book about the General. In the years that followed, these included memoranda, letters, speeches, and similar documentary manifestations of his thinking.

My first position in the Sears parent personnel department involved responsibility for the research and planning by which Clarence Caldwell, then director of retail personnel, sought to give organizational expression to General Wood's concern for developing and conserving the company's human resources. Work along this line fostered a curiosity to understand more clearly the whys along with the whats. On numerous occasions beginning in the early 1940s, I endeavored to analyze and interpret in writing the significance of the managerial behavior of Wood and his key officers; this effort took the form of statements issued as official company policy, internal memoranda (sometimes over my signature but more typically over Caldwell's), speeches prepared for Caldwell and other officers, and, from about 1948 on, speeches given by me or papers published under my name.

I accumulated these materials, along with those mentioned above, in file boxes and transfer cases and carried them with me as I moved from one position to another in Sears, and later as I moved from Sears to management consulting to teaching. (My wife, Mildred, was both amused by and tolerant of my packrat habits; we changed residences often, and wherever we went the files went, too.) Finally, in 1977—not fully retired but somewhat relieved of daily work pressure—I was able to begin the sorting and classifying that formed a necessary prelude to the writing I had been planning so long to do.

In addition to having my own papers to draw from, I have had the privilege of free access to the official Sears Archives, an entity which I established in 1955 and which in the last quarter century has managed to acquire and preserve an impressive body of materials bearing on the company and its history. Particularly valuable for my purposes were transcripts of interviews with active and retired officers recorded as part of the company's Oral History Project and now permanently filed in the Archives.

Notable among the materials in the Archives are the proceedings of the various On-to-Chicago meetings conducted by the company. These were gatherings of all company executives from the level of store manager or equivalent up to and including senior officers. The proceedings of these meetings are preserved in the Sears Archives and provide an invaluable source of information for students of corporate management and business history.

In assembling materials for this book, I have conducted an oral history project of my own. Over the past five years, I have tape recorded extensive interviews with retired officers and senior executives of Sears, each of whom worked closely with General Wood. The people I spoke with have added materially to the wealth of information at my disposal.

On publication of this book, I shall deposit all of my personal Sears papers, including interview transcripts, in the Sears Archives, where I hope they may be of use to the company and to future historians and students of business and management. At the time of this writing, however, they are still in my possession, and are identified in the notes by "(author's files)."

Two other sources of information that proved particularly useful to me were the "Reminiscences" of General Wood and J. M. Barker, recorded respectively in 1961 and 1951 by the Oral History Collection of Columbia University (the Wood document is copyright 1972; the Barker document, 1980). I have quoted and cited frequently from both documents by kind permission of The Trustees of Columbia University in New York City.

Other documentary sources consulted are identified in the Notes following. Especially important is *Catalogues and Counters*, the definitive (as of 1950) history of Sears, Roebuck and Co. by Boris Emmet and John E. Jeuch.

Unless otherwise indicated, all *Annual Reports*, letters, memoranda, communications, unpublished materials, copies of speeches, etc., cited in the Notes are currently housed in the Sears Archives.

All factual statements for which no authority is cited are based on my personal knowledge, and I accept personal responsibility for them.

Notes

Notes to Prologue

1. Sloan, *My Years at General Motors*.
2. David G. Moore, memorandum to me, ca. 1949–50 (author's files).

Notes to Chapter 1, "Robert E. Wood: The Early Years"

1. Details of Wood's family background and early life are drawn from three sources: "The Reminiscences of General Robert E. Wood" (1961), pp. 1–3 hereafter Wood, "Reminscences"; "General Robert E. Wood, President," *Fortune*, 17 (May 1938), 66–69, 104–10; and an interview with Mary Hardwick Wood, widow of General Wood, 9 February 1979 (author's files).
2. Unless otherwise indicated, this and subsequent passages quoting Wood in this portion of the chapter are from his "Reminiscences," pp. 3–8. As in all materials quoted herein, punctuation and syntax are rendered verbatim. Bracketed words and/or phrases have occasionally been added for the sake of clarification.
3. Wood, *Monument for the World*, p. 15.
4. McCullough, *Path between the Seas*, p. 465.
5. Interview with Mary Hardwick Wood. It is interesting to note that while Wood showed no concern for his own safety, he delayed his marriage and bringing his bride to Panama until 1908, five years after they met. By that time the Herculean efforts of Colonel William C. Gorgas had eliminated yellow fever from the Canal and brought other epidemic and endemic diseases under control.
6. Interview with Wood by Frank S. Cellier, 5 June 1967, pp. 1–2. Cellier was a member of the Sears corporate personnel staff who set out in the late 1960s to write a book on General Wood. In pursuit of this objective, he conducted extensive tape-recorded interviews with General Wood and other senior Sears officers, including notably James M. Barker. Cellier's untimely death prevented completion of his project, but transcripts of his interviews are pre-

served in the Sears Archives. These have proved most helpful at several points in the writing of my own book.

7. Wood, *Monument for the World*, p. 34.
8. McCullough, *Path between the Seas*, pp. 538–39.
9. Wood, *Monument for the World*, p. 36.
10. Information and quotations from his period of Wood's life (1915–19) are from his "Reminiscences," pp. 19–36.
11. Except as otherwise noted, the account given here of Wood's Montgomery Ward experience is based on tape-recorded interviews with Edward Pennell (E. P.) Brooks at his home, Buxton Farm, Millboro, Virginia, 29–30 April 1977. I had previously recorded an interview with Brooks at my home in Sanibel, Florida, 8 March 1977. A third extensive interview with Brooks was also recorded in Sanibel 11 March 1979. (All author's files.) Most of the Brooks citations in this book are from the 29–30 April 1977 interview because this took place at his home where he had ready access to his records, which he found useful to consult from time to time. The 8 March 1977 and 11 March 1979 interviews contain rich, elaborative detail. Brooks was employed as a young man by Wood at Ward's and followed him to Sears, where he held a number of important posts in the retail and buying organizations. These culminated in the position of factory vice-president from which he retired in 1951 to become founding dean of Sloan School of Industrial Management at the Massachusetts Institute of Technology.
12. Interview with Louis Pfeiffle, 4 February 1967 (author's files).
13. *Montgomery Ward & Co.*, part 1. This eleven-part tabloid-form publication was issued in connection with the company's celebration of its centennial. Courtesy Montgomery Ward & Co.
14. Leslie Kountze, unpublished manuscript. Courtesy Leslie Kountze.
15. Except as otherwise indicated, this and subsequent information on the policy debate of the period is drawn from *Montgomery Ward & Co.*, parts 5 and 7.
16. "Miss Richardson," as she was always known within the Sears organization, was assigned to General Wood as his secretary when he was appointed acting quartermaster general in 1918. She accompanied him to Ward's and subsequently to Sears, where she remained with him until his retirement in 1954.

Notes to Chapter 2, "Sears, Roebuck and Co.: The Mail-Order Years"

1. Information on the founding and early history of Sears is drawn from three sources: Sears, Roebuck and Co., *Annual Report*, 1940, which contains a special "Historical Supplement"; Emmet and Jeuch, *Catalogues and Counters*; and Sears, Roebuck and Co., *Merchant to the Millions*.
2. For an excellent account of Rosenwald's life and work, see Werner, *Julius Rosenwald*.
3. Emmet and Jeuch, *Catalogues and Counters*, p. 52.
4. Information on the early years of Ward's is from *Montgomery Ward & Co.*, part 2.

5. Sears Catalog, 1896.
6. Montgomery Ward's Catalog No. 13 (Spring/Summer 1875) stated unequivocally: "We guarantee all our goods. If any of them are not satisfactory after due inspection, we will take them back, pay all expenses, and refund the money paid for them." Quoted in *Montgomery Ward & Co.*, part 1.
7. Sears, Roebuck and Co., *Annual Report*, 1940, "Historical Supplement."
8. Elmer Scott, memoir, p. 20 (Elmer Scott Papers, Dallas Historical Society, Dallas). Scott was employed by Sears from 1895 to 1913 and was the first general manager of the Dallas mail-order plant. He was an early pioneer in the development of modern personnel practices and was intimately involved with Doering in the design and implementation of the schedule system.
9. Emmet and Jeuch, *Catalogues and Counters*, pp. 132–33. The record is silent as to whether the pneumatic tube system was provided by Nussbaum's old company.
10. There is some possibility that Scott may have been familiar with Taylor's work or perhaps with the writings of Henry Towne or some of the early exponents of the "scientific" approach to management. Scott read widely and was obviously influenced in his concern for employee welfare by the "progressive" spirit of the times, and the ideas of men such as Taylor and Towne would have appealed to him had he known about them. However, nothing is found in his memoir or his other papers in the Dallas Historical Society to suggest that he had any contact with or knowledge of these men and their work.
11. Werner, *Julius Rosenwald*, pp. 74–75.
12. Emmet and Jeuch, *Catalogues and Counters*, pp. 172, 194.
13. Werner, *Julius Rosenwald*, p. 76. The author goes on to note that the stock sold to Goldman, Sachs for $10 million in 1909 was worth $200 million in 1928.
14. The Dallas plant was not Rosenwald's idea and in fact he opposed it, but he acquiesced in its establishment and his judgment in doing so proved sound.
15. Emmet and Jeuch, *Catalogues and Counters*, p. 211; Werner, *Julius Rosenwald*, pp. 228–31.
16. Emmet and Jeuch, *Catalogues and Counters*, p. 205.
17. Ibid., p. 214.
18. The account given here of Rosenwald's philanthropic and civic endeavors is based on Werner, *Julius Rosenwald*.

Notes to Chapter 3, "General Wood: The Sears Years"

1. Unless otherwise indicated, materials for this account of Wood's move to Sears is from interviews with E. P. Brooks, 29–30 April 1977.
2. Boris Emmet and John E. Jeuch, *Catalogues and Counters*, p. 295.
3. Endicott to Wood, 6 October 1924 (Endicott's syntax rendered verbatim here and in all quotations following). (Robert E. Wood Papers, Herbert Hoover Presidential Library, West Branch, Iowa.)
4. Wood to Endicott, 3 October 1924 (Wood Papers).
5. Endicott to Wood, 6 October 1924 (Wood Papers).

6. Ibid.
7. "On Saturday morning, October 18th, I saw Mr. Rosenwald at his residence in Highland Park and told him I had decided to accept the vice presidency of Sears, Roebuck & Co. I told him I would leave the terms in his hands. He gave me the following: Salary $40,000.00 a year; Bonus on the same terms as the other officers of the company, Mr. Adler and Mr. Doering.

"He also stated that he would make a personal arrangement with me by which he would turn over to me a minimum of one thousand shares of Sears, Roebuck stock on the basis of $100 per share, this minimum to be considerably increased if he could make the proper arrangements. He stated that he would give me a memorandum of this after I reported for duty.

"Stock and bonus arrangements are to be kept absolutely confidential and not told even to Mr. Adler or Mr. Doering."

Memorandum for file, signed by Robert E. Wood and witnessed by Jennie M. Richardson (Wood Papers, 14 November [*sic*] 1924). Rosenwald and Wood subsequently entered into an agreement for Wood to purchase, over a five-year period, 2,500 shares of Sears stock at $100 a share, a figure well below the current market price in the mid-$150s (Agreement signed by Julius Rosenwald and Robert E. Wood, 24 December 1924, Wood Papers).
8. Endicott to Wood, 27 October 1924 (Wood Papers).
9. Cf. Wood to Endicott, 14 January 1925 (Wood Papers).
10. Interview with Brooks.
11. For Lessing Rosenwald's account of these events, see Emmet and Jeuch, *Catalogues and Counters*, pp. 330–31.
12. This and the following quotations are from Wood to Endicott, 6 January 1928 (Wood Papers).
13. Interview with Brooks.
14. This and the following quotation are from Wood to Lessing Rosenwald, 3 July 1929 (Wood Papers).
15. Interview with Wood by Cellier, p. 4.
16. Wood's "Reminiscences," p. 79.
17. Wood to Roosevelt, 27 January 1933 (Wood Papers).
18. Wood to Wallace, 26 May 1933 (Wood Papers).
19. Wood to Roosevelt, 24 October 1934, and Wood, "Memorandum to the President," 14 October 1936 (both Wood Papers). See also Wood's "Reminiscences," pp. 79, 80, 82, 106.
20. Wood to Wallace, 31 May 1938 (Wood Papers).
21. Wood to Roosevelt, 17 June and 13 October 1937 (Wood Papers)
22. Wood, "Memorandum to the President"; Wood to Marvin H. McIntyre, 31 December 1937; and Wood to Roosevelt, 26 January 1938 (all Wood Papers).
23. Wood, "Our Foreign Policy," address before the Council on Foreign Relations, Chicago, 4 October 1940.
24. Wood freely recounted his discussion with Lindbergh with his Sears associates and other business friends.
25. Interview with Robert S. Adler, 29 November 1979 (author's files).
26. Interview with Douglas J. Peacher, 9 July 1979 (author's files). Peacher re-

ports a conversation he had with Wood ca. 1941. Although Peacher is quoting Wood from memory many years later, he is emphatic that the statement as given is accurate if not necessarily verbatim.

27. Wood's "Reminiscences," p. 84.
28. Wood to Colonel J. C. O'Laughlin, 27 February 1946 (Wood Papers).
29. Wood, "Address to Annual Dinner, Association of Cotton Textile Merchants," New York, 2 February 1950 (author's files).
30. Cf. Wood's "Reminiscences," pp. 93–95. See also his memorandum of 21 June 1944 suggesting procedures for the early termination of procurement contracts in anticipation of the end of the war.
31. Wood's "Reminiscences," p. 95.
32. Wood, memorandum to Barrows, Barker, and the outside directors, 5 April 1945.
33. Sears, Roebuck and Co., *Annual Reports*, 1946–53.
34. Sears, Roebuck and Co., *Annual Reports*, 1946 and 1953; Montgomery Ward & Co., *Annual Reports*, 1946 and 1953, Chicago.
35. Comparative data for 1924 and 1953 from Sears, Roebuck and Co., *Annual Report*, 1953. Other data furnished by Sears.

Notes to Chapter 4, "The Business Purpose"

1. Wood's "Reminiscences," p. 40.
2. Ibid., p. 4.
3. Interview with Mary Hardwick Wood.
4. Wood, "Address Before Convention of National Life Insurance Companies," Chicago, 5 September 1950.
5. Ibid.
6. Drucker, *Management Tasks, Responsibilities, Practices*, p. 64.
7. Wood, memorandum to Sears Board of Directors, 3 August 1940.
8. Wood, "Talk to Buyers," Chicago, 5 November 1936.
9. Wood's "Reminiscences," pp. 53–54.
10. Interview with Brooks, 29–30 April 1977.
11. Quoted in "50 and 100 Years Ago," *Scientific American*, 233 (September 1975), 12.
12. Sears Catalog, Fall 1934.
13. Wood to Wallace, 24 July 1934 (Wood Papers),
14. Wallace to Wood, 28 July 1934 (Wood Papers).
15. These and the two succeeding quotations are from Wood, "Talk to Buyers."
16. Wood, "Address to Annual Dinner, Association of Cotton Textile Merchants."
17. Wood, address before On-to-Chicago meeting, Chicago, 4 May 1950 (author's files).

Notes to Chapter 5, "The Buying Strategy"

1. Wood, "Talk Given at Meeting of Buyers," Chicago, 1 March 1924. Courtesy Montgomery Ward & Co.

2. Interview with Brooks, 29–30 April 1977.
3. Interview with Barker by Frank S. Cellier, 16 September 1968, p. 4.
4. The quotations in this paragraph are from an interview with Wood by Frank S. Cellier (undated but apparently recorded between June and September of 1967), pp. 5, 6.
5. D. M. Nelson took Adler's place as merchandising vice-president when Adler retired, but it was Houser, not Nelson, who was the chief architect of Sears buying strategy from 1928 on. Houser succeeded Wood as chairman of the board when Wood retired in 1954.
6. Wood, "Talk to Buyers," Chicago, 5 November 1936.
7. This and the two succeeding quotations are from Houser, "The Whys and Wherefores of Sears Merchandise," address before On-to-Chicago meeting, Chicago, 30 March 1939.
8. Gudeman, "Sears Basic Buying Practices," presentation to a group of Sears merchandising executives, Chicago, 23 April 1947.
9. Interview with Pfeiffle, 4 February 1979 (author's files).
10. The quotations in this paragraph are from interviews with Brooks, 29–30 April 1977.
11. Wood, "Talk to Buyers."
12. Houser, "The Whys and Wherefores."
13. Interview with Arthur Rosenbaum, 8 July 1979 (author's files).
14. Houser, "The Whys and Wherefores."
15. This and the three succeeding quotations are Gudeman, "Sears Basic Buying Practices."
16. Wood's "Reminiscences," p. 54.
17. Ibid., p. 54.
18. Interview with Brooks.
19. Wood, address before On-to-Chicago meeting, Chicago, 4 May 1950.
20. The quotations in this paragraph are from the Burleigh B. Gardner, "Study of Source Relations, Preliminary Report" (author's files). This report is undated, but Dr. Gardner has consulted his records and determined that it was prepared in 1948. Gardner was at that time (and still is) president of Social Research, Inc.
21. Interview with Wood by Cellier, 5 June 1967, p. 14.
22. This episode was related to me by Harry Wellbank on 1 May 1979.

Notes to Chapter 6, "The Selling Strategy"

1. Interview with Brooks, 29–30 April 1977.
2. Information provided by Lenore Swoiskin, Sears archivist.
3. Wood, address before the Boston Conference on Distribution, Boston, 20 September 1937.
4. This account of retail development at Montgomery Ward during the years 1925–29 is drawn from two sources: Latham, *1872–1972*, pp. 70–74; and *Montgomery Ward & Co.*, part 7.
5. Interview with Brooks.

6. Emmet and Jeuch, *Catalogues and Counters*, pp. 344–45.
7. Wood's "Reminiscences" p. 57.
8. Cyril Deutsch, letter to me, 7 November 1979 (author's files). Deutsch was a longtime Sears retail manager.
9. Interview with Louis Pfeiffle, 4 February 1979.
10. Interview with Brooks.
11. Ibid.
12. Ibid.
13. Interview with Barker by Cellier, 11 September 1964, pp. 3–4.
14. "The Reminiscences of J. M. Barker (1951)," pp. 92–93, in the Oral History Collection of Columbia University, hereafter Barker's "Reminiscences."
15. Interview with Brooks.
16. Emmet and Jeuch, *Catalogues and Counters*, p. 350.
17. Interview with Brooks.
18. Cf. Barker's "Reminiscences," pp. 89–90.
19. Ibid., pp. 95–96.
20. Ibid., p. 92.
21. Interview with Barker by Cellier, 2 September 1968, pp. 14–15.
22. Barker's "Reminiscences," pp. 99–100.
23. Interview with Pfeiffle.
24. Wood, "Tobé Award Speech," New York, 10 January 1951.
25. Emmet and Jeuch, *Catalogues and Counters*, p. 653.
26. Barker's "Reminiscences," p. 93.

Notes to Chapter 7, "Organizational Policies"

1. For a more detailed description of the Sears organizational structure under Wood, see Chandler, *Strategy and Structure*, pp. 252–82. See also Emmet and Jeuch, *Catalogues and Counters*, pp. 358–73.
2. Interview with Louis Pfeiffle, 4 February 1979. Pfeiffle was one of these four.
3. E. P. Brooks, "Sears in Perspective," *Sears World* 1 (Spring 1958); also interview with Brooks, 29–30 April 1977.
4. Wood to Rosenwald, 3 September 1929.
5. George E. Frazer, "Sears, Roebuck and Co., Proposed Definitions of Responsibility," a report submitted 3 January 1930. This is referred to in text as the Frazer Report.
6. Ibid., pp. 6–7.
7. Ibid., p. 40.
8. G. E. Humphrey to Wood, 26 June 1930. Quoted in Chandler, *Strategy and Structure*, p. 252.
9. Wood to Rosenwald, 29 February 1931.
10. Wood to Rosenwald, 4 August 1930.
11. Wood, memorandum to all territorial officers, 21 December 1931.
12. Carney to Wood, 16 December 1931.
13. Barker to Wood, 31 December 1931.
14. Wood to Carney with copies to functional and territorial officers, 16 January 1932.

15. Barker's "Reminiscences," pp. 101–2. See also Wood to A. E. Cushman, 12 May 1964. Cushman was then chairman of Sears. In his letter, Wood voiced his response to a May 1964 *Fortune* article criticizing his 1932 dismantling of the territorial organization.
16. Barker to Wood, 2 January 1935. This fifteen-page memorandum gives a detailed account of the operations of the office of retail administration under Barker's direction.
17. Humphrey to Wood, quoted in Chandler, *Strategy and Structure*, p. 252.
18. Wood, memorandum to officers and retail policy committee, 27 October 1938.
19. Wood, address before On-to-Chicago Meeting, 30 March 1939.
20. Wood, "Tobé Award Speech," New York, 10 January 1951.
21. Our conversation took place ca. 1947.
22. Interview with Brooks, 29–30 April 1977.
23. Humphrey as quoted by Brooks in interview.
24. Interview with Barker by Cellier, 11 November 1968, p. 32.
25. Cf. Worthy, "Organizational Structure and Employee Morale," pp. 169–79.
26. For a more complete description of the parent merchandising and retail organizations and the way they worked, see Worthy, *Big Business and Free Men*, pp. 94–98, 108–12.
27. Emmet and Jeuch, *Catalogues and Counters*, pp. 487, 653.
28. Ibid., p. 595.
29. Wood, memorandum to Sears directors, 3 August 1940.
30. Cf. Wood, memoranda to directors, 3 August 1940 and 29 August 1941, and Barker, memoranda to Wood, 26 June 1944 and 23 September 1947.
31. Wood, "Talk Given at Dinner for Directors, Officers, Supervisors, Factory Managers, etc. at the Chicago Club," Chicago, 24 March 1947.
32. Wood to McConnell, 1 June 1949 (author's files).
23. McConnell, memorandum to officers with copies to senior executives, 7 June 1949 (author's files).
34. Caldwell, address to On-to-Chicago meeting, Chicago, 6 May 1950 (author's files).
35. Caldwell to McConnell, 26 February 1952 (author's files).
36. Wood, memorandum to officers and retail policy committee, 27 October 1938.

Notes to Chapter 8, "Manager Policies"

1. Wood, memorandum to territorial officers, 21 December 1931. Quoted in Chandler, *Strategy and Structure*, pp. 154–55.
2. Interview with Barker by Cellier, 16 September 1963, p. 13.
3. This account is based on a story often told to me and in my hearing by Caldwell.
4. Wood, address before National Personnel Conference, Chicago, 17 June 1948 (author's files).
5. Interview with Louis Pfeiffle, 4 February 1979.
6. Wood, address before On-to-Chicago meeting, 30 March 1939.
7. From my speech, "Management Development: The Extent and Nature of

Company Activity," delivered before the American Management Association, New York, 27–28 May 1952 (author's files).

8. Houser, *Big Business and Human Values*, p. 5.
9. Conference among Drucker, Houser, and myself, 2 March 1957 (author's files).
10. Emmet and Jeuch, *Catalogues and Counters*, p. 555.
11. Cf. Sears, Roebuck and Co., Department 707, "Retail Personel Projects and Plans for 1939," pp. 10–12 (author's files).
12. Ibid., p. 11.
13. From my report to Caldwell, "Three-year Program Training and Related Activities," 7 December 1944 (author's files).
14. Sears, Roebuck and Co., Department 707, "Post-War Personnel Program," p. 45 (author's files). This document is undated, but internal evidence combined with my own recollection as a member of the Post-War Planning Committee indicate that it was written in the latter part of 1944.
15. Caldwell, "Personnel Discussions," On-to-Chicago meeting, 27–31 March 1939.
16. Sears, Roebuck and Co., Department 707, "The Retail Personnel Program for 1940 (With Review of Operations During 1939)," p. 13 (author's files).
17. Ibid., pp. 13–14.
18. Wood, "Talk before Meeting of Supervisors and Members of the Buying Force," Chicago, 27 December 1933.
19. Caldwell, address before On-to-Chicago meeting, 28 February 1940.
20. Burleigh B. Gardner, "A Study of Opportunity at Sears: A Preliminary Report," ca. 1948 (author's files).
21. Ibid.
22. Department 707, "The Retail Personnel Program for 1940," p. 2 (author's files).
23. Wood, On-to-Chicago address, 1939.
24. Department 707, "The Retail Personnel Program for 1940," pp. 8, 13 (author's files).
25. Department 707, "Post-War Personnel Program," p. 17.
26. Ibid., p. 33
27. Wood, On-to-Chicago address, 1939.
28. Wood, address before On-to-Chicago meeting, 4 May 1950.
29. Sears, Roebuck and Co., Department 707, "College Training Program 1928–1940," a report submitted 10 October 1941 (author's files).
30. Gardner, "A Study of Opportunity at Sears."
31. Cf. the outline of Caldwell's talk to merchandise field men, 26 July 1945 (author's files).
32. Caldwell, address to On-to-Chicago meeting, 6 May 1950.

Notes to Chapter 9, *"Employee Policies"*

1. Wood, "Tobé Award Speech," New York, 10 January 1951.
2. Wood's "Reminiscences," pp. 67–68.

3. Ibid., p. 62.
4. Data on appreciation of Sears stock courtesy Sears, Roebuck and Co., data on Dow Jones Industrials from *The Wall Street Journal*, 84 (3 November 1924), and 143 (23 April 1954).
5. Interview with Wood by Cellier, 5 June 1967, p. 18.
6. Wood to Lessing Rosenwald, 7 April 1930.
7. Diligent search has failed to turn up a copy of the original 1935 "Bulletin 0–399," but numerous revised versions were issued on various dates between then and 1941 when it, together with other operating bulletins and statements of employee relations policies, were codified and incorporated into a comprehensive *Personnel Manual* published in that year. Cf. Sears, Roebuck and Co., "Employee Wage and Hour Policy Bulletin 0–399 Revised April 24, 1940," the last and most complete of this significant series (author's files).
8. My responsibilities at this time included administration of retail wage and hour policies; the account given here is based on my recollections reinforced by a review of papers in my personal files.
9. Department 707, "Post-War Personnel Program," p. 76.
10. Ibid, pp. 81–82.
11. McConnell, memorandum to all officers of the company, 14 February 1949.
12. Cf. my "Discovering and Evaluating Employee Attitudes" (American Management Association, Personnel Series No. 113, 1947), and "Attitude Studies as a Tool of Management" (American Management Association, General Management Series No. 145, 1950. (Both are in author's files.)
13. The survey results discussed in this section and the quoted materials are from Worthy, "Factors Influencing Employee Morale," pp. 61–73.
14. Ibid. See also my "Organizational Structure and Employee Morale," pp. 169–79; "Some Aspects of Organization Structure in Relation to Pressures on Company Decision-Making," Industrial Relations Research Association, Proceedings of the Fifth Annual Meeting (December 1952), pp. 66–79; and *Big Business and Free Men*, especially chapters 6 and 7.
15. Sears, Roebuck and Co., "What Do Employes [*sic*] Like About Sears?" 1 June 1948 (author's files).
16. There was no need for Wood to put his wishes on this score in writing; by word and deed, he left no doubt in anyone's mind as to where he stood and what he wanted done.
17. These and other details on Shefferman and his career are from Shefferman, *Man in the Middle*.
18. Ibid., pp. 10–11.
19. Ibid., p. 166.
20. Ibid., p. 18.
21. Ibid., pp. ix-x.
22. Tudor, *Hearings before the Select Committee on Improper Activities in the Labor Management Field* (McClellan Committee), 25 October 1957 (Washington, D.C.: Government Printing Office, 1957), p. 6045.
23. Ibid., p. 6043.
24. Ibid., pp. 6045–46.

25. Kennedy, *The Enemy Within*, p. 219.
26. Survey conducted by Social Research, Inc. (author's files).
27. My memorandum to Caldwell, 2 February 1951 (author's files). This memorandum and accompanying report present a detailed analysis of the extent of union organization for the period "prior to 1941" through 1950. Data are arranged by year, by territory, by union involved, and by type of company operation. Figures cover only the retail, mail-order, and parent branches of the company and do not include factories or other subsidiary operations. The data are definitive for the period covered and probably changed little in the three remaining years of General Wood's tenure.

Notes to Chapter 10, "Public Policies"

1. Barker's "Reminiscences," p. 120.
2. Interview with Barker by Cellier, 11 September 1968, pp. 27–28.
3. Barker to D. M. Nelson, 15 November 1939.
4. Ibid.
5. Ibid.
6. Sears, Roebuck and Co., *Annual Report*, 1936.
7. Wood, Address before On-to-Chicago meeting, 30 March 1939.
8. Wood, "Social Responsibility of the Retailer," address before the American Retail Federation, Washington, D.C., 18 July 1939. The copy of this address in the Sears Archives is dated 9 June 1939, which is apparently the date Wood finished preparing it. The address was actually delivered 18 July.
9. Wood, address before On-to-Chicago meeting, Chicago, 4 May 1950.
10. Cf. Wood, "Social Responsibility of the Retailer."
11. Cf. Wood, On-to-Chicago address, 1939.
12. Wood, "Social Responsibility of the Retailer."
13. Ibid.
14. Emmet and Jeuch, *Catalogues and Counters*, pp. 633–34.
15. Ibid., pp. 623–24.
16. Ibid., pp. 624–25.
17. This information is drawn from the personal papers of Robert V. Mullen, former executive director of the Sears-Roebuck Foundation. Courtesy Robert V. Mullen.
18. Emmet and Jeuch, *Catalogues and Counters*, pp. 633–34.
19. Condon, address before On-to-Chicago meeting, 6 May 1950.
20. Ibid.
21. Emmet and Jeuch, *Catalogues and Counters*, p. 634.
22. Condon, address before On-to-Chicago meeting.
23. Condon, "Report to Board of Directors," 1952 (month and date not reported) (Mullen Papers).
24. This and the following quotation are from Endicott to Wood, 1 March 1948.
25. Robert V. Mullen, "How Sears Pays Its Debt to the American Farmer," 1950 (place of speech, audience, and exact date not recorded) (Mullen Papers). Also, Condon, address before On-to-Chicago meeting.
26. Condon, "Report to Board of Directors."

27. Emmet and Jeuch, *Catalogues and Counters*, p. 641.
28. Condon, address before On-to-Chicago meeting.
29. Mullen, "How Sears Pays Its Debts."
30. Condon, address before On-to-Chicago meeting.
31. Interview with J. C. Haynes, Atlanta, 9 August 1979.
32. Mullen, "How Sears Pays Its Debts."
33. Condon, address before On-to-Chicago meeting.
34. Mullen, "How Sears Pays Its Debts."
35. Ibid.
36. Condon, address before On-to-Chicago meeting.
37. Sears-Roebuck Foundation, *Where Are They Now?* a brochure published in 1962 (Mullen Papers).
38. Emmet and Jeuch, *Catalogues and Counters*, p. 632.
39. Interview with Haynes.
40. This account of the "Church of the Year" program is drawn from the interview with Haynes. See also Condon, "Report to Board of Directors," 22–23 March 1953.
41. Condon, address before On-to-Chicago meeting.
42. This description of the National Grange Community Service Contest is drawn from my personal recollections, reinforced by a telephone interview with Mullen, 4 January 1981.
43. Condon, address before On-to-Chicago meeting.
44. Interview with Mullen.
45. Mullen, "Remarks on Launching of Women's Club Program," address before General Federation of Women's Clubs, Washington, D.C., 27 January 1955 (Mullen Papers).
46. Cf. Wood to Barker, 4 March 1936.
47. Information on the Sears associate and agency systems is drawn from a telephone interview with Ralph Schindler, 24 March 1979 (author's files). Schindler administered both systems.
48. Wood to Endicott, 6 January 1928.
49. Wood, memorandum to Sears board, 3 August 1940.
50. Ibid.
51. Cf. Barker to Wood, 26 June 1944.
52. Wood, memorandum to Sears board, 21 November 1947.
53. Wood, address before National Personnel Conference, Chicago, 17 June 1948 (author's files).
54. Price quotation for January 1925 from *The Wall Street Journal*, 85 (3 January 1925).
55. Wood, On-to-Chicago meeting, 1950.
56. Interview with Mullen.
57. Interview with Haynes.
58. Ibid.
59. I accompanied Condon to St. Paul and was present during this conversation.
60. I was the Sears representative, and the cufflinks are still among my prized possessions.

Notes to Chapter 11, "Entrepreneurial Policies"

1. Interview with Barker by Cellier, 17 September 1968, p. 20.
2. Wood's "Reminiscences," pp. 74–75.
3. Barker's "Reminiscences," p. 149.
4. The Allstate Insurance Companies, *Annual Report*, 1950 (internal document).
5. Cf. Emmet and Jeuch, *Catalogues and Counters*, p. 442.
6. Interview with Meyer, 23 January 1981 (author's files).
7. Ibid.
8. Wood to Endicott, 4 June 1929.
9. Interview with W. Wallace Tudor, 23 August 1979 (author's files). Tudor worked closely with Wood during the early years of the Latin American venture and was elected corporate personnel vice president and director in 1956.
10. Interview with Meyer.
11. Wood, "Talk Given at Dinner for Directors, Officers, Supervisors, Factory Managers, etc. at the Chicago Club," Chicago, 24 March 1947.
12. For an excellent and objective account of Sears first six years in Mexico, see Wood and Keyser, *Sears, Roebuck de Mexico*. This report gives a vivid description of Sears impact on the Mexican economy and society.
13. Ibid., p. 34.
14. Ibid.
15. Ibid., pp. 50–51.
16. Sears, Roebuck and Co., *Annual Report*, 1954.
17. Charles A. Meyer, response to telephone inquiry, 1 August 1983.
18. Wood and Keyser, *Sears, Roebuck de Mexico*, pp. 50–51.
19. Sears, Roebuck and Co., *Annual Report*, 1960.
20. This account of the early contacts between Sears and Simpsons and of the founding of Simpsons-Sears is based on interviews with Douglas J. Peacher, 9 July 1979; James W. Button, 7 July 1981; and Arthur M. Wood, 6 July 1981 (all author's files). Wood (no relation to the General) was vice-president and general counsel of Sears at the time of the formation of Simpsons-Sears and was later chairman and chief executive officer of Sears.
21. Interview with Peacher.
22. Sears, Roebuck and Co., *Annual Report*, 1952.
23. Interview with Peacher.
24. This account of the course of relations between Sears and Waltons is based on the interview with Arthur M. Wood. At the time of the Waltons-Sears venture, Wood was general counsel of Sears and was directly involved in the negotiations which led to the establishment and subsequent dissolution of that enterprise.
25. Sears, Roebuck and Co., *Annual Report*, 1955.
26. Ibid.
27. Sears, Roebuck and Co., *Annual Reports*, 1946 through 1955 inclusive. See especially those for 1951 and 1955, which include summary discussions of the expansion program.
28. Ibid., 1951 and 1955.

29. Ibid., 1951.
30. Interview with Wood by Cellier, 9 September 1967, p. 6.
31. Cf. *Montgomery Ward & Co.*, part 8.
32. Sears, Roebuck and Montgomery Ward, *Annual Reports*, 1946 and 1954.

Notes to Chapter 12, "The Politician"

1. Wood, untitled talk to parent merchandising staff, undated but from internal evidence ca. July 1932 (Wood papers).
2. Ibid.
3. Wood, memorandum to all store managers, 27 May 1938.
4. Wood to McConnell, quoted in McConnell, memorandum to retail field officers, group managers, and district managers, 19 July 1938.
5. Wood, memorandum to Sears officers, 11 March 1942.
6. Wood's "Reminiscences," p. 106.
7. Ibid., p. 79.
8. Wood to Roosevelt, 27 January 1933 (Wood Papers).
9. *American Heritage Dictionary of the English Language* (Boston: Houghton-Mifflin, 1978).
10. Hugh Hough, "General Robert Wood of Sears Dies at 90," Chicago *Sun-Times*, 7 November 1969.
11. Pflaum, "The Baffling Career of Robert E. Wood," pp. 68–73.
12. Wood, "Tobé Award Speech," 10 January 1951.

Notes to Chapter 13, "Personal Sketches"

1. Interview with Mary Hardwick Wood, 9 February 1979 (author's files).
2. Interview with Meyer, 23 January 1981 (author's files).
3. Interview with Arthur Rosenbaum, 8 July 1979 (author's files).
4. Interview with Mary Hardwick Wood. See also Wood's "Reminiscences," p. 61, where he speculates, "I think I could have gone on in history."
5. Interview with Barker by Frank S. Cellier, 17 September 1968, p. 11.
6. Ibid., pp. 5–6.
7. Barker's "Reminiscences," pp. 269–70.
8. Ibid., p. 270.
9. Interview with Mary Hardwick Wood.
10. Interview with W. Wallace Tudor, 23 August 1979 (author's files).
11. Ibid.
12. Wood, address before On-to-Chicago Meeting, 30 March 1939.
13. Wood, "Talk Given at Meeting of Buyers," Chicago, 1 March 1924.
14. Wood, "Talk with Buyers," Chicago, 5 November 1936.
15. Interview with Barker by Cellier, 16 September 1968, p. 14.
16. Alexander Eban, tape-recorded editorial conference, Chicago, 1958. In addition to Eban, participants included Brooks, Sanford Cobb, and myself. Courtesy E. P. Brooks. The day and month of the conference is not recorded, but its

purpose was to discuss preparation of an article by Brooks which appeared in the spring 1958 issue of *Sears World*, I:3.

17. Wood, "Speech Given on Accepting Merit Award Presented by the Rotary Club of Chicago," Chicago, 24 July 1951.
18. Deutsch, letter to me, 7 November 1978 (author's files).
19. Interview with Douglas J. Peacher, 9 July 1979 (author's files).
20. Boynton, letter to me, 24 September 1978 (author's files).
21. Ibid.
22. Interview with J. Howard Wood, 19 March 1979 (author's files).
23. Wood's "Reminiscences," p. 3.
24. Interview with Frederick P. Boynton, Jr., 9 July 1979 (author's files).
25. Interview with Brooks, 29–30 April 1977 (author's files).
26. Ibid.
27. Interview with Boynton. The same story is recounted in the interview with Brooks.
28. Interview with Boynton.
29. Ibid.
30. Interview with Robert E. Brooker, 2 August 1983 (author's files).
31. Interview with Tudor.
32. Sanford Cobb, conversation with me, 2 March 1981. Cobb is a retired Sears executive.
33. Interview with Tudor.
34. Conversation with Cobb.
35. Interview with Brooker.
36. Deutsch to me, 7 November 1979 (author's files).
37. Interview with Burleigh B. Gardner, 30 March 1978 (author's files).
38. Ibid.
39. Ibid.
40. Interview with Barker by Cellier, 12 September 1968, pp. 22–23.

Notes to Chapter 14, "The Legacies"

1. Emmet and Jeuch, *Catalogues and Counters*, pp. 301, 595; Sears, Roebuck and Co., *Annual Report*, 1954.
2. Wood, memorandum to officers of the company, 14 October 1948. The memorandum transmitted a copy of "Democratic Principles in the Business Management," a speech I had delivered before the Industrial Management Institute of Lake Forest College, Lake Forest, Illinois, on 27 May 1948. Wood enjoined his key officers to read the speech, pass it along to their key people, and "try to see that the principles set forth are put into practice."
3. Wood, address before On-to-Chicago meeting, Chicago, 4 May 1950.
4. Ibid.
5. Interview with retired Sears executive, anonymous here to avoid possible embarrassment (author's files).
6. Interview with Barker by Cellier, 16 September 1968, p. 68.

7. Ibid., p. 10.
8. Ibid., p. 22.

Notes to Epilogue

1. Sears, Roebuck and Co., *Annual Reports*, 1954, 1971, and 1978.
2. The Consumer Price Index stood at 80.5 in 1954, 121.3 in 1971, and 195.4 in 1978 (1967 = 100). *Statistical Abstract of the United States* (Washington, D.C.: Government Printing Office, 1980), p. 486.
3. Sears, Roebuck and Co., *Annual Reports*, 1955 and 1975.
4. Cf. "Sears Identity Crisis," *Business Week*, No. 2410 (8 December 1975), pp. 52, 58.

Bibliography

Asher, Louis E., and Edith Heal. *Send No Money*. Chicago: Argus Books, 1942.

Boorstin, Daniel J. "A Montgomery Ward's Mail-Order Business." *Chicago History*, 2 (Spring-Summer 1973).

Columbia University Oral History Collection. "The Reminiscences of James M. Barker," 1951.

————. "The Reminiscences of General Robert E. Wood," 1961.

Chandler, Alfred D., Jr. *Strategy and Structure: Chapters in the History of Industrial Enterprise*. Cambridge, Mass.: MIT Press, 1962.

Cohn, David L. *The Good Old Days*. New York: Simon and Schuster, 1940.

Doenecke, Justus D. "General Robert E. Wood: The Evolution of a Conservative." *Journal of the Illinois State Historical Society*, 71 (August 1978).

————. "The Isolationism of General Robert E. Wood," in *Three Faces of Midwest Isolationism: Gerald P. Nye, Robert E. Wood, and John L. Lewis*, ed. John N. Schacht. Iowa City: The Center for the Study of Recent History of the United States, 1981.

Drucker, Peter F. *Management Tasks, Responsibilities, Practices*. New York: Harper & Row, 1973.

Emmet, Boris, and John E. Jeuch. *Catalogues and Counters: A History of Sears, Roebuck & Company*. Chicago: University of Chicago Press, 1950.

Houser, Theodore V. *Big Business and Human Values*. New York: McGraw-Hill Book Co., Inc., 1957.

Kennedy, Robert F. *The Enemy Within*. New York: Harper & Brothers, 1960.

Latham, Frank B. *1872–1972, a Century of Serving Customers: The Story of Montgomery Ward*. Chicago: Montgomery Ward & Co., 1972.

Leys, Wayne A. R. "Ward and Sears, Expansion and Business Judgement," in *Ethics for Policy Decisions*, Ch. 18. New York: Prentice-Hall, 1952.

McCullough, David. *The Path between the Seas*. New York: Simon & Schuster, 1977.

Mahoney, Tom, and Leonard Sloan. *The Great Merchants*. New York: Harper & Row, 1966.

Montgomery Ward & Co.: The First Hundred Years. Chicago: Montgomery Ward & Co., 1972.

Pflaum, Irving. "The Baffling Career of Robert E. Wood." *Harper's*, 208 (April 1954), 68–73.

Sears, Roebuck and Co. *Merchant to the Millions*. Chicago: Sears, Roebuck, 1940.

Shefferman, Nathan W. *The Man in the Middle*. New York: Doubleday & Co., 1961.

Sloan, Alfred P., Jr. *My Years at General Motors*, ed. John McDonald with Catherine Stevens. New York: Doubleday & Co., 1964.

Weil, Gordon. *Sears, Roebuck, USA*. New York: Stein and Day, 1977.

Wood, R. E. *Mail Order Retailing Pioneered in Chicago*. New York: Newcomen Society of England, American Branch, 1948.

———. *Monument for the World*. Chicago: Encyclopedia Brittanica, Inc., 1963.

Wood, Richardson, and Virginia Keyser. *Sears, Roebuck de Mexico, S.A., First Case Study in an NPA Series on United States Business Performance Abroad*. Washington, D.C.: National Planning Association, 1953.

Worthy, James C. *Big Business and Free Men*. New York: Harper & Brothers, 1959.

———. "Factors Influencing Employee Morale," *Harvard Business Review*, 28 (January-February 1950), 61–73.

———. "Organization Structure and Employee Morale," *American Sociological Review*, 15 (April 1950), 169–79.

———. "Sears, Roebuck: General Robert E. Wood's Retail Strategy," *Business and Economic History Papers* (presented at the Twenty-Sixth Annual Meeting of the Business History Conference, 6–8 March 1980, Paul Uselding, editor).

Index

291

Ward, A. Montgomery, 26
Ward's. *See* Montgomery Ward & Co.
Warner, W. Lloyd, 158
Washington, Booker T., 37
Weinberg, Sidney, 53, 198
Werner, M. R., 36
West Point, 4, 5, 11
West Side plant (Chicago), 28–31
Wheeler, Burton, 230
Whirlpool, Inc., 71
Wilkie, Wendell, 51
Wilson, Woodrow, 33
WLS (World's Largest Store) radio, 178
Women's Clubs program, Sears, 190
Wood, Arthur M., 215, 265, 266, 285*n*20,
  *n*24
Wood, J. Howard, 238
Wood, Lillie Collins (mother), 3, 4
Wood, Mary Hardwick (wife), 5, 9, 179,
  240, 241
Wood, General Robert Elkington: ability to
  mobilize support for his policies, 223,
  225; affection of employees for, 237; affinity with Midwest, 3, 13, 230; alleged
  anti-Semitism, 48, 49; and the America
  First Committee, 48–50, 231; on the automobile, 82–83; aversion to overhead
  of, 113, 114, 127, 231; belief in large
  families, 238; boyhood of, 3–4; on character, 235; compared to Sewell Avery,
  xiv, 53, 219, 243; concern for customers'
  needs, 60, 61, 62; concern for human
  values, xiii; on corporate social responsibility, 64, 173–74, 176; on the customer,
  194–95; death of, 53; on decentralization, 120, 127–28; desire for independent authority of, 255; distinguishing
  characteristics of, 224; distrust of debt,
  219; distrust of Eastern financial interests, 49, 51, 229; distrust of formal organization, 121, 122, 129, 224; at the Du
  Pont Company, 9, 255; education of, 4;
  encouragement of employees by, 227; as
  entrepreneur, 197–220; failure to provide
  for his own succession, 129–30, 251–
  53, 256; fascination with census data and
  demographic figures, 59, 66, 90, 91,
  202, 233; fondness for children, 238–39;
  on his Fort Assiniboine experience, 5; at
  General Asphalt Company, 9–10; health

of, 5, 6, 234; on Hubert Humphrey, 230;
  as impediment to adaptive change at
  Sears, 257–58; inability to predict performance, 242, 253; influence of George
  Goethals on, 8; influence of Sears environment on, xiv, xv, 40–41; intelligence of, xv, 232, 233, 234; interest in
  retail stores, 15, 16, 17, 18, 36, 39, 81;
  interest in the South, 179; interest in
  young people, 144; on the interests of
  business, 63–64; on the lack of previous
  business experience, 58–59; and Latin
  American trips, 208; leadership style,
  223, 237; legacies of, 248–50, 258–59;
  leisure activities, 234–35; management
  style, 24; managerial philosophy, xiii, 98,
  117, 118–21, 131, 134–35; on marketing, 60; on meeting customers' needs,
  62–63; memory for figures, 232; on merchandising, 60; at Montgomery Ward,
  xiv, xv, 13–18, 66, 67, 73, 255; moral
  values of, 235; and the New Deal,
  46–47, 51, 228, 230–31; on "no frills"
  stores, 92; opposition to American involvement in World War II, 48, 49–50,
  231; opposition to unions and collective
  bargaining, 160–61, 163, 168; and organized labor, 47; at the Panama Canal,
  6–9, 255; participation of, in opening of
  retail stores, 88; on the personnel function, 115, 133; on his Philippines experience, 5; political instincts of, 76, 173,
  196, 254; political involvement of,
  46–48, 49–50, 50–51, 228, 229; as
  politician, 223–31; populist leanings of,
  229, 230, 231; on his pride in Sears,
  64–65; on the problems of Sears size,
  124, 125, 192–94; on production, 73; on
  promotion from within, 141; on rationale
  behind Allstate Insurance Company, 19;
  reprimands, manner of handling of,
  244–45; retirement of, 51, 53; on the
  role of the buyer, 69, 79; on his role as
  Sears president, 131; on sales, 92; on
  Sears as an agent of social change, 60; on
  Sears as an American institution, 65; on
  Sears personnel department, 133; on
  Sears sources, 79, 80; on the stockholder,
  63, 64; store visits by, 150–51, 208, 223;
  on strategy, 267; summary of Sears growth

Note on the Author

JAMES C. WORTHY spent the greater part of his career with Sears, Roebuck and Co., where he held various positions in the corporate personnel and public relations departments and rose to the position of vice-president. He was subsequently managing partner of the central region of Cresap, McCormick and Paget, management consultants. On retiring from that firm, he joined the faculty of Sangamon State University in Springfield, Illinois, as professor of public affairs and management. Since 1978, he has held an appointment as professor of management at the J. L. Kellogg Graduate School of Management of Northwestern University, Evanston, Illinois.

His business and educational experience has been interspersed with governmental assignments. He was an assistant deputy administrator of the National Recovery Administration during President Franklin D. Roosevelt's first term, and an assistant secretary of commerce, on leave from Sears, in the early years of the Dwight D. Eisenhower administration. In addition, he held appointments to an industry advisory panel of the Wage Stabilization Board under President Harry Truman and to President John Kennedy's Commission on Campaign Finance. He was also a commissioner of the Chicago Medical Center.

He was educated at Lake Forest College and Northwestern University, and holds honorary doctor of laws degrees from Lake Forest and the Chicago Theological Seminary.

Professor Worthy has written and lectured extensively on business, management, politics, and government. He is a fellow of the Academy of Management (United States) and of the International Academy of Management.

Over the years, he has taken an active part in civic and professonal affairs. Among other things, he has served as a member of the Illinois State Board of Higher Education and chaired the two committees on governance which designed the unique governing structure of the Illinois public university system.